William Gibson

The Abbé de Lamennais and the Liberal Catholic Movement in France

William Gibson

The Abbé de Lamennais and the Liberal Catholic Movement in France

ISBN/EAN: 9783744653671

Printed in Europe, USA, Canada, Australia, Japan

Cover: Foto ©ninafisch / pixelio.de

More available books at **www.hansebooks.com**

THE
ABBÉ DE LAMENNAIS

AND THE

LIBERAL CATHOLIC MOVEMENT IN FRANCE

BY

THE HON. W. GIBSON

LONGMANS, GREEN, AND CO.
LONDON, NEW YORK, AND BOMBAY
1896

All rights reserved

CONTENTS

CHAPTER		PAGE
	INTRODUCTORY	1
I.	A RESTLESS YOUTH. ORDINATION	8
II.	THE ESSAY ON INDIFFERENCE	44
III.	THE AUTHOR GOES TO ROME	76
IV.	POPE OR KING	92
V.	THE REVOLUTION OF JULY 1830	116
VI.	THE 'AVENIR'	154
VII.	APPEAL TO ROME. CONDEMNATION	195
VIII.	THE VOICE OF THE PEOPLE	219
IX.	PHILOSOPHIC RECONSTRUCTION	273
X.	A LIFE OF SUFFERING AND DEVOTION. '48	298
XI.	CLOSING SCENES	333

Erratum

Page 165, line 26, and page 194, line 25, *for* confessional *read* confession

THE ABBÉ DE LAMENNAIS

INTRODUCTORY

L'homme devient de plus en plus religieux.—COMTE.

'MAN tends to become more and more religious.' When the great French philosopher, founder of the Religion of Humanity, gave utterance to this profound thought, he had already witnessed the progress of the movement to which he owed his place in the history of human aspiration; and he did but sum up the results, so far as they were known to him, of the constructive efforts which have marked the present century, and of which his own system was the most striking example.

Towards the end of the preceding period a cold blast of analytic and irreligious criticism had passed over the thinking world, leaving behind it a state of things wherein 'the soul of man [had] become void, and into the void [had] entered the seven devils of secularity.' The Past as a living actuality had been swept away, or remained only as a heaving mass of decomposing material, lifeless yet life-giving, from which none but a master-hand might dare to construct the Future. It was fortunate that the very forces of destruction, working on minds and brains, had provided for this, and had evolved, not one, but a series of thinkers, each of whom contributed something to the work. In France alone there are many names not unworthy of notice; but of these I must be content to mention, as forming in themselves a kind of continuity in thought, De Maistre, Bonald, Chateaubriand, Lamennais, and Comte.

Following the local and personal exaggerations, as well as the apparent failure of the Revolution, it was natural that the earlier of this series of writers should have given to their work, superficially at least, the character of a reactionary movement. But we should bear in mind that in reality a return to the dead past was impossible; and that they, and especially De Maistre with his profound insight into human nature, were not unaware of this. Had it been otherwise they could have had no message for their time, and consequently would have been starved by neglect out of the world of life and movement.

Pondering on this fact, wandering in thought over the ground made holy by the footsteps of these great men, studying them not only in their work but in their character, I was especially impressed by the fact that in one of them at least a severe and ruthless logic, a by no means scanty fund of cynicism, and a somewhat pronounced development of the critical faculty were strangely mingled with a wild and stormy temperament, a temperament in which a daring, persistent energy was often rudely broken down by uncouth, almost incomprehensible attacks of exaggerated melancholy, explaining at once the value and the deep pathos of his life. This determined me in my choice of him as the central figure in the present study.

Thinking of this, and remembering what I had read of the dreamings and strugglings of his young days, and of the place which witnessed them, I felt that I should find something to inspire me in the wild, rugged scenery, the gloomy colouring, the angry battlings of wind and water round the little tide-washed town in Brittany which gave birth to him.

And I thought of St. Malo, built on a rock in the midst of the water, protected from the violence of the sea by a solid rampart of granite rising sheer from its foundation of primæval stone—thought of its history, of its legends, of its tutelary Virgin thrown up fully formed by the angry deep and set over the great gate, fit guardian of the storm-lashed town. I remembered the Rocher du Naye with its barbarous drownings of criminals tied up in weighted sacks and thrown over to perish in the waves below, whose last gurgling cries are said to still mingle with the low, sad moanings of the wind at night-time, as it makes its way in at the gates under the ramparts, and hugging the houses, winds along the narrow streets, and creeps under the doors, causing the shuddering inmates to draw closer round the fire. I thought of the fishermen going year by year to the fisheries in Iceland and Newfoundland, leaving in

March and returning to shelter in October and November; of Jacques Cartier, the discoverer of Canada; of the corsairs, of Duquay Trouin ... of Chateaubriand.

So strong, indeed, was the impression made upon me by this thought, that I determined to go to the place; there, in the midst of granite rocks and winter storms, to pen the first pages of this work.

I have a room overlooking the sea, which is wild and stormy. The windows are rattling with the wind, which is howling round the house. When first I came to it it was already dark, and as I opened the door the candle flickered and nearly went out. There was a low, weird moaning in the chimney from the storm without. Every now and then a blast would seem to shake the whole house, and there was a clattering on the window panes which reminded me unpleasantly of rain, but which I afterwards discovered to have been caused by fine particles of sand, blown up from the shore. Pulling aside the curtain, and peering out into the darkness, I could see a part of the rampart, a few yards from me, faintly lighted by the uncertain rays of a flickering street lamp, while over the top of it was just visible what seemed to be a sandy shore, studded here and there with rugged points of protruding rock. Further out, a little to the right, was a huge black mass of granite, the sides of which, from time to time, were almost hidden by cloud-like tongues, rising and falling. Along the shore was a curving line of uneven whiteness forming as it were the border of a moving mass of dull grey, gradually toning off into the deep, impenetrable blackness of the night. This, with the howling of the wind, and the clattering of the sand against the panes of glass, enabled me to form a kind of mental picture of the scene which awaited me in the morning. But the picture was nothing to the reality.

Tired from my journey, I slept soundly and late. I was awakened by the loud banging of a door, accompanied by the noise of the falling of fragments of broken glass. Jumping out of bed, I ran to the window. Pulling back the curtain I saw a sight which, from its grandeur, I shall never forget, and which, from its immensity, I hardly dare to describe. The sea, which was of a rich dark emerald green, as far as the eye could reach, was rent into great banks of giant swell, not smooth or regular, but torn and broken in angry, restless, heaving, foaming contest, writhing, as it were, in furious agony under the full blast of the storm, dashing themselves into a thousand foaming fragments, over the sharp points of rock which seemed to protrude everywhere from the surface of the water.

I opened the window. Invigorated by the fresh salt smell of the sea, and by the delightful odour of the torn and broken seaweed, soothed by the harmonious mingling of the voices of the people walking on the rampart, with the wild roaring of the tempest, I was soon lost in silent contemplation of this seething mass of inorganic matter, lifeless yet moving, heaving, breaking, thundering in mad confusion. I watched them, these enormous, broken mounds of rolling water, as, plunging and hissing in their reckless hurrying towards the coast, the crests of them were frayed by the wind into dense floating clouds of smoke-like spray. I listened to the splashing and the roaring of the surf on the shore, and to the dripping of the water from the storm-lashed parapet. Then looking towards the solitary rock, where, alone and defiant, stands the tomb of Chateaubriand, I saw the waves as they hurled themselves in their mad fury against the solid masses of granite, checked in their wild career, rush with a roar round the cavernous hollows at the base, or else, rising majestically, sweep up the rough surface of the rock, until, as if spent in fruitless efforts, the mighty volumes of water could go no further, seemed to pause, and, crashing down again over the loose boulders into the sea below, filled the air with a deafening noise. I saw them, stopped in their upward course by some sharp, uncouth corner of the jutting cragg, broken into a thousand fragments, while, here and there, they found their way, in single streams, to cracks and crannies, worked in the rock by centuries of briny turmoil, and thus, dashing on and mingling with the wind which howled in every cleft and hollow, transformed themselves into flakes of frothy foam, and then, caught up by some angry partial gust, faint echo of the raging storm without, they were torn from their momentary resting place, and blown far inland, there to dissolve, lost in the general warring of the elements.

And as I watched this heaving, foaming, plunging mass of tormented water, seething and hissing in the endless contest of the waves, suddenly breaking through the dense though quickly moving darkness of the heavens, a ray from the pale winter sun, flashing down, glanced on the rich emerald of the sea, and, passing on, showed it at every point in turn, varied in snowy white and watery green, veiled, at times, by quickly rolling mists of smoky spray. Then, creeping by, it swept along the ramparts, lighting up for a moment the scattered groups of awestruck watchers, and sank again, leaving all cold, and dark, and wild and stormy as it was before.

On such a day as this, more than a hundred years ago, there stood on these walls, holding the hand of his companion, a little boy of eight years old. His thin, pale face was turned towards the sea, as he watched with deep, sad eyes the fierce battlings of wind and wave, and listened to the angry roaring of the waters. He looked and listened, and in his child-like mind he seemed to ponder some thought beyond his years; then, turning scornfully towards the groups of men and women standing round, he said to his companion, 'Ils regardent ce que je regarde, mais ils ne voient pas ce je vois.' He little thought that the scene he gazed on was a picture of his own life.

Meditating on this, I drew back and closed the window, and I felt that I was prepared to enter, with a better understanding and a deeper sympathy, into the career of Félicité de Lamennais.

CHAPTER I

A RESTLESS YOUTH.   ORDINATION

FÉLICITÉ ROBERT DE LAMENNAIS was born at St. Malo on June 19, 1782, in the house which is now No. 3 Rue St.-Vincent. Anyone seeing it for the first time, and knowing nothing of its history, would naturally conclude that this large solid building, standing back from the street, and entered by a courtyard, in striking contrast to its neighbours, must have been owned by a family of some local importance; and so it was. Tradition tells us of the Roberts, 'that in character they were doggedly persevering and energetic, a bold and resolute race of men, who had been known on occasion, impelled by their indomitable nature, to resort to strange extremities.' Féli's[1] father, Pierre-Louis Robert de la Mennais, made his fortune as a shipowner, and he seems to have made patriotic use of his wealth—so much so, indeed, that the Estates of Brittany demanded for him, from Louis XVI., letters of nobility, quoting as their reason, besides innumerable instances of disinterested public action, the special fact that he had once saved the town from starvation, by providing corn at his own expense. The request was granted, and M. Robert was ennobled

[1] The name by which he was familiarly known among his friends.

in 1788, receiving as his coat of arms the suitable emblems, an anchor and an ear of corn. It was probably about this time that he added to his family name the designation of *de la Mennais*, a Breton word meaning *mountain*. His wife had been a Mademoiselle Lorin, and was, through her mother, of Irish extraction.[1]

From the first Féli was weak and fragile. He nearly died soon after his birth of an internal disease which troubled him all his life. We are told by one who had special facilities for getting to know the family traditions, that

> his features recalled in many ways those of Madame Lorin. He resembled her in his broad high forehead, his thin oval face and high cheek bones, his grey eyes, his thin lips, his slender body. He was under the average height. Of an extraordinary and feverish vivacity, resulting from a nervous, excitable temperament, he was, in childhood, domineering, irritable, and subject to fits of anger, which were often ended by fainting. He kept aloof from the other children, and rarely joined in their games; a vague feeling of superiority seemed to incline him to solitude.

When he was seven years old he was suddenly deprived of that softening influence so necessary in early life, a mother's love and sympathy. Madame de la Mennais died in 1789. In after years he used

---

[1] 'There were,' says M. Roussel, 'six children. . . . Louis-Marie was born on September 12, 1776; Pierre-Jean on June 24, 1778; Jean-Marie on September 8, 1780; Félicité on June 19, 1782; Marie-Joseph on February 25, 1784; and Gratien-Claude on May 2, 1785.

'Marie, in 1814, became the wife of Ange Blaize, and had several children, amongst others Augustine, who in 1836 married M. Elie de Kertanguy.'

to say that he could only remember two things about her, that he had seen her 'recite her rosary and play on the violin.' After this he became still more sad and reserved, though he seems, from time to time, to have broken through the monotony of his gloomy and isolated existence by unexpected outbursts of daring self-assertion, as in the scene he described to a friend in later life, when he spoke to him 'of an adventurous drifting on the sea in a boat furtively untied, and of the emotions caused him by this perilous defiance of the treacherous waters.'

Nor was the Revolution without its influence in the formation of his character. M. de la Mennais, who had, as we have seen, received very special marks of favour from the government of Louis XVI., seems to have gone, outwardly at least, with the times. After the fall of the unfortunate monarch, he is said to have scandalised the good people of St. Malo by hanging out of one of his ships, as a sign, an emblem of the head of the ex-king, dripping with blood. For this and other, perhaps more substantial, acts of patriotism, he was rewarded by a reputation for good citizenship, and even obtained under the Directory a certificate of civic virtue, valuable at a time when the unquiet state of Brittany rendered its chief towns liable to constant visits from Republican armies, accompanied by proconsular proscriptions of leading citizens. On the other hand, there is evidence which tends to show that the republicanism of the wealthy shipowner was not very deep-rooted—in fact, that it had for its principal motive the preservation of life and property. Had any of his Republican friends been present, on certain days, in a small upper room in the Hôtel de la Mennais, they would have been somewhat taken aback by the unexpected picture which would have presented itself to them. There, in the early hours of the morning, they would have seen a group of kneeling worshippers, from time to time timorously glancing round, or starting at the slightest movement in the street below, while, in their midst, standing before an improvised altar, a non-juring priest was saying Mass. They might have noticed one of the sons of the house, Jean-Marie, performing the office of server, while his younger brother, Féli, sat by the door and listened anxiously for the slightest sound.

Remembering this in after life, associating with his earliest thoughts at a time when, at the dawning of intelligence, the mind expands, in sympathetic longing to every new impression, these stealthy communings with God, threatened by the jealous watchfulness of a vigilant police, the labours of the venerable priest, carried on at the risk of his life, it is not surprising that the young Féli should have conceived an incurable hatred of the Revolution.

Yet this was not the most serious result of the disorganised state of society in which he grew up. The whole system of education, which had been largely in the hands of ecclesiastical bodies, had been shattered in the over-hasty progressiveness of the early revolutionists, and the administrative confusion which reigned everywhere, together with the continuous warring of parties in Paris, made impossible, for a time at least, the establishment of anything to take its place. This being so, the boy's education was undertaken by his uncle Robert des Saudrais.

The task does not seem to have been an easy one. The self-willed Féli was industrious enough, but he liked to set about a thing in his own way. In learning Latin, for instance, he seems to have objected to the technical preliminaries. Looking over one of his early note-books, M. Blaize came upon some amusing evidences of these youthful strugglings.

'Noé eut trois fils, Shem, Cham et Japhet: Noemus habuit tres filius, Shemus, Chamus et Japhetus.—Ces arbres sont très bien fleuris: Hi arbores sunt optimi floridi.—Ce thème a été fait par moi: Hic scriptio factus est ab ego.' And at the bottom of the page: ' My uncle is angry with me, because I will not read over my rules before doing my work.' Opposite is an epigram on the monks: 'Facere officium talitar qualiter, sinere tempus ire ut vult ire, et semper benedicere de domino Priori.' And underneath: 'Panurge, who could speak ten languages, knew of sixty-three ways of making money, the most honest of which was stealing it.' In the same note-book there is a suggestive English quotation: 'You must know that i am very well descended: my ancestors have made some noise in the world. For my mother cried oysters, and my father beat a drum : i am told we even had some trumpeters in our family.'

When Féli's rebelliousness proved more than he could cope with, his uncle used to lock him up in the library, a punishment which he soon came to like, and which he tried to earn as often as possible, with the result that, at an early age, he read everything without restriction. Diderot, Voltaire, Rousseau, were studied with eagerness, but the last seems to have made the deepest impression on him. It is not, then, surprising that, when, at the age of twelve, an attempt was made to prepare him for his first communion, he should have poured forth, at the second lesson of the catechism, such a volume of incredulity that the good priest retired gasping with astonishment and grief.

Of the next few years of his life but little is known.

One day [says M. Forgues, the friend of his last years] he spoke at some length of a trip to Paris with his father, under the Directory. It had come back to his memory *à propos* of some discussion on liberty and its compatibility with order. In this respect the Paris of 1796 had made a deep impression on him. 'Never,' he said, 'has the like of it been seen,' and he described the gaiety of a people given over to itself, the absence of all constraint and of all police, or, at least, of any that made itself felt, opinions uttered freely everywhere, the arena of journalism open to all who wished to enter it. 'So much so,' he added, 'that I myself, at the age of fourteen, managed to get one or two articles into some obscure paper.'

We are also told that, with his faith, he lost the

innocence of his first years. He seems to have struck out wildly in every direction, seeking vaguely and without guidance for an outlet for that burning thirst for action which followed him through his whole career, goading him on. His father, who had lost the greater part of his fortune in the troubles of the Revolution, and who had not much to leave him, wished him to learn to earn a living for himself. He set him to work in his office, with the intention of ultimately making over the business to him. Féli submitted to this, but he spent all his spare time in study and in other forms of intellectual activity. He conceived a passion for mathematics, languages, and music. He belonged to a musical society at St. Malo, where he excelled in playing the flute. Nor did he despise the noble art of fencing, and he became skilled with the rapier. He even fought a duel, and it is on record that he wounded his adversary. From time to time he seems to have determined to settle down to his work, and schemes for making his fortune were matured in his brain. There is a published letter in which he speaks of a privateer fitted out by some friends of his; he has a share in it, and believes that it will bring in a large booty. But, on the whole, he seems to have been bored with business, and, indeed, with his home surroundings. He had reached the age of nineteen, and was in the full swing of this kind of life when he said: 'Ennui was born in the family circle, on a winter evening.' In fact, so utterly disgusted had he become with the inanity and aimlessness of his existence that he wrote a letter to a cousin of his, setting forth the idea of emigration to the colonies, where he might succeed in working out a career for himself. Fortunately this half-formed resolution was not acted upon, and he remained to fulfil his mission to France and to the world.

What that mission was to be he knew not, and as yet no thought of it had entered his mind. He had already, it is true, found employment for his pen, but those early articles of his, could they be traced, would probably hardly repay the trouble of looking for them, while the poetical attempts which have come down to us, and whose constant theme is love and nature, a fact which is suggestive enough, have no particular merit in themselves, and contain very little that is interesting from a biographical point of view. On the other hand, there is one little work which must be mentioned here, throwing as it does considerable light both on the author's state of mind at this period and on the influences which had contributed to the formation of his character and the evolution of his thought. It is a criticism of a harmless custom which sprang, indirectly at least, from the Revolution.

As soon as the Consulate had restored the administrative regularity and respect for law which had been somewhat shaken by the series of upheavals through which France had passed, the wealthy bourgeois municipalities, composed of respectable citizens, who had been fortunate enough to come out of the process alive, and with their pockets not quite empty, began to congratulate themselves on what had happened, and to speak and act as if the whole movement had been carried out by and for themselves. One of the most curious results of this was that the later months of the consular *régime* and the early years of the empire were marked in most of the French towns by the renaming of streets, an inexpensive though effective way of doing honour to the heroes of philosophy and literature. At some time, probably in 1805, the municipal council of St. Malo decided to follow the example of its neighbours. This was the occasion of a scathing satire from the pen of Féli. It is not known how or where it was published, but a fragment of it was found, in manuscript, among the papers of the late Superior of the Oratory at Rennes, and has been given to the public by M. Roussel in a recent work.

'A curious report,' says the author, 'has come to us from St. Malo. It is said that it has been proposed to exhume all that the town has produced in notable men of every variety, and to post up one of them in every street.' The honour, it is true, is a doubtful one, but admitting the wisdom of the plan proposed by the council they should be careful in their choice. Now, it has been suggested that ' to the La Bourdonaies, the Cartiers, the Dugué-Trouins, there should be added a man whose family has for some time enjoyed a well-merited esteem, the whole of which he has unselfishly left to them, for assuredly he has kept none of it for himself: I speak of La Mettrie.' It was suggested at the council that he was 'a fool, a mountebank, a vile minion of the Court, without morals, without religion, without a God.' It was answered that he was a philosopher, and that the accusations about him were scandals invented by the priests. . . . 'I am not a priest, so perhaps I may be allowed to give my opinion.

But no; I prefer that you should have that of Voltaire, for neither, I think, was he a priest. 'Have you,' he wrote, 'have you ever heard speak of a doctor called La Mettrie, an honest atheist, a celebrated glutton? His ideas are in a constant firework state, incessantly going off like squibs. He has just got published at Potsdam a work *in which he condemns virtue and praises vice, invites his readers to every kind of immorality*, and this with the best intentions in the world. . . . . God preserve me from employing him as my doctor: he would give me some sublimated corrosive instead of rhubarb, innocently enough, and then would laugh at the result.'

I wish, gentlemen, that I could stop here; I really feel what your tenderness for your illustrious compatriot must make you suffer, for the man who speaks is not a *dévot*. But you may reassure yourselves: I shall be discreet; just one more passage.

Then follows another quotation from the same writer, after which our young author continues:—

Few, perhaps, are aware to what we owe these fine testimonies of the great Lama of Ferney. Oh, miracle of philosophic providence! La Mettrie, as a simple doctor, would only have poisoned his fellow-countrymen; but La Mettrie, become a citizen of the world, owed himself to the human race, and he paid his debt by his writings. But what was the origin of this high destiny? Alas! a woman's head; and yet there are people who say that women have no heads. The father of our philosopher, one day, like the stork in the fable, determined to entertain his friends. La

Mettrie, who apparently did not like plain broth, and who, though a simple assistant at a hospital, had developed a taste for experiments, thought he would strengthen the soup with the leavings of a dissection at which he had been present in the morning. The head of a woman, adroitly slipped into the pot, while the cook was looking the other way, prepared for her a great surprise, and, for the guests, a dish novel enough at least in those days. But there is no accounting for tastes: this soup was not liked . . . . . and our young anatomist, nobly incensed, and, perhaps too, a little frightened at the reception his first experiments met with in his native place, prudently retired to Berlin, where a fatal fit of indigestion soon proved, in spite of his reasonings, that he was neither a *plant nor a machine.* Now, whatever may be said to the contrary, without the head and without that journey, La Mettrie had probably remained unknown to Voltaire and to Europe.

Then follows a quotation from Diderot, in the middle of which the manuscript suddenly breaks off, leaving us to imagine as best we may the further developments and the conclusion of this fantastic little squib. Of its immediate influence on the population and on the municipal council history tells us nothing, but there is a fact which is more eloquent than history. It is immortalised on stone and may still be seen at the corner of the Rue la Mettrie at St. Malo.

But, whatever may have been its fate with the public, the pamphlet was certainly appreciated by one whose opinion its author had learned to respect, and who probably looked on it as the first step in the career of a Voltaire or of a Rabelais—M. des Saudrais, or 'Tonton,' as he was familiarly called by the two brothers. There is a letter from him in 1806 to the younger of them, in which he says: 'I have read your little satire, my dear Féli. Nothing could be better. It is clear and precise. That is the *multa in paucis* I recommended to you. He who can write thus knows his subject.' And further on in the same letter: 'This little work, which I am sending back to you, is really the best thing you have done. Je crois que tu irais loin sur ce chemin-là, et, peut-être, au bout du chemin. But your health, your health ! . . . . . Who is hurrying you? Your whole life is before you. . . . . . "I have done nothing to-day." Have you not lived ?'

These last words indicate a change which was coming about in the life and prospects of the young De la Mennais, who had finally resolved to settle down to his books and to give up all idea of succeeding his father in his business, thus inaugurating those years of painful toilings and battlings with himself and with the world from which, after many alternations between doubtful victories and almost hopeless defeats, after more than one recurrence of those terrible fits of despondency which crushed him to the earth, and held him for days and weeks, as it were, lying in the dust, he was finally to emerge suddenly, and in the full glory of his genius, as a writer and as a thinker. At the moment at which we have arrived he was on the eve of his first great struggle.

I have already alluded to the touching picture of Jean-Marie de la Mennais serving at Mass, in the silence and mystery of a small upper room, under the

Terror. From his earliest childhood, no doubt, no obstacle seems to have crossed his path, or to have turned him aside for an instant from his vocation. When, in the early years of the Revolution, he heard that the bishop was about to fly the country, he said to him: 'Monseigneur, you are my bishop, I want to be a priest, and I will follow you!' And he was only kept back with difficulty. It was he who was the cause of his father's house becoming a refuge for the holy man, who fulfilled there the office of his ministry all through those trying times. He had met him walking about disguised as a fisherman, and had asked him to come in, adding: 'Won't you stay always with us? I will serve your Mass every day. I, too, want to become a priest. I shall devote myself to this religion which they wish to destroy.' When the bishop came back from exile it was told him that Jean de la Mennais wished to prepare for ordination. As they happened to be in Paris the good man took him to the Rue Vaugirard, and, bringing him into a church, he said to him: 'We are in the chapel of what was formerly the abbey of the Carmelites. On this very spot, just nine years ago, a number of priests and bishops were cut down or shot, in hatred of the faith. Here you can see the marks of blood which have not yet disappeared, and the executioners are still living. Do you think that they will not begin again?' And Jean answered: 'With the grace of God, Monseigneur, I shall have strength.' In December 1801 he received sub-deacon's orders, and three years later he proceeded to the priesthood. In the same year he persuaded his brother, who had reached the age of twenty-two, to make his first Communion.

Soon after this his health broke down through over-work as a vicaire at St. Malo. His father advised him to go with Féli to Paris, where they might see a good doctor. They passed the spring of 1806 in the capital, and they were told that both of them were suffering from over-work. In July they returned to St. Malo, in which place they got gradually better. They had been recommended 'country air, a *régime* of milk, much exercise, and very little intellectual work.' It is needless to say that this last piece of advice was lost on them. Their uncle *Tonton* had constantly to write to them to warn them against over-reading, against trying to furnish their minds before they had formed them, pointing out to them the advantage of the *multa in paucis* alluded to in the letter quoted above. What was the result of their imprudence we are not told, but we are not surprised to find the Abbé Jean writing in August 1807 : 'We have retired (Féli and I) to a country house of ours, situated some miles from Dinan, and we have forbidden ennui to come near us. So far it has not dared once to knock at our door. But health has not been so docile. However, I am not worse than I was, and the doctor thinks that not to be worse is to be better.'

It is not too much to say that this illness led to the conversion of Féli. We can imagine him, tired and disgusted with the variety and the aimlessness of the life he had led, meditating on the past, or, perhaps, turning his thoughts vaguely to the future as he lingered in the shady woods at La Chênaie, wandering over the soft greensward, picking his way among the mossy roots of the trees while he listened to the rustling of the autumn leaves and to the soft murmuring of the wind in the branches. We can think of him in the evening as he strolled with his brother by the pond at the bottom of the garden, where no human voice could reach them, and where their conversation was undisturbed by any sound save the cracking of the twigs under their feet, the twittering of the birds in the trees, the tapping of the wood-pecker, the croaking of the frogs in the pond, the incessant buzzing of the gnats, or the humming of the myriads of winged insects which swarmed round the falling leaves, or worried, in thirsty expectancy, the fading petals of the dying flowers. What a contrast to the life he had been leading! To the noise and din, to the excitement of the world he had left behind him! Add to this the arguments, the reasonings, the enthusiasm, the burning sympathy, above all the example of his holy brother, and it is not difficult to understand the change which came over his mind. And, to Féli de la Mennais, no half measures were possible. When he turned his back upon the past, his whole nature seems to have been shaken by a violent reaction. Unfortunately, there is no immediate evidence of what took place, but there are two letters, written soon afterwards, which we cannot read without a shudder at the terrible, almost hopeless struggle to which they bear witness. The first of them is dated March 17, 1809. In it he says:—

Oh! Too deeply have I loved the bitter joys of the world, the consolations of the world, the hopes of the world! Now, I wish only for the cross, the cross alone, the cross of Jesus. . . . I shall live on Calvary in a spirit of love, of denial of self, of sacrifice. Oh! what a life! What a sweet, what a happy life! My only desire is to be crucified with Jesus by suffering, by contradiction, by contempt, in rebuffs, in ingratitudes and hatreds, in outrages, in persecutions, in everything which may crucify my heart and my flesh. . . . I must drink long draughts from the holy cup of humiliation. My God! My God! Once more, the cross, the cross and nothing but the cross!

The second letter is undated, but M. Roussel places it somewhere between 1808 and 1810. The Abbé Bruté had evidently written to him about some work of his, possibly the 'Réflexions sur l'état de l'Eglise.' We can imagine what this pious though perhaps too mystical priest had said to him; indeed, it is written in every line of the answer:—

Ah! you are right; a single page, a single line, a single word of St. François de Sales or of the 'Imitation' is worth more than all these controversial pamphlets, which can but crush and dry up the soul. . . . Pray, my tender brother, pray, I implore you, for the miserable wretch, who should be, nay, who is, I say it in the deepest sincerity, filled with confusion at having even thought of raising his voice in the Church, for him whom the ancient Church would hardly have admitted to the number of its penitents, and whose life cannot be long enough to expiate a single one of his sins. . . . Oh! This is the result of my bad beginning, this is the consequence of my first wanderings. Where shall I stop? Alas! God knows. . . . Who shall grant me to enter like you, my dear friend, that night of faith, where are lost the vain phantoms of self-love and imagination! Who shall pour on my dried-up lips some drops of those pure, life-giving waters which spring up eternally from the fountain of love! O sweet fountain, fountain of gladness, of happiness and of peace, I see thee far off, as through a mist, and my heart, in its misery, is worn out with desire and faints in the ardour with which it would plunge and be lost for ever in thy mystical depths.

Dear friend, I do not know what will become of me. . . . I wish to remain in the hands of Providence as a little child. . . . Nevertheless, it seems to me that solitude would be good for me; I think I hear a voice which calls me to the desert: others shall decide, and for me it only remains to say from the depths of my soul: *Ecce venio ut faciam, Deus, voluntatem tuam.*

What a background of internal misery and of black, hopeless despair is here revealed to us. This sudden resolution, half formed it is true, yet afterwards supported by all the intensity of his deep, impressionable nature, gave his friends reason to fear for his mental stability, and it is not improbable that the strain might have proved too great, and that some fatal catastrophe might have ensued, had not his inborn passion for work turned these outbursts from the smouldering fires of immature genius, for a time at least, into other and safer channels.

Before entering into a description of his life and work at La Chênaie, it will be necessary to mention a circumstance of considerable import in the development of this story. In February, 1809, the Abbé Jean wrote to Bruté from St. Malo, asking him whether the ordination was to take place in the first week in Lent, as his brother wished to make his arrangements. He added: 'Papa does not know of his resolution, and will not hear of it till the moment is come for carrying it out . . . please keep my brother's secret till you hear from me again; speak of it only to God.' After this we hear that Féli received minor orders on December 23, 1809. His state of mind did not allow him to go further, and, for the present, the matter remained at this point. This fact being noted, we may return to La Chênaie.

It has been said of Lamennais that, though a wide, he was not a deep reader, that there was no order or method in his studies, and that his work all along bore traces of the time when, as a punishment, he was locked into the library by his uncle. This I should be inclined to doubt, for reasons which I shall now lay before my readers; but there is one criticism which is not without a certain amount of truth. 'Forced,' says M. Ferray,[1] 'to live in the wilds of Brittany . . . in the uncouth solitude of La Chênaie, he did not learn to know society with the diversity and the wealth of detail which it presents to the observer.' If, however, he neglected this important element in mental training, and, as we shall see, with the most fatal results on his later career he did his best to make up for it in other ways.

Fumbling [says M. Forgues] among the piles of documents which, by his will, have come into my hands, when I

---

[1] Professor of Philosophy in the Faculté des Lettres at Lyons, quoted by Ricard.

examine those in which the coarse, bluish paper and the faded ink indicate a far-off origin, I find traces of implacable study. I hold in my hand a translation of the *Œdipus Tyrannus*; the margins are covered with notes :— θοάζειν, to hasten to seat oneself. Ten lines on θοάζειν. The next note-book, a model of caligraphy, is an extract from Viger's 'Principal Idioms of the Greek Language.' Here is a table of conjugations. The energetic aorist or paragogic future of Erpenius appears in it beside the apocopated future. Then comes a plan for an Arabic grammar. . . . Another manuscript bears the title: *Rules for the changes of the vowel points in masculine substantives*; these masculine substantives are Hebrew. The next treats of accents, after Buxtorf—the tonic and euphonic accent, the ὀξύτονος and the παροξύτονος of the Greeks, which the Hebrews called . . .

In 1809 we find him writing to the Abbé Jean on a series of fundamental questions. It is evident that he has faith in his brother's superior knowledge. He asks :—

Geology : What must we think of these superimposed strata, formed of shells which differ from the known kinds in proportion as they are distant from the surface of the ground? *Chronology :* Which text must we follow, the Hebrew or the Septuagint? *Creation :* Can we do without the system of Deluc, which treats the six days as six indefinite periods of time? *Criticism :* What are the works which are essential, and those which are merely useful, and in what degree? What does M. Garnier think of Masclef's system of reading? Is the knowledge of Masoretic points indispensable? Note the best books on Oriental languages. Plan of study, method, &c.

In the same year he asks his brother to send him 'the *Essai sur la première formation des langues, &c.*,

translation from the English of Adam Smith, also the *Recherches sur la langue et la philosophie des Indiens*, analysis and translation from the German of F. Schlegel.' In another letter he says :—' Send me Guarin's Hebrew Grammar, 2 vols. in 4to. I have been using your room since yesterday. I can hear nothing there but the wind and the noise of my own footsteps. . . .' These extracts (and they might be multiplied indefinitely) are, I think, sufficient evidence that his reading was neither shallow nor wanting in method. On the other hand, there is sometimes a certain apparent lightness of treatment in dealing with works which he has hardly looked at, or which he has seen reviewed, resulting, not so much from want of profundity as from a quickness of perception and over-confidence in himself, which is not necessarily a grievous fault. Witness this letter to M. Querret; it is dated 1814 :—

What is this book on probabilities by M. de Laplace? Have you read it? As it is very probable that I shall not do so, I should like to know what one ought to think of it, and, above all, whether his theory can be usefully applied. I imagine that he has tried to bring under his system moral and historic probabilities, and perhaps even supernatural facts, so that his book, or his formulæ, may be looked on as a kind of geometrical profession of faith. It seems to me that his subject must force him to go thus far: if he has fallen short of this, he has more common sense than I gave him credit for. It is a pity that the newspapers do not contain more about scientific works. One would like to follow the human mind in all its paths even where it is mistaken, to observe it in any of the forms it may take, though these are sometimes curious enough. Between ourselves, how supremely entertaining are its great efforts and its little devices for hiding from itself its profound ignorance and its utter helplessness. One laughs at them, or at least one smiles, and one is inclined to say with the poet: *Homunculi quanti sunt cum recogito !* [1]

But Féli de la Mennais did not confine his studies to the domain of history, languages, physical science, and Biblical criticism. He relieved the monotony of his work by turning from time to time to the writings of the great French, and sometimes of German, metaphysicians. In the Malebranches, the Descartes', the Leibnitz', he found congenial food for that taste for speculation which was a second nature to him. This was comparatively harmless, so long as he wandered in those regions which are the only legitimate domain of purely abstract thought, but it became very dangerous when he attempted to descend with it to the earth and to apply it to the practical things of this world. Thus we are not surprised to find a warning letter from his uncle 'Tonton' :—

What a thing it is [he writes] to be able to stir up passion! Yours for Bonald quite gives him over to me. 'I should not like him,' you say, 'to transform his monarchy into a despotism.' But that is the kernel of his whole doctrine; it is just there that I find the weak point in his system. . . . No doubt his book will live, but it will not be widely read. . . . Even when he is right, his rightness is too inaccessible and too absolute. It is the fault of metaphysicians . . . . they always think that they have got *the* truth. . . . How could they question what is infallibly demonstrated to them? And yet, these infallible demon-

---

[1] Plautus, *Captivi* (prologue).

strations are often but illusions. . . . There is not a single great metaphysician who could not be cited in proof of this assertion. . . . It is only natural. They leave things and run after *causes*. . . . They build as well on the void as on the solid, and out of nothing as when they use matter. However . . . . these people have a right to astonish us by the breadth and by the depth of their conceptions, and when they unite with this, as did Malebranche, that force of imagination, that magnificence of expression, we must admire and be silent . . . . for, where genius passes, it draws you, it drags you along, and it carries you where it will. . . . Your logic, my dear Féli, is very rigid, very severe, and very ruthless. Could you not soften it a little ?

But these days of preparation were not all passed in such congenial occupations. In 1807 the Abbé Jean had been appointed Vicar General of the diocese of St. Brieuc, and, as soon as his health permitted it, he had gone to the scene of his new duties, leaving to his brother the sole responsibility for the management of La Chênaie. Thus the labours of maturing genius were picturesquely varied by details of house and farm work, as well as by the usual practical anxieties entailed in looking after the property. We smile when he tells us that he has had to cut down the wages of all the servants, that they have not grumbled very much, and when he continues writing to his brother :—

I have just settled with the gardener of whom I spoke to you, and who was brought here by the man who fulfils the same function at La Buparais. This last would have liked to come to us himself, but he could not resist the entreaties of Madame de la Buparais, who wanted to keep him. Ours is a young man of twenty-four. He has been earning in his present place 156 francs, and he has had half the product of the vegetables. We shall have no vegetables to sell, and can only pay him 140 francs. He seems satisfied, and I think we shall like him.

Then there is a pleasant odour of fresh-cut wood, prosaically mingled with bricks and mortar, in the following :—

I shall not send any wood to St. Malo, for the bad would not sell there, and we want the good for the chapel. . . . I have drawn a little plan of the last, which you shall see; I think it will do. It would not be a long business with workmen who had any activity in them; but ours are slowness itself, especially the masons. Tempus et patientia. . . . Please find out how much the plasterer in St. Malo charges by the *toise*, if they are supplied with everything; also how much plaster is required for a *toise* of ceiling; as it is expensive, I am having lime mixed with it.

We cannot but be amused at this woeful description of the unpleasant results of riding over the rough country roads :—

I have just come from Plesder, very headachy. Really our parish is too far off. On Friday I doubted whether I should be able to go over there to-day, I was so broken and flayed, and besides I had begun to spit blood, but that did not last. . . . . That was the trouble I spoke to you of, and I should have taken care not to mention it had the least trace of it remained. The worst of all ce sont mes fesses, à qui, pour comble de malheur, je ne puis dire leurs vérités en face.

On the other hand, this period is not wanting in literary interest. To it belong the *Réflexions sur l'état de l'Eglise en France*, 1808; the *Guide spirituel*, 1809, and the *Tradition de l'Eglise sur l'institution des évêques*, the publication of which was deferred for reasons which will presently appear. These works were the joint production of the two brothers. The raw material, as a rule, was supplied by the Abbé Jean, while the arrangement and composing were done by Féli. Of the *Guide* it is sufficient to say that it was the result of a long familiarity with the meditations of a Benedictine mystic of the sixteenth century. The *Réflexions* appeared at the time when Napoleon was preparing for his great conflict with the Church and with Pius VII., and it may be regarded as the first indication of the ardent Ultramontanism which was afterwards to characterise the writings of De la Mennais. The authors suggested a series of reforms, calculated to breathe new life into the dry bones of official State Catholicism, and it is not surprising that the book should have been badly received by the Imperial Government, in spite of its incidental praise of 'the man of genius who has just restored to France monarchy and religion.' It was seized by the police.

The *Tradition*, as its title suggests, was occasioned by a later phase in the struggle.

The story of the brutal conduct of Napoleon, and of the heroic resistance of the Holy Pontiff, who maintained his ground till he was literally broken in mind and body, has so often been told that it need not be repeated here; but there are one or two circumstances of which I must remind my readers. Failing in his attempt to win over the Pope, the Emperor resolved to try what he could do with the bishops, who were more directly under his sway, and most of whom were his nominees. He called them together in what he called a national council, and used what means he could to force them into giving their sanction to the measures he proposed to them. When they resisted he bethought himself of the odious device of calling on them separately for their signatures, but even here he was hardly more successful. We can imagine the enthusiasm with which the news was received by those French Catholics who, while pining for freedom, had not dared openly to make their voices heard in the ominous silence which reigned everywhere. It was now that Féli wrote to his brother (La Chênaie, 1811) :—'How Providence plays with human passions, and with the power of men who are called great! There was one who had forced the world to bow before him, and, suddenly, some poor bishops saying simply "I cannot" broke that power, which thought that nothing could stand before it . . . in his very capital, at the seat of his empire. How grand! How divine!' He then asks Jean to bring him a rosary, and adds: 'Aie soin de le faire choisir tel que les Gloria patri soient aisés à reconnaître au tact.'

But Napoleon was in earnest. The Pope had refused to institute his bishops, and he was determined to proceed without him. When the Archbishop of Paris died he tried to get someone to take his place. Unfortunately it was no easy matter to find anyone willing to accept the honour and dignity of the position at the expense of his conscience and his reputation, and the Emperor was somewhat embarrassed.

But help came from an unexpected quarter. Cardinal Maury, who had distinguished himself in the Constituent Assembly by his faithfulness to the monarchy and to the Holy See, who had emigrated to Rome, where he had used his influence in bringing down ecclesiastical censures on the different phases of the Revolution, and who had been rewarded for his zeal and devotion with a cardinal's hat, now came forward and declared himself willing to accept the position. As a result, there was offered to the world the scandal of an archbishop repudiated by the Pope and unrecognised by his clergy. These events called forth from the brothers De la Mennais the *Tradition de l'Église sur l'Institution des Évêques*.

As in the case of the other works I have mentioned, the materials had been for the most part collected by the Abbé Jean, while the composing was done by Féli, and this part of the work was by no means easy, for the writer had not as yet attained to that knowledge of, or confidence in, his own powers which marked him in his later life. For the moment his brother is all, he is nothing. Thus he writes in 1811:—

> It seems that each day only brings with it a deeper conviction of my perfect ineptitude. I can neither study, nor compose, nor act; I can do nothing. This absolute incapacity is beginning to reconcile me to the utter uselessness of my life. I cannot bury in the ground or put out to interest a talent which I have not received. What am I fit for? Suffering perhaps; that must be the way in which I am intended to glorify God. But I must not complain of my lot.

In 1810 he had written :—

In speaking of St. John Chrysostom, I have brought in very well I think what Dom Constant says of the liberalism of the first Popes . . . I have got to Nestorius, and I am at page 90. I could never have finished at St. Malo—I see this more and more every day—and even here I am not getting on very brilliantly. The thing that drives me wild is the uniformity of the whole business; one must continually keep saying the same things, and then there is the difficulty of bringing all this into any kind of shape; but that is in the nature of the work.

And in the same year there is a letter written in wild distraction :—

Since you left I have hardly begun the last division of the first part. I cannot get on. After having sweated profusely for an hour I find myself precisely at the same point. Besides, the subject itself stops me. We must talk over it together before I do anything more.

When the book was finished its publication was prevented by the imperial police, who could not look with favour on this marshalling of accumulated facts in support of the rights of the Pope in the institution of bishops. It did not appear till after the fall of Napoleon in 1814. When it was given to the public it drew the attention of the world to the intrepid champions of the spiritual power, exciting the enthusiasm of the clergy and the suspicion of the governing classes; but as a literary work it does not seem to have had much success. There is probably a delicate vein of condolence in the words of the Abbé Teysseyre in September of that year when he wrote: 'I no longer hear anyone speak of your work;

finding it impossible to refute it, they wish to forget it.' Nevertheless, this book was of great personal importance to its author; in a sense it became the instrument of fate which drew him, perhaps in spite of himself, to a step, the results of which, as a blessing or as a curse, were to follow him through the rest of his life.

Napoleon returned from Elba in the spring of 1815, and it was felt that it would not be long before measures were taken against the author of so daring an attack on his policy. To shield his brother, whose responsible position at St. Brieuc made him an easy object for attack, Féli retired to London, where he lived for some months under the assumed name of Patrick Robertson. Of his doings in the English capital many interesting anecdotes are told, and of these not the least entertaining is the one in which it is related that when he was recommended to a lady as tutor to her children she hardly waited to hear what he had to say for himself, but dismissed him at once because, as she said, 'he looked too stupid.'

But it is from a more serious point of view that this residence in a Protestant centre is especially interesting.

Coming thus to a strange country, and finding himself among a people so different to that to which he had been accustomed, and of whose language he had but an imperfect knowledge, it was natural that he should have sought the society of those of his compatriots who were living there in exile like himself.

It was in this way that he came to know a number of French ladies of noble blood whose fortunes had been lost in the Revolution, and who lived, for the sake of economy and for greater facility in the exchange of social and spiritual sympathy, in a kind of religious community. These good people introduced him to their director, the Abbé Carron, who obtained, almost immediately, an unbounded influence over him. As a result of this, and also perhaps through an awakening of antipathy to his Protestant surroundings, easily understood in his impressionable temperament, Féli de la Mennais became much more thorough in his Catholicism than he had been when living in the midst of his own people. There are signs in his correspondence of an ardent apostolic zeal which led him to praiseworthy, though not always very practical, attempts to convert to the true faith members of the heretical population in the midst of which he found himself. In September 1815 he wrote to the Abbé Jean to tell him that he had met in the house he was staying at a boy of thirteen who had taken a fancy to him, and whose parents had consented to his becoming a Catholic, provided that the trouble and expense of educating him was taken off their hands :—

> I have given them no answer [he continues], but I have spoken to M. Carron, who says that though one should neglect nothing where the saving of a soul is concerned, nevertheless such a burden would weigh very heavily on us. . . . In case you should think that the thing cannot be done with prudence, please write to me and say that the political situa-

tion in France and the uncertainty of your residence at St. Brieuc do not permit you to take on yourself an engagement of this nature.

Is it necessary to state that this idea was never carried out? Much more touching and more characteristic is his connection with Henry Moorman. This young man became firmly attached to him, and eventually was received into the Catholic Church. His parents opposed the change, and tried to prevent all intercourse with the young Frenchman. Moorman seems to have rather enjoyed the idea of a clandestine correspondence. He wrote to Féli, telling him that several of his letters had been intercepted, and suggesting that he should disguise his handwriting. He even went so far as to hint that he might imitate a female hand on the envelope, and impress a pretty name on the seal. We can imagine the indignation of the young apostle, and the vehemence of his reply. This episode, however, did not end their friendship, and we are glad to hear that when Henry died, a few years afterwards, De la Mennais received a touching letter of sympathy from his father, showing that all, if not forgotten, was at least forgiven.

But to return to the Abbé Carron.

It will be remembered that Féli had received minor orders in 1809, and that this step had been preceded by a painful attack of gloomy and mystical despondency which had prevented his going any further. After that event he had settled down to his work, and this for the time had saved him, though some of his letters still bore traces of a morbid brooding over the worldly past. At the period we have reached another crisis was approaching. In April 1814 he had written to the Abbé Jean: 'I need someone who can direct me, who can strengthen me, who can support me; someone who understands me, and to whom I can say absolutely everything. On this, perhaps, depends my salvation.'

And in London he had met such a guide. On August 10, 1815, his brother wrote to M. Querret: 'I heard a short time ago from Robertson; he began, in the middle of July, a retreat, after which M. Carron had promised to decide on the course he ought to pursue; I pray God with all my heart that he may enlighten them both, but I am glad that I have nothing to do with the decision.' His director as well as his friends in France pressed him to take the irrevocable step, and yet Féli seems to have hesitated. A final and decisive conflict was raging in his perplexed and already wearied soul. Most of those whom he respected advised him to go on, but his brother stood by silent, while he himself drew back, and became more and more timid as the time for actual decision drew near. And it is this which gives a vividly pathetic interest to his correspondence at this date, and to some valuable letters brought to light by M. Alfred Roussel.

There is a piece of news which is long in coming [wrote the Abbé Teysseyre to the two brothers: the date of this letter is unknown, but it must have been written while Féli was still in France], and it is that the youngest of you, walking in the glorious footsteps of his elder brother, has contracted those sweet and holy obligations which will bind him irrevocably to his Saviour and the Church. . . . If some difficulty still stands in the way of the generous longing of his heart, let him come to us [to St. Sulpice]. . . . Yes, let him come, and we will prepare for him chains of love, but so beautiful, so light, so glorious, that they themselves must make him feel the liberty, the peace, and the joy of the children of God and of the ministers of the Lord. One of our fervent seminarists told us the other day that he had spent part of his time of meditation in wondering how one could love in this life anything but God; what would he have thought if he had been told that a soul, singularly favoured by God, had hesitated for so long to engage himself in His service?

Already in June 1812 he had written: 'Remember me to your brother. I am almost angry at your not being able to tell me that he is a priest.' In the previous year, 1811, there is a letter from Féli himself to the Abbé Jean. Speaking of a friend of theirs, he says:—

This peace of mind moves me deeply, I can hardly understand it; not that I cannot conceive that it may be possible, by faith, to put oneself above the pains of the body . . . but the wounds of the soul, the secret agony of a sick heart, in which the softest feelings are embittered, and which has no strength but to torment itself, these are incompatible with the tranquillity we admire, and leave no hope but in the eternal peace of the tomb. Unable to work, I have suffered much in these last two days. When I think of this increasing disposition to a barren and gloomy melancholy, the future frightens me; and it matters not which way I turn my eyes, the horizon threatens me; dark, heavy clouds break off from time to time, and lay waste everything that stands in their way; for me there can no more be any season but the season of storms. However, God is always a Father, even when He strikes.

And now a storm had burst upon him. The Abbé Bruté, the intimate friend of the brothers, was on his way to America, where he was to devote himself to a missionary life. He had gone off without seeing Féli, and he was still oppressed with the painful memories of leave-taking, and by the thought that perhaps he might never return, when he wrote from on board ship, November 12, 1815 :—'Féli, Féli—has he come back? Is he, will he soon be a priest? Does he still hesitate? Could it be possible? Has our sweet Jesus too many friends, too many priests in these times?' Was it possible to resist such pressure? By nature he was sympathetic and impressionable, and he only desired someone whom he could respect, whom he could lean upon, who could decide for him. His friends were unanimous in trying to induce him to take the irrevocable step, while the Abbé Jean alone was silent, and even he, perhaps, was hoping in secret for the decision which the others invoked in words. He did not resist. He returned to France in November 1815, and he was ordained subdeacon in 1816. Upon this, his brother, who had hitherto held aloof, now that the doors of the world had finally closed behind him, took the wisest course and cordially joined in leading him on. Thus, on January 4, 1816, he wrote to M. Querret, announcing the fact, and he added:—

Who could have said, last March, that he was going to England only to come upon the man whom God destined to lead him to the foot of the altar, and to bring him to a determination from which he had seemed for some time to be getting every day further and further away? Oh, Providence, this is one of Thy miracles! . . . How goes it with your political state of mind? Is it bright? Mine is black, black as ebony. Féli's is darker still.

In March Teysseyre wrote to Jean :—

Living in obedience, in spite of his natural bent, and without consolation, he has been drawn to this step as a victim. He has all the merits of love, but he has tasted none of its sweetness. . . . It is this which has led me to entertain his idea of joining the Jesuits at Rome. . . . If such a resolution had come from himself, if I had had any ground for supposing that his imagination had had the least part in it . . . I should have been in doubt about it. But, on the contrary, he had ceased to think of it for some time, and it is M. Carron who has re-awakened the idea in his mind.

It will be remembered that when he had been suffering from an attack of melancholy in 1807, Féli had hinted at a desire for solitude. He then thought of the Trappists. He had now come to the more practical idea of joining the Jesuits, who had just been restored, and who were tolerated in France, in spite of the laws against religious orders. Fortunately, this project was not carried out. He was ordained on March 9, 1816. A short time previously he had written to his sister, Madame Blaize :—' I certainly have not followed my own inclination in deciding on an ecclesiastical career. But we must try to make the best of this short life. What we give to God is little enough; nothing, in fact, and the reward is infinite.'

The Abbé Carron had tried to console him. In February he had written:—'I think, my dear friend, that it is not wise to ask God for crosses, and that we should limit ourselves to demanding the love of suffering, leaving it to Him to expose us to what He considers not to be beyond our strength. . . . But why, my Féli, this melancholy? Is not the life of a good Christian passed, as it were, in continual festivity? Does not the very thought of God give us joy?'

After the ordination matters do not seem to have improved. 'The only thing,' he wrote, 'which remains for me to do, is to make myself as comfortable as possible, and to try to go to sleep at the foot of the post to which they have fastened my chain.'

Utterly sick at heart, he tried to find comfort by going to live in Paris, with the Abbé Carron and his flock, who had returned to France. It is to this fact that we owe some painful letters from Teysseyre to the Abbé Jean. Here is an extract from one of them:—

I hasten, my dear friend, to set your mind at ease about your brother, who, I believe, has written you a letter more calculated to break your heart than to console it. He is going through a severe crisis, temptations of every kind. He is, like the prophet, hanging by a single thread over the abyss of despair. . . . He pushes his obedience so far as to say Mass nearly every day, *in spite of the horror which he seems to have of the priesthood*; and we are doing everything to occupy and divert his mind. . . . Write to him kindly, and encourage him to work with me at a great work on Indifference, the translation of the famous manuscript of Leibniz.

Speak to him, as from yourself, of a little project we have formed . . . of a society of young men trained for the defence of religion. He is saved if we can occupy and divert him, without leaving him time to breathe or to dwell on his own thoughts. . . . Enter as little as possible with him into discussion on the priesthood—a few words only, full of tenderness. . . .

Shortly before the final consummation, but when the choice was no longer open, this same M. Teysseyre had written to Feli :—

Alas! poor imperfect mortals, we said our first Mass on Mount Tabor; to you it will be given to say yours on Calvary. Your soul, perhaps, will be as the soul of Jesus in His agony, *sad unto death*. Abandoned in appearance by God and man, you will be tempted to cry out, in plaintive longing, as did our Lord: '*I thirst*'—'*My God, why hast Thou forsaken Me?*'

And this first Mass? As in the case of the ordination, no detailed account of it has come down to us, but one fact has remained which is not without its significance, for he himself became our authority for it when he afterwards declared that, as he held the newly consecrated Host in his trembling hands, he heard distinctly a voice which said to him: 'I call on you to carry my cross, nothing but the cross. . . . Remember!'

CHAPTER II.

THE ESSAY ON INDIFFERENCE

THE Abbé de Lamennais,[1] for so we must now call him, was not a man to allow himself to remain for long in a state of helpless and inactive despondency. Though there may possibly seem to be a vein of grim irony in the statement, it yet remains true that he was known among the *Feuillantines*, as the flock of M. Carron were called, as 'le jovial Mennais.' This may be accounted for partly by a very natural desire to hide from himself and others the gloomy state of his feelings in his ordinary every-day intercourse with those amongst whom he lived, and to reserve those painful outpourings from his inmost soul to more intimate moments of conversation with his closest friends, with those who had advised him to take the step, and who could therefore sympathise with him. But it may also be explained by the fact which has come down to us through one of his earliest biographers, that his moods, though extreme in their intensity, were of short duration. This writer, quoted by M. Roussel, tells us that 'one day, when he had cruelly and unreasonably scolded a servant, he begged the poor terrified girl's pardon,

---

[1] Shortly after the period at which we have now arrived, he adopted this form of his name in signing his letters.

and added : "What would you have! You know I sometimes lose control over myself, and if I had not got into a furious passion, I should have fainted."' In any case he seems to have settled down gradually to his normal occupations and to have reconciled himself by degrees to his new position. As before, he found refuge in his work, and in preparing for the contests which had inevitably to arise in the peculiar circumstances of the Restoration.

In the case of Napoleon, his opposition had been fundamental. He had hated the Emperor as being an impersonation of the Revolution. This could not be said of the monarchy, for he was an ardent Royalist, and believed that the only safety for France was in its being governed by a *legitimate* ruler. His opposition, therefore, was now directed, not against the theory, but against the practical working of the new Government, against the compromises with the previous *régime* which were forced upon it by the necessities of the case. Thus, so early as March 1815, before his departure for London, he wrote to a friend, criticising the educational legislation of the ministry. 'Have you seen,' he wrote, 'this beautiful ordinance, drawn up by the Protestant Guizot, and signed by the most Christian king? Nothing is wanting in it but religion.' And also to his brother at about the same date: 'Cursed be the daughter and the mother, the old and the new University! Cursed be the fabricators of this infernal intrusion! Cursed be those who have given it birth, or who shall contribute to the developing of it!

Cursed be the superiors, cursed be the subordinates, cursed be the whole of the infamous rabble!' After Waterloo the Abbé Jean wrote to Querret: 'I no longer fear the man from the Isle of Elba; he is played out . . . but who would not tremble at seeing, on the one hand, the feebleness of those who govern, and, on the other, the extreme corruption of the governed? . . . The Jacobins are beginning, unblushingly, to raise their heads.'

On August 10, 1815, Féli wrote to him from London:—

Great God, what times we live in! I foresee calamities, revolutions, and interminable wars. The infamous conduct of the allies is not calculated to inspire hopefulness in anyone who can see a little beyond the present. They are working, as if of set purpose, to dethrone the monarch whom they have brought back to us on their bloody bayonets. That man can no longer be viewed by the nation in any other light than as the instrument or the pretext of its disgrace and of its misfortunes. The title deed of his restoration has been signed in French blood, by the light from the burning of our towns and villages. Only a foreign army can keep him upon his throne; and if that army remains in France, if this organised plundering continues, in a word, if they treat us as Bonaparte treated Spain, we have but one example to follow, that of the Spaniards; for no misfortune can happen to a people which is not preferable to loss of honour and of independence. On the other hand, supposing that nothing of this kind come about, that the enemy retires, that internal peace is restored, and that power is consolidated in the feeble hands in which it has been placed, what can we reasonably hope for from an administration, wild, uncertain, drunk with all the principles which have tormented society for the last twenty-five years; from a king who is good, but who is so blind as to misunderstand both men and things, to place his person under the protection of murderers, and the State under the safeguard of institutions which France, for any good they have brought it, owes to the reign of Terror or to that of Napoleon. Certainly, one need not be either a prophet or the son of a prophet to foresee the results of such inconceivable madness. And who would not be frightened at these demagogic ravings, which seem suddenly to have seized a part of the nation, men, women, children, infatuated worshippers of their own frightful and laughable sovereignty? For myself, whichever way I look, I see things which make me tremble and shudder. The whole human race seems to be rushing to its destruction; it is in its death agony, and, like a wounded man, it staggers and rolls over in its own blood.

It was in no very friendly frame of mind, then, that the Abbé de Lamennais looked around him when he came to Paris and settled down, in M. Carron's house, to work and to observe. In religion, as in other departments of life, the old landmarks had disappeared. A scientific and synthetic spirit had slowly undermined the analytic and deductive methods which had at one time held undisputed sway. Bacon had finally triumphed over the schoolmen, while the once brilliant star of Descartes had paled before the rising sun of Diderot and the Encyclopædists. And the new point of view had, in a few superior minds, produced its enthusiasms and even its martyrs. Lavoisier had asked for a short respite from the guillotine for the purpose of concluding an experiment; and Condorcet had spent those last awful moments when, under sentence of death, he was probably meditating suicide, in consigning to paper some calmly philosophic thoughts on the social phenomena which were the cause of his own misfortune. But with the mass of the people this state of things had meant simply a loss of ideal and the growth of a vaguely synthetic instinct which had to be appealed to in dealing with the highest questions. Chateaubriand had recognised this when he turned for support to the æsthetic sense, and Bonald when he based himself on the traditions of mankind, while De Maistre had already shown signs of that immense constructive faculty which was to make his name immortal. On the other hand, the needs of a period of transition had been entirely misunderstood by the great genius who, at a critical moment, held in his hand the destinies of the most progressive country in Europe. Indeed, it may be said, without exaggeration, that to the Concordat of 1801 is to be chiefly attributed the unhealthy spirit which has reigned in France ever since.

This policy of Napoleon was inherited by the Restoration, and it is hardly necessary to say that the idea of a *State Church*, which had seemed almost respectable as part of a scheme for a world empire, became contemptible when it reduced religion and its ministers to the position of mere salaried agents of a monarchy which owed its very existence to the intervention of foreign powers. Thus it happened that when men were longing for a doctrine which might appeal to the highest instincts, which might offer itself as a solution of the problems that had now become of surpassing interest, a venerable institution was forced to present itself to them as a miserable caricature of its own glorious past. Can it be wondered at that they smiled when they were told that the Catholic religion was the religion of the great majority of Frenchmen, and that they looked on the existence of a creed in their legal formularies principally as an excuse for having none of their own? Superficial statesmen, it is true, saw in the general apathy only a reason for congratulating themselves on the absence of that fanaticism which had so often appeared in history with baneful results; but those who were gifted with a deeper insight into the meaning of things recognised in it a dangerous disease which, unless it were checked in time, would undermine the moral fibre of the nation. At other times, and notably during the Revolution, there had been much difference of opinion in religious matters; but then men had been sincere, and where they had ceased to believe they had begun to hate. This may have been unpleasant, but at least it was healthy. In the first years of the Restoration there was no bitterness against religion, and the guillotine was replaced by a shrug of the shoulders. The Terror had tried to suppress thought, and had but added strength to it by concentration; the Empire and the early Restoration endowed it, and, as a result, it became tame, and almost died of inertia. Men spent their days in work and their evenings in pleasure, and did not bother themselves about questions to which they could only hope for an official solution. History and the sciences were taught, under careful supervision, in the State University, while theology was clothed in the worn-out formulæ of Gallican orthodoxy by the salaried ministers of the State Church, and the precepts of religion were frigidly mumbled to sparse and apathetic congregations, in buildings set aside for that purpose by the Government.

And yet, as has been suggested, there were not wanting in that society the germs of a healthier state of things. The point of view, it is true, had changed, and the old metaphysical methods, even could they have been pursued freely, would have met with no response in an age which had become thoroughly scientific and synthetical in its ways of thought. What was wanted was a teacher who could point out the fact that religion, *as a social factor*, could no more be ignored in dealing with society than the law of gravity in the domain of physics or of astronomy, and who, strictly adhering to this principle, could show the way to a doctrine without which it was impossible for the religious instinct to express itself.

In the first years of the Restoration it did not seem likely that such a teacher would arise. The majority of the clergy willingly bowed their heads to the yoke imposed upon them by a legitimate monarch, while the lucrative posts offered by the University silenced opposition on the part of candidates for promotion in a more purely intellectual sphere. This, with the apathy of the educated laity, gave the Government every reason to hope that their policy had been successful, and that their dominion in every department would be peacefully recognised, when suddenly, in 1818, two works were given to the world, and these were followed in 1819 by a third. They went, each in its way, to the heart of the question.

Appearing thus almost simultaneously, the effect of these works in disturbing the ominous quiet of the religious atmosphere was considerable. They were entitled: *Essai historique sur les libertés de l'Eglise Gallicane; Essai sur l'Indifférence en matière de religion*, and *Du Pape*. The first was a defence of that system of State Churches which the ministry were endeavouring to establish; it was written by Grégoire, the former constitutional bishop of Blois, and, as it made a liberal and republican State a necessary condition for the successful working of the theological principle it advocated, it came into the controversy as a powerful blow to the monarchy from the side on which an attack was least expected. The last was the great masterpiece of De Maistre, in which he laid down with deep philosophic insight a complete basis for that ultramontane theory which was so much dreaded by those in power. But the second was by a comparatively unknown author, and it revealed to the world the fact that a new and dangerous champion had appeared in the Catholic camp.

In April 1817 the Abbé de Lamennais had written to his brother about a book he was engaged on: 'You will form an opinion on it when you see it.

Many a time I have felt inclined to give the whole thing up, and should have done so had not Teysseyre persuaded me to go on. In any case I do not deceive myself about what I am doing, but it is something to be able to think that Providence may cause a bad book to produce some useful results.'

And again, on November 30, 'I cannot work at my second volume. Often I feel a kind of regret at having done the first. If it were still unwritten, I should not begin it.'

The cause of these anxious misgivings was the *Essai sur l'Indifférence*, which placed its author at once in the first rank of contemporary writers. Coming, as it did, in the midst of the prevailing security, this first volume read like a withering satire on the utter rottenness of society. Its scope and its object are suggested in the opening paragraph:—

The century which is most hopelessly diseased is not that which is passionate in error, but rather that which neglects, which disdains truth. There is still vitality, and consequently hope, where violence is seen; but, when all movement has ceased, when the pulse no longer beats, when the heart has become cold, can we fail to recognise the signs of approaching dissolution?

Then follows a ruthless criticism of the state of things in France:—

Convinced [says the writer in one passage], convinced in spite of itself, of the necessity of connecting earth with heaven and man with his Creator, the statecraft of to-day enters the sanctuary and brings forth from it the Supreme Being who is adored there. It clothes Him in rags of purple, puts a reed into His hand, on His head a crown of thorns, and it shows Him to the people, saying : ' Behold your God ! ' Can it be wondered at that religion, thus humiliated and dishonoured, is received with indifference? After eighteen hundred years of fighting and of triumphs, Christianity at length meets with the same fate as its Founder. Summoned, so to speak, to appear, not before a proconsul, but before the human race, the question is put to it : *Art thou a king?* Is it true, as these accuse thee, that thou pretendest to rule over us? Then comes the answer: It is you who have said it; *I am a king*. I reign over minds by enlightening them, and over hearts by guiding their movements, and even their very desires; I reign over society by the good that I have done. The world was buried in the darkness of error, *I came to bring truth to it*; hence my mission : *he who loves the truth hears me*. But this saying has already ceased to have a meaning to perverted reason ; it must be explained to it. *What is truth?* asks the stupid, absent-minded judge ; and, without waiting for an answer, he goes out, declares that he *finds no fault* in the accused, and, washing his hands, gives religion over to the multitude to become, first their plaything and then their victim.

There is a vein of deep sarcasm in such a passage as the following :—

Among the pagans there was not a temple which had not its sacred revenues, not a divinity whom its adorers had not made independent by endowing his altars ; but the God of the Christians, hardly admitted to a temporary salary, figures every year in an insulting budget as a pensioner of the State. . . . Statecraft may smile complacently at the sublime outcome of its maxims ; it may congratulate itself on the peace which it has succeeded in establishing between hostile religions; this does not excite our wonder, but our tears. Peace, profound peace, reigned also over those dismal plains where Germanicus found, in mournful proximity, the bones of the Germans and of the soldiers of Varus.

Defining indifference, as 'the extinction of all feeling of love or hatred in the heart, through the absence of any judgment or belief in the mind,' the author subjects it to a severe analysis, classifies it in all its manifestations, pitilessly drags it forth and holds it up to ridicule in all the hideous absurdity of its manifold expressions. He sets forth, for instance, the proposition that *religion may be looked upon as a mere political institution, necessary only to the people*, and, devoting two chapters to a merciless drawing out of all its consequences, he says, amongst other things:—

I appeal to experience: what is it that has introduced irreligion to our cottages? Reasoning? No, but example; the fear of appearing credulous. . . . And certainly philosophy is strangely confident, if it seriously hopes to divide the human race into two classes, one of which is to believe for the security of the other, and is to receive in payment nothing but sarcasm; of which one is to recognise no duty but inclination, while the other is to renounce its inclinations for duties which are recognised to be chimerical; of which one is to laugh at what the other is complacently to respect; so that, on one side is to be found, with independence, everything which man hopes for in this world; and on the other, with slavery to prejudice, all that he fears and hates, and this with ridicule as a reward. What a happy, what a profoundly judicious arrangement!

Turning then to writers who, in one form or another, had advocated indifference, his heaviest blows are reserved for J. J. Rousseau and the profession of faith of the Savoyard vicar. 'If [after examining into the foundations of things] we go wrong,' had said the author of 'Émile,' 'we shall have deprived ourselves of a great excuse before the tribunal of the Sovereign Judge. Will He not rather pardon the error in which we were brought up than that which we dared to choose for ourselves?' And to this comes the pithy answer :—

A son, they say, can never be wrong in following the religion of his father. Thus, in religion, birth decides everything. In one country it is your duty to be a polytheist, in another to adore only one God. . . . Christian in Europe, Mussulman in Persia, idolater by the Congo, you will offer on the banks of the Ganges divine honours to Vishnu. Your father, who was a little credulous, worshipped a stone, or an onion. Keep up this touching domestic devotion, for a 'son can never be wrong,' &c.

Thus passage after passage is cited, and proposition is confronted with proposition, from this masterpiece of the Genevan writer, till the impression is produced on the reader that he is witnessing the dissection of a body, beautiful in form, but saturated with some fetid poison or habitual paradox, which, when stirred, causes all else to be lost in its own foulness. And yet, curiously enough, there is something in the style and method of the Abbé de Lamennais which forcibly suggests the influence over him of the author of 'Émile.' There are whole pages which might have found their place in that work, while certain passages almost make us forget that we are not dealing with the eighteenth century writer. Perhaps even the very bitterness of the attack is but an evidence of a secret liking.

As we approach the concluding arguments of this volume, the shadows become deepened, and dark, threatening clouds begin to gather on the horizon. It is useless, contends the writer, for monarchy to think that it can strengthen itself by sacrificing the highest interests to the Revolution. A terrible example of a similar policy and its results were but recently given to the world.

Then, on the ruins of the altar and the throne, over the bones of priest and sovereign, began the reign of force, the reign of hatred and of terror; a frightful fulfilment of the prophecy : 'A whole people will hurl itself, man against man, neighbour against neighbour, and, with a great tumult, the child will rise against the old man, the populace against those in power; for they have opposed their language and their inventions to God.' To describe that terrible scene of disorder, of crime, of dissolution, and of slaughter, that orgy of doctrines, that confused clashing of interests and of passions, that mingling of proscription with impure feasts, those cries of blasphemy, those sinister songs, that low, persistent knocking of the hammer of destruction, of the axe striking its victims, those horrible detonations and those roars of joy, dismal echo from a vast massacre, those widowed cities, those rivers fouled with dead bodies, those temples, those towns in ashes, murder and lust, tears and blood—one would have to borrow its tongue from hell, as some monsters have borrowed its furies.

Then, further on, is a significant note of warning :—

What is power in society if not the right to command, which presupposes the duty of obeying. But he who commands is higher than he who obeys, so much so that it is impossible to imagine a greater superiority; for it does not imply a mere difference in nature. An angel, by his nature, is higher than man; yet man, strictly speaking, owes nothing to an angel. If an angel were to clothe himself in flesh and to appear on the earth, why should I obey him? I can see, on the one hand, no right, and on the other, no duty. Every created being is, by nature, independent of every other, and if the highest of celestial spirits were to come of his own accord, and with no sanction but his will, to dictate laws to man, and to acquire dominion over him, I should see in him but a tyrant, and in his subjects only slaves. What, then, are we to think when a man arrogates to himself sovereignty over his fellow men, his equals in right, and often his superiors in intellect, in enlightenment, and in virtue? Is it possible to conceive a more iniquitous, a more insolent usurpation, or a more degrading servitude? Certainly, I do not hesitate to say with Rousseau: 'It is only after prolonged perversion of feeling and of ideas that it becomes possible for a man to recognise a master in one like to himself.'

And finally, as a conclusion to the whole argument, 'Glory to God in the highest, peace on earth to men of good will. . . . But, to those whose will is so perverted that they refuse to listen to the divine word, to love infinite goodness, to obey immutable order—*war, eternal war.*' . . .

I leave it to my readers to imagine the effect produced by a work of which the Gallican Frayssinous said: 'This book would awaken the dead.' But, there is an incident connected with its publication which is not without a humorous interest. It will be remembered that Grégoire's work, which appeared almost simultaneously with it, though equally disconcerting to the Government, was opposed to it in fundamental principle, advocating, as it did, Gallicanism, with the establishment of a republic as a necessary condition. On February 10, 1818, the

Abbé de Lamennais wrote to his brother Jean : 'I am getting them to send you fifteen copies of the Essay, together with Grégoire.' This note was followed on the 13th by another : 'Through a misunderstanding, which is very disagreeable to me, they have forwarded to you fifteen copies of Grégoire's *Essai* instead of mine. This will mean the loss of at least a hundred francs.' And then we breathe again, for we are told, in a letter of the 15th of the same month : 'Happily the Grégoires had not been sent off, and the bookseller has kindly consented to take them back.'

On the other hand, this year of triumph was also a year of sadness, for it witnessed the death of the Abbé Teysseyre (who had watched over him and encouraged him in his work), of his younger brother Gratien, and of Henry Moorman. After a short stay with the Abbé Jean at St. Brieuc, he retired to La Chênaie, with the intention of occupying his mind in dealing with the immense problems which had been raised in his first volume. He had already demonstrated the necessity of religion as a social factor, and the absurdity of the prevailing indifference, but a more difficult task still lay before him. It was necessary to discover a criterion of truth, or rather of selection, by which it might become possible for men to choose something ultimate and real amongst the thousand competing doctrines which had appeared in the course of the long evolution of the religious instinct in man. He thoroughly realised that the old metaphysical methods were worn out, not only as actual proofs of the existence of a God, but as processes of thought which would win for themselves serious consideration, in an age which was entirely given over to physical science. The traditional first principles of what was called Catholic philosophy were no longer accepted outside the circle of theological disputations, or, if ever they were dragged forth into the world, they served only to demonstrate the futility of the system which was based on them, and often to shatter the faith of the hapless believer who was officially informed that everything depended on them. On February 1, 1820, Féli de Lamennais wrote from La Chênaie to the Abbé Jean :—

> I have received from Turin a curious letter, written by a person who does not give his name. Having been brought up a Christian, he began to read the apologists for religion, with the idea that it would strengthen his faith. As a result he no longer knows what to believe. He says, and he is right, that he must begin by proving, not that there is a God, but that he himself exists.

In 1818 he had written to the Abbé Bruté :—

> I shall work out a new system of defence for Christianity against infidels and heretics, a very simple system, in which the proofs will be so rigorous that unless one is prepared to give up the right of saying *I am*, it will be necessary to say *Credo* to the very end.

In this spirit, then, he set to work, and as a result he brought out, between 1820 and 1823, the remaining volumes of the 'Essai sur l'Indifférence.'

In the opening chapter the author sets himself, in a few terse and pithy arguments, to demolish the cobwebs of philosophic dogmatism which still lingered in the schools. The process of deduction may be absolutely conclusive. Our logic may be faultless, but it

is without a basis; it rests on gratuitous hypotheses, and its value is measured by theirs; for whence do we conclude that there is any necessary relation between truth and certain operations of the mind? . . . When, therefore, Descartes, wishing to escape from his systematic doubt, establishes the proposition: '*I think; therefore I am*,' he crosses an immense gulf, and lays in the midst of nothing the foundation stone of the edifice which he undertakes to build.

And in another passage :—

How is it that people will not recognise that nothing could be demonstrated without the help of truths already certain? This being admitted, it is contradictory to pretend to demonstrate a first truth; and, consequently, far from certitude resting on demonstration, no demonstration would be possible without an anterior certitude, on which its validity absolutely depends. Thus dogmatists begin by assuming that they are already in possession of what they are in search of. . . . Recognising this contradiction, many of them admit the necessity of presupposing what they call first principles. . . . If you ask them what constitutes a first principle, they answer: What every one believes invincibly. But the madman is absolutely convinced of the error which characterises his madness. Individual conviction, then, is not sufficient for discerning truth from error, or for ascertaining first principles. . . . Must we plunge, then, into the silent depths of universal scepticism? . . . Nature does not permit it. . . . Whether man wills it or not, he *must* believe, because he *must* act, because he *must* fulfil the law of self-preservation. If he were to listen only to his individual reason, he would learn only to doubt of everything, even of himself; it would reduce him to a condition of absolute inaction; he would perish before he succeeded in proving his own existence.

How, then, are we to escape from this difficulty? Let us examine human nature from a non-metaphysical point of view.

There is a series of truths which is formed in our understanding in spite of ourselves, and of which it is impossible to doubt; they come to us either through our senses or through some other channel. Such are all truths necessary to our preservation, all those on which is based the ordinary intercourse of life, the practice of the arts and the pursuit of indispensable callings. . . . Why is it that we do not question a multitude of truths which science has established? It is because we are absolutely incapable of doing so, or because we know that, if we were to doubt them, we should be declared mad, ignorant, or stupid by other men; and this constitutes human certitude. Common consent, *sensus communis*, is for us the seal of truth; there is no other. . . . Every created being who dares to say *I am*, gives utterance, not to a judgment, but to his faith in an impenetrable mystery, and does but stammer, without understanding it, the first article of the symbol of intelligences.

If, then, we are to arrive at a conclusion in religious matters, we must make use of those methods which have been proved successful in other things. Astronomy and biology have been examined in the sequence of their phenomena, and they have yielded up their secrets; so now society must be studied in all its manifestations. Wandering among the ruins of the historic past, searching amid the traditions of mankind, we shall be answered by the voice of humanity, as we have been answered by space and time by the planets and by the phenomena of life.

Following up this thought, the Abbé de Lamennais invites us to descend with him into the arena of history.

It would be impossible in the space at my disposal to give any adequate idea of the real weight of this powerful work, for its strength depends on the mass of evidence with which the writer endeavours to crush opposition. No doubt there are inaccuracies: he depended on the knowledge of his time; but these are lost in the vast accumulation of facts which overwhelm the hapless objector, and compel him to admit that, convicted in his isolation, he stands condemned before the tribunal of the human race.

'Ask Cicero,' says the author in one place—

whether the soul is immortal, and he answers that by his reason alone he 'can form only conjectures. What is most likely? That is the great question.' But presently, raising his eyes and looking over the whole world, his doubts disappear, and he boldly gives utterance to these words, which will be repeated through all time: 'Basing ourselves on the agreement of all nations, we believe that souls are immortal; for the unanimous consent of the peoples ought to be looked upon in all things as a law of nature.'

And again, speaking of truth:—

We shall not seek it in the isolated mind of man, but in the reason of society. We shall examine the beliefs, the traditions of the human race, we shall note down its decisions; and if any objector presents himself, we shall point out to him two roads, one of which he must follow: the dark, solitary way of private judgment, which ends in nothing, and the social way of authority, which leads to life or even to God, and we shall say to him as our only answer: Choose.

Then, seizing the objector, and holding him fast by the fascination of boldness and of erudition, he compels him to stand and look while he unrolls before him the history of human thought and aspiration, only desisting when he has completely driven home the proposition that *Christianity began with the world*.

One after another the root doctrines of the Catholic religion are shown to have existed, in one form or another, in all the mythologies which have appeared in the course of the evolution of man. The gods and heroes were worshipped, but they were intermediary beings, and the idea of a Supreme God never entirely disappeared. So, in Homer, we find (1) that there is one Supreme God who is called (*passim*) *the father and the sovereign master of gods and men, the architect of the world, the prince and governor of the universe, the first God and the great God*; (2) that all nature is peopled with subordinate intelligences, who are the ministers of the supreme Divinity. . . . So also in the beautiful hymn of Cleanthes :—

Hail, glorious King of the immortals, adored under different names, eternally all powerful, author of Nature, who governest the world by thy laws! It is permitted to mortals to invoke thee, for we are thy children, thy image, and as a feeble echo of thy voice, we who live but for a moment and who crawl on the earth. I will ever praise thee, always will I sing of thy power. The whole universe obeys thee. . . . Thy invincible hands are armed with the thunderbolt; it falls, and Nature trembles. Thou guidest the common reason, thou penetratest and makest to germinate everything that is. Great King, nothing is done without thee, neither on the earth, nor in the heavens, nor in the deep sea, except evil, which is the work of foolish mortals. Bringing into agreement contrary principles, defining the limits of each, and fusing happiness and misfortune, thou maintainest harmony; of so many different parts thou formest a single whole, ruled by constant order, which mad, sinful men trouble by their blind desire. . . . Author of all good, father of men, deliver them from this baneful ignorance, dissipate the mists which cloud their souls, give them to know the wisdom by which thou governest the world, that we may honour thee worthily. . . . For no act is greater for man or for the gods than the celebration, in justice, of universal law. (3rd century B.C.)

And in another place he quotes from Rémusat a translated passage from the writings of the Chinese philosopher Lao-tseu :—

He whom you look at and whom you cannot see is called *I*; he whom you listen to and cannot hear is called *Hi*; he whom you seek with your hand but cannot touch is called *Wei*. These three beings are incomprehensible, and together they make but one. The highest is not more brilliant, the lowest is not more obscure. It is a chain without interruption, and which cannot be named.

He then continues :—

M. Remusat observes on this passage, that the three characters which form the words *I*, *Hi*, *Wei* have no sense; that they are simply signs of sounds foreign to the Chinese language, whether pronounced as a whole or only in their initials *I*, *H*, *V*, which the Chinese cannot isolate in writing; and he demonstrates that the name *I-Hi-Wei*, or *I H V*, is identical with the name Jehovah. . . .

In fine, searching among the traditions of all the nations, the harmony is broken by no dissentient voice. Teotl among the Mexicans, Pacha-Camac with the Peruvians, Ormuzd in Persia: the Creator of the universe was worshipped by the Irish as Kean Kroithi, and by the ancient Britons as *Hu*, surnamed *Gadarn*, the powerful. Whichever way we turn we are met by the same result, and there is no escaping from the conclusion unless we would isolate ourselves from the human race. 'It is enough,' he says, when he has caused his reader's brain to throb with the vast accumulation of evidence which is scattered up and down the pages of this work :—

What need have we of further witnesses? Even if all the generations, rising from their dust, were to come to us of themselves and to say, 'This was our belief,' could we have greater certainty that the knowledge of a God, one, eternal, Father of all that is, was never absent from the world? It is the universal faith, the faith of all the centuries and of all the nations. What astounding unanimity! What wonderful harmony! It is imposing, this voice which rises from every corner of the earth and of time towards the God of eternity.

Apart, in the shadow, another voice, a sinister voice, has been heard; it seemed to come from a sepulchre, and to have broken itself amongst the bones; it was as the voice of the dead. The peoples have listened to the dismal sound; low murmured blasphemies have reached them; they have said, 'It is the cry of the atheist,' and they have shuddered.

To these traditions, which deal with fundamental things, may be added all those which tell us of the canonisation of saints, of heroes, of ancestors; the consecration of life in the choice of a profession, as in the case of the monk, the priest, or the young warrior; the sanctity of the marriage tie, in one form or another, in all but the most degraded; the consciousness of sin and the practice of baptism. On this last the author says:—

> The idea that we are born impure and sinful was, from the highest antiquity, so profoundly impressed on the minds of men, that there existed, in every people, expiatory rites to purify the child on its entry into life. Usually this ceremony took place when a name was given to it. With the Romans the day was the ninth for boys, and the eighth for girls. It was called *lustricus* on account of the lustral water which was used for the purification of the new born. The Egyptians, the Persians, the Greeks had a similar custom. At Yucatan the child was brought to the temple, where the priest poured on its head the water which was set apart for this, and gave him a name. In the Canaries this function was fulfilled by women instead of priests.

Then comes a quotation from Humboldt on Mexico:—

> The midwife, calling on the god Ometeuctli and the goddess Omecihuatl, who live in the dwelling of the blessed, poured water on the forehead and breast of the new born; after having pronounced different prayers, in which the water was described as the symbol of the purification of the soul, the midwife called up some children, who had been invited to give a name to the new born. In some provinces they now brought fire and pretended to pass the child through the flame, as if to purify it by fire as well as by water. This ceremony recalls customs whose origin, in Asia, is lost in the highest antiquity. Not less curious is a custom found among the Hindoos. The name is written on the child's forehead, and after having plunged it three times into the water of a river, the Brahmin cries, in a loud voice, 'Oh God, pure, one, invisible, eternal and perfect! We offer thee this child, issue of a holy tribe, anointed with an incorruptible oil and purified with water!'

And so the argument continues. No corner is left unsearched, no stone is left unturned which may yield up to the observer some choice treasure of historic or traditional antiquity. Turning, for instance, to the practice of praying for the dead, he triumphantly demonstrates that at no period in the religious evolution of man has this been other than a fundamental principle, and that never, at any time since the beginning of the known world, has there been a nation or a tribe which could not say with the deepest conviction, 'It is a holy and wholesome thought to pray for the dead.'

But when the Abbé de Lamennais has led his readers through the traditions and beliefs of every branch of the human family, when he has demonstrated to them the universality of every distinctive doctrine and of every practice in the Catholic religion, from the existence of God to the veneration of relics, he is confronted by the main difficulty of his undertaking.

These beliefs and practices may have existed amongst all the peoples from the highest antiquity, and many of them may have been practically universal, but each of them had, in different parts of the world, been incorporated in a body of doctrine which may be described as national and local. Many of the peoples had so exaggerated the purely human side of religion, the honour due to great men, to gods and heroes, as to obscure the central principle, the idea which should have given unity to the whole; in fact, they had become idolaters, and, as a result, a considerable amount of moral anarchy had been introduced through the want of any adequate idea of goodness and badness in the gods selected for public and private worship. On the other hand, a nation like the Jews, while holding strictly in the long run to the principle of unity, had allowed the softening and humanising elements in religion to fall into the background, thus permitting a cruel and ultra-national spirit to grow up amongst them, and this almost destroyed the social efficacy of religion—at least from a broadly human point of view. Add to this the fact that most of the Asiatic religions were utterly clouded in an unpractical and other-worldly mysticism, and it becomes extremely difficult to extract from the tangled mass of human traditions a doctrine which may be dignified by the name of religion, and which may have a social efficacy. It might be possible for the learned, for the critical, by setting aside all that is local, all that seems to be inconsistent with the general tendencies of religious evolution, to construct for themselves a system more or less suited to their individual wants; but a religion so formed could have no social value, the continuity with the past would be broken, and ordinary men would see in it only one more curious product of the ever restless human brain.

Feeling this difficulty, the author of the *Essai* refers us back to the principle from which he started. *It is not good for a man to be alone* had been the constant theme of his early chapters, and he reminds his readers that this principle, too, has always been recognised as fundamental in the history of the human race. In all the old mythologies and cosmogonies the working out of their position as religions was based on the fact that, as it is impossible for a man to *live* alone or to *act* alone, so it is impossible for him to *think* alone. 'They say,' says the author of *Émile*, 'that Socrates invented morality. Others before him had put it into practice: he only put into words what they had done; he simply turned their examples into precepts. Aristides had been just before Socrates had explained what justice was; Leonidas had died for his country ere Socrates proclaimed patriotism as a duty.'

At no time did religion depend for its sanction on the individual reason; its real force always lay in a kind of social instinct which made it easier for a man to believe than to disbelieve. Every nation, every tribe, had its gods or its ideas about God, while there was no family which had not its tutelary divinities, and to doubt of or to criticise these would have been to undermine the very foundations of society. But when those foundations had been weakened by other causes, when the growth of commerce, the development of conquest, and the increase of international intercourse had done their work—when men had become thoroughly alive to the fact that there were other gods and other systems than their own, there arose the sophists, the critics, the philosophers, and in the most enlightened countries the ancestral constructions slowly crumbled away. For how was it possible to hold to antique ideals and principles, however venerable, when others had been discovered equally well attested and systematised out of all possibility of general unity by their too purely national development? Great statesmen, Roman emperors, tried to solve the difficulty by the creation of a world empire, and at its centre there began to form itself a kind of international pantheon, where devotees from every nation might find gratification for their own particular spiritual needs. But, setting aside the fact that such an idea was glaringly irrational and could only impose on the most ignorant, the whole imperial system was ephemeral, and, in reality, represented a greater principle which was germinating in the mind of man. And that greater principle found its fulfilment in Christianity. Men turned their thoughts vaguely, tentatively, to a universal society, which might sum up within itself those traditions which had been handed down from all antiquity, but which now seemed likely to perish; and, when things seemed most hopeless, they discovered that such a society was already in their midst. For Christianity from its earliest beginnings was founded on this principle of universality. 'My kingdom is not of this world.' 'Many shall come from the east and from the west,' etc., etc. And it appealed to the traditions of the human race. Christ himself constantly referred the Jews to their sacred writings, and His example was followed by the apostles in dealing with the peoples to whom they preached the gospel. In fact no one could say with greater truth than a Christian: *Homo sum, humani nihil a me alienum puto.*

But this state of things did not come about at once, it took time to draw out the virtue that was hidden in the new religion. 'Did anyone believe,' says the author, 'that Christianity had always been what it is to-day, the thing he believed in would not be Christianity.' Beginning among the Jews, and having for its first exponents members of the chosen race, it was but natural that its earliest colouring should have been almost exclusively Jewish. But as the field of its operation was widened, as it spread itself abroad over the pagan and heathen world, it gradually absorbed, by a system of comparison and selection, all that was durable in the civilisations with which it came into contact. And so it has gone on ever since; so it will continue to the end of time. Every newly discovered civilisation, every newly converted people, every forward step in the older nations of the Christian world leads to some fresh development— some further adaptation to the needs of place and time. Thus all the various streams of tradition, many of them lost in the impenetrable mists of prehistoric antiquity, find their way sooner or later to the Catholic Church. Christianity is not a book, still less is it a system of metaphysics; but about those problems which, if left unsolved, must eternally torment mankind, it tells its adherents just enough to save them from that terrible disease of anarchic and therefore futile speculation which dissipates those energies that might be so usefully employed in other spheres. It demands of the individual a sacrifice, but this sacrifice differs in nothing from those which he recognises as necessary in other things. He must constantly refer back to *his only possible criterion*, the universal consent of mankind, the dictates of which are summed up and formulated by the Catholic Church, and this in its turn is the ultimate expression of human society, not that it has reached its full development—that cannot be till the end of time; but outside this organisation there can be no evolution, and any apparent growth must be ephemeral, and must lead to mental anarchy and consequently to social inaction.

For man [says the author of the *Essai*] cannot live in isolation; try to conceive him freed from all dependence, and you will conceive a mere negation. Outside nothingness all things are linked together, and there is nothing which does not lean for support on something else. Minds, like bodies, have no life but that which they receive on condition that they share it. Not a being but owes itself to other beings, for it is indebted to them for everything that it is.

And, in another place:—

The mind, the *heart*, even the senses, or the body, in a word, the whole man, naturally desires to perpetuate himself, for it is in his nature to wish to live, and it is not in his power to wish anything else.

In the state of unnatural isolation in which *philosophy* places him, all his efforts at self-preservation tend to destroy him. In himself, man produces nothing; life is the gift of the Sovereign Being—creatures transmit it, and that is all. Now, to transmit is to communicate what one has received. To receive and to give up, it is in this that life consists, and by this means it is preserved. This being so, there can be no life outside of society, and society considered in its intellectual aspect, is essentially composed of three persons—

the first, who receives; the second, from whom he receives; and the third, to whom he transmits what he has received.

Everything in man which has a special mode of life, the mind, the *heart*, the senses, or the body, is subject to this universal law of union and dependence.

What happens when a man is alone?

The mind wishes to live, to fulfil the law of self-preservation; to live for it is to know or to possess truth. When it receives it, it is passive; when it communicates or transmits it, it is active; but, in either state, it must be united to another mind which acts on it, or on which it acts. Being unable, when alone, to receive or to transmit, and yet wishing to live, it tries to multiply itself or to create in itself the social persons necessary to the preserving and to the perpetuation of its life: a vain attempt, a sterile effort in a mind which, seeking to fertilise itself, hopes to bring forth without having conceived. This kind of depravation, this loathsome vice of the intelligence, weakens it, wears it out, and leads to a curious sort of idiocy called *idéologie*.

Thus, whichever way we turn we are driven to the same conclusion. *Man cannot live alone*, the law of self-preservation compels him to seek expression for himself in society; but the only possible society in religious matters is the Catholic Church. Consequently . . .

Such, in its general outlines is the argument of this powerful book. Its importance may be estimated by the fact that, not so long afterwards, its methods were pursued from a wider standpoint, and its conclusions more fully drawn out by the great genius who gave to the world the system which culminated in the *Religion of Humanity*. But we must be careful of exaggeration. The only science with which the

Abbé de Lamennais was thoroughly conversant was mathematics, of which he had, before his ordination, been professor at St. Malo. As a consequence of this, he lays too much stress on tradition, and not enough on tendency, on evolution. This tradition, for him, is an absolute criterion of *truth* in its plain statements, and not in the *underlying* truths which have to be developed in due course by the progress of the human mind, by the increase of experience, and by the demands of a growing organism. He recognised the necessity of evolution, but the process did not carry him much further than the gathering up and systematising of *fully formed* doctrines already existing in the world. He had no knowledge of the embryological fact that '*every function is successively executed by two (sometimes more) organs; of which one is primitive, transitory, provisional; the others, secondary, definitive, permanent.*' And this further one: '*That . . . the embryo of the higher animals successively renews its organs and its characteristics through a series of metamorphoses which give it permanent conditions, not only different, but even directly contrary to those which it had primitively.*' In consequence of this, his treatment of society as an organism is very defective, and it is here that the founder of Positivism is immeasurably his superior. It is only when we bear in mind the time of its appearance, and the antecedents of its author, that we can estimate the real greatness of the 'Essai sur l'Indifférence en matière de Religion.'

Inspired by his genius, Lamennais had become

conscious of the fact that the knowledge which underlies religion cannot be *essentially* different from that which forms the basis of any science. But he had not realised the full import of his discovery. Like his predecessors and contemporaries, he strove after the absolute, thus vitiating the argument in which he sought to correct their obvious errors. We shall see how time and experience led him to alter his opinion.

CHAPTER III

THE AUTHOR GOES TO ROME

It is not to be wondered at that so bold an attack on the traditional methods should have raised a storm in the theological world. It was generally considered, amongst the older clergy, that the author had undermined the only possible basis of religion; that, in his criticism of individual reason, he had destroyed that very authority whose prerogatives he had wished to defend. Thus, in August 1820, Frayssinous wrote to him: 'I am sure you will not mind my telling you of the impression your second volume seems to have made on the clergy in general. They are unanimous on the strength and talent of the writer; but they are frightened at the new philosophy it contains; they fear that you may, on the one hand, have weakened the ordinary motives of credibility, and, on the other, exaggerated the scope of authority.' In October he received a letter from his old friend and adviser the Abbé Carron, who told him that the authorities at St. Sulpice criticised the book, as undermining the foundations of human certitude; he also suggested that he would have done well to consult some one more experienced than himself before entering on so dangerous a subject. This may be looked upon as a last warning from the venerable priest, who died soon afterwards. The answer, which is dated November 1, 1820, is characteristic :—

I thank you a thousand times, my dear Father, for your pious and tender letter. You need not fear that I shall ever be hurt by your criticisms and by your advice. I understand the feeling which inspires them, and they can but increase my affection for you. Coming to the matter itself, I think I did everything which prudence demanded of me, in showing my work to some whom I thought, and whom I still think, the most capable of judging it. Here the clergy, with some exceptions, approve of it. . . . At first I received nothing but objections ; now justifications are being sent to me from every side. It is clear to me that my adversaries do not understand me. . . . *If the principles for which I contend are rejected, I cannot conceive of any sound method for the defence of religion*, nor any decisive answer to the unbelievers of our time. . . . But I know, and I admit, without hesitation, that I may be wrong; and that is why (this in the strictest confidence) I have sent a petition to Rome to have my book examined. My request has been received with kindness. . . . I can say with the deepest sincerity, that I have not been more moved by the criticisms than by the praises which have been heaped upon me. . . . All this noise does not reach my soul, so you need not pity me. My tranquillity has not been disturbed for a moment by these clamourings. I will even go farther : if the judgment of Rome is favourable to me, I shall rejoice for religion's sake ; if it goes against me, I shall be glad for my own. *I have decided in that case to write no more*, and I shall be the happiest of men ; for I shall be able conscientiously to enjoy that rest which, in my opinion, is the only good thing in this world. . . . Pray for your poor son.

Féli de Lamennais did not know himself. To him rest was never possible, driven as he was by that inner force which throughout his life compelled him to work and act, whether he would or no. But this letter is interesting from another point of view. It reveals to us a very legitimate confidence in himself, which was natural, and in fact necessary, in a writer who had undertaken to think out a system of defence for religion, and this, I think, is combined with all that could be demanded in humility and submissiveness to lawful authority; yet curiously enough, Monseigneur Ricard, in his interesting and deeply critical volume on the founder of the *Mennaisian School*, seizing on the two passages which I have placed in italics, remarks: ' Thus then, on the one hand, *never before his time has religion been solidly* defended, and, on the other, if Rome does not agree with him, he will not retract, he will break his pen.' On the first point I would answer that the sentence following the first italicised passage would in itself be a decisive refutation of this interpretation of the writer's meaning, even were it unsupported by protests like the following, which is taken from the 'Défense de l'Essai sur l'Indifférence': ' "Why," they say, " do you seek for new proofs of religion ? Why are you not content with the old ones ? " Why ? Because new objections have been brought—because the position of men's minds is no longer the same. . . .' The second point I leave to the judgment of my readers.

But Lamennais was mistaken in thinking that he was proof against the clamours of the world, however much he might affect to despise them. His was one of those impressionable natures which require sympathy, and he was deeply wounded by many things which were said in the course of the controversy. There seems to be evidence of this in a letter published by M. Roussel. The recipient, the Abbé Hay, was an old friend of his and of the Abbé Jean: 'M. l'Abbé, your principles in matters of religion, of conscience, and of honour differ so essentially from mine, that it is my duty to inform you that there can no longer be anything in common between us. F. de Lamennais.' This was written in March 1824.

On the other hand he derived comfort from the adherence of his brother, who described the new system as *our philosophy*, and from that of the great mass of the young clergy, which convinced him that the future was with the doctrine of the *Essai*. Then again, in a letter dated August 1823, to his friend the Abbé Rohrbacher, he mentions a fact which must have been very reassuring to him: 'I have received, from the most distinguished men of learning, expressions of the liveliest satisfaction at the part of my work which especially interests them. The light which has already been thrown on things by the study of traditions seems to promise a new kind of triumph for religion. The mass of material furnished by India and China is enormous. We are at the beginning of a great epoch.'

Thus the name of Lamennais was in every mouth, and his position was assured in the foremost rank of contemporary writers. A portrait of him was circulated, and it found its way to an old friend. The Abbé Bruté wrote, probably in 1824 :—

I have just returned from a visit to M. Bouillon. The sight of Féli's portrait . . . I did not recognise it—well done, you say, from every point of view. . . . I thought of our sixteen years of separation. How time works! That face, now so decided, was so childish, so weakly, so good; here it is all genius, I think. I have been singularly disappointed, to have come twice without seeing him—and I saw you so easily—to go away thus, perhaps for a last separation. I was like a child, and in passing by the Luxembourg I felt tears coming into my eyes.

M. Roussel thinks that this curious letter was written to the Abbé Jean.

Late in the spring of 1824, the author of the *Essai* went to Switzerland to recruit. Neither the climate nor the scenery seems to have agreed with him, for he wrote in May from Geneva to Mdlle. de Lucinière, one of the Feuillantines:—

I hate above all things the town from which I write. Everything here gets on my nerves, and I would rather a hundred times live among the Turks than in the midst of this abominable population. The rest of Switzerland is hardly better. I doubt whether there is in the world any country where one could get more bored. As to natural curiosities, mountains, valleys, lakes, torrents, waterfalls, these are things which do not take long to see, and which then have no further charm. I put it to you, is not a pointed rock with a little snow on the top a wonderful thing? I must say I prefer my fire-wood. And besides, the climate is very severe. We have had winter weather almost constantly since I left home. As I do not know how many months I shall have to wait before the season changes, I think it will be safer to go to seek summer in Italy, to imitate Hannibal in crossing the Alps. I shall do so towards the end of the month.

He kept his word, and the summer of this year found him in the Eternal City. The Pope, Leo XII., received him kindly. The doctrine of the *Essai* had already been examined by three Roman theologians, and had been formally approved by the Master of the Sacred Palace. Lamennais was now admitted to a private audience, and the report went round that as he came into the room he noticed that it had for its only ornaments a crucifix, a picture of the Madonna, and his own portrait.[1] Everywhere he was received as befitted the greatest defender of the faith in modern times. On July 13 he wrote to Mdlle. de Lucinière :—

I do not yet know how long I shall remain here. My reception could not have been better, and they are pressing me to stay longer than I originally intended. . . . I have seen the Holy Father twice, and he has treated me with great kindness. Just now he is in good health, and I thank God for it. . . . We must pray for him, for he is a good and worthy Pope, besides being a man of very great merit. . . . The heat here is stifling. . . . I may mention that Italian cooking is detestable from our French point of view. I feel the want of some good soup, a respectable piece of boiled beef, and a good roast joint. An edifying wish, is it not, from the capital of the Christian world.

In the same letter he mentions 'M. Wiseman, a young English ecclesiastic,' by whom indeed it was to be delivered at its destination. Lamennais had now reached the age of forty-two, while the future cardinal was still in his twenties, so that there can-

[1] It appears, from a letter written at the time of the death of Leo XII., that he did not learn till that occasion that the Pope's room was thus decorated.

not have been much in common between the two men; nevertheless this chance acquaintance seems to have ripened into a closer friendship, and it is to this that we owe an interesting description of the French writer which may be fittingly inserted here. It is to be found in the *Recollections of the Four last Popes.*

How he did so mightily prevail on others it is hard to say. He was truly in look and presence almost contemptible: small, weakly, without pride of countenance or mastery of eye, without any external grace; his tongue seemed to be the organ by which, unaided, he gave marvellous utterance to thoughts clear, deep, and strong. Several times have I held long conversations with him at various intervals, and he was always the same. With his head hung down, his hands clasped before him, or gently moving in one another, he poured out, in answer to a question, a stream of thought. . . . He at once seized the whole subject, divided it into its heads, as symmetrically as Fléchier or Massillon; then took them one by one, enunciated each, and drew his conclusions. All this went on in a monotonous but soft tone, and was so unbroken, so unhesitating, and yet so polished and elegant, that if you had closed your eyes, you might easily have fancied you were listening to the reading of a finished and elaborately corrected volume.

Then everything was illustrated by happy imagery, so apt, so graphic, and so complete. I remember his once describing, in glowing colours, the future prospects of the Church. He had referred to prophecies of Scripture and fulfilments in history, and had concluded that, not even at the period of Constantine, has perfect accomplishment of predictions and types been made; and that, therefore, a more glorious phase yet awaited the Church than any she had yet experienced, and this, he thought, could not be far off.

'And how,' I asked, ' do you think, or see that this great

and wonderful change in her condition will be brought about?'

'I cannot see,' he replied; 'I feel myself like a man placed at one end of a long gallery, at the other extremity of which are brilliant lights shedding their rays on objects there. I see paintings and sculpture, furniture and persons, clear and distinct, but of what is between me and them I see nothing; the whole interval is dark, and I cannot describe what occupies the space.' . . .

On another occasion his answer was more explicit. He had been discoursing eloquently on England, and what had to be done there in our religious struggles. He had described the way in which prejudices had to be overcome, and public opinion won over. He was asked—

'But what, or where, are the instruments with which such great and difficult things have to be wrought?'

'They do not exist as yet,' he answered. 'You must begin by making the implements with which your work has to be performed; it is what we are doing in France.'

But we must return to the Abbé Jean.

While his younger brother in these brilliant beginnings was convincing himself and the world of the genius that was in him, this exemplary priest, quietly and unobtrusively, had been labouring at St. Brieuc for the salvation of souls. For some years, during an interregnum, the entire responsibility for the management of the diocese had rested on his shoulders. In fulfilling the arduous duties of his position he had realised the necessity of mutual help, of organisation with a view to social action, and he had founded, besides innumerable confraternities of children, the *Daughters of Providence* (a teaching order of women) and the *Brothers of Christian Instruction*. This last, which was his greatest and most enduring work, was afterwards destined to immortalise his name in every part of the Catholic world. In 1819 Mgr. de la Romagère had been installed as bishop of St. Brieuc, and he had appointed the Abbé Jean de Lamennais his vicar-general, but the pronounced Gallicanism of the bishop and the extreme Ultramontanism of the priest had made it impossible for the latter to hold his post for long, and he had resigned, notwithstanding the entreaties of the venerable prelate. In 1822 he had accepted the office of vicar-general to the Prince de Croy, Grand Almoner of France, Archbishop of Rouen, and had come to Paris, where he was with difficulty persuaded to change his old snuff-stained cassock for a new one, more suited to the atmosphere of the Court. He performed the functions of this office, which practically involved the nomination of bishops to the French Sees, till its abolition in 1824. Had he chosen, he might then have been raised to the episcopal dignity, but we are told that he 'energetically refused seventeen offers,' so wholly had he given himself up to the development of the work of his *Congregation of Brothers*.

When Féli returned from Rome in the autumn of 1824, Jean was still in residence at the Grand Almonry, and he very naturally offered him a room on his way through Paris. But the author of the *Essai sur l'Indifférence*, and of divers articles in the independent papers, was not in good odour with the Court, and the Prince de Croy wrote to his friend M. de Senfft to ask him to hint to Lamennais that he would do well to leave. The effect of such a communication on the irritable abbé is easier to imagine than to describe.

He wrote at once to the archbishop, apologising for his imprudence, and he added :—' Three weeks ago the Sovereign Pontiff begged me earnestly to accept a room at the Vatican. I thank you for having made me realise so soon that there are differences both in men and in countries.'

This incident, trivial though it may seem, was of considerable importance in bringing home to him the real meaning of the controversy which he had forced upon the world. The opposition to the doctrine of *common consent* did not come so much from Catholicism itself as from particular phases in it. He had been well received in Rome, while even in France his opinions were rapidly making their way with the younger clergy—that is to say, with all those who could afford to look with equanimity on the undermining of the artificial arrangements on which the welfare of religion was supposed to depend. The danger was on the side of the official classes, lay and clerical, whose public position made it impossible for them to appreciate, even had they dared to do so openly, an independent or militant attitude.

Lamennais was not a Republican, still less was he a Revolutionist. Witness a graphic passage in an article for January 21, 1823 :—' A king, a scaffold, hell revelling in blood, the earth in silence and in terror ; heaven opening to receive the just and then closing again : that is the 21st of January.' His ideal was a monarchy absolute in all matters of state, but strictly subordinated to the spiritual power: an important condition when we remember that, with him, religion was the most perfect expression of the voice of the peoples. Thus, he contemptuously speaks of Louis XVIII. as 'a descendant of the monarch whose soul gave utterance to this profound saying: *L'Etat, c'est moi*' (*art*. 1823). For he recognised that the general corruption of the *ancien régime* had not spared even the most sacred things. In 1822 he had said: 'The Revolution was a fact; it was fully accomplished at the period which is generally assigned as its starting point. Men mistook putrefaction for death, and perhaps that is why all those who have attempted a restoration have thought it sufficient to embalm the corpse.' Then what could be more scathing than this description of the typical government official or venal deputy? 'He modestly approaches the regulator of his legislative reason, leans over and whispers into his ear, then pricks up his own so as to take in, without losing anything, the answer to this profound and delicate question: "*Monseigneur, what is true to-day?*"'

By his Royalist friends, by those who saw in the monarchical principle the only true solution of social difficulties, he was looked on chiefly as a staunch defender of the good cause. Thus the Baron de Vitrolles had written to him in 1822: 'I love to see you, in the midst of these agitations, performing the great and noble task which you have imposed upon yourself, the strengthening of that religious barrier which should stand in the way of the new ideas.' Up to a certain point, as my readers will see from the passages to which I have alluded, this opinion was justified. Legitimate monarchy seemed the only means of escape from those frightful forms of tyranny which Frenchmen had but too recently experienced, and, with Lamennais, the distance which separated an opinion from a conviction was never very great. But, what these friends did not realise in him, was the intensity of the religious point of view. To men like Vitrolles, religion was a *barrier*; to the author of the *Essai sur l'Indifférence* it was everything. Hitherto he had dreamt of an alliance between the two principles, but now, on his return from Rome, a new idea began to germinate in his mind. He was deeply impressed by the contrast between the serenity of the atmosphere in the capital of the Christian world and the clashing of sordid interests in the comparatively narrow arena of French officialism. Thus the political ideal receded further and further into the background, leaving the other gradually to work its way towards complete mastery over his mind.

Nor did those in power attempt in any way to deal with this growing feeling of indifference, and even of hatred, to the existing state of things. It would be hard to find in the history of diplomacy anything more thoroughly attested than the fact that Leo XII. proposed to promote Lamennais to the dignity of the cardinalate; and it is asserted that the proposition came to naught through the opposition of the French Government. His letters during the year 1825 show signs of a growing tendency to cut himself adrift from things which he came to look upon as of a purely ephemeral importance, and to identify himself more and more with the one lasting social organisation, the Catholic Church. Thus he wrote in March 1825 to his friend the Marquis de Coriolis :—

I do not believe that anyone has ever been more an object of abuse and clamour than I have been for some time past, and all because I said what I thought of two prelates in influential positions who, for the greater glory of God and the advantage of religion, had judged it expedient publicly to make a semi-abjuration of Christianity. I feel every day what I should have believed impossible—a growing contempt for the men of our time. I should never have thought that human nature could descend so low. . . . It is in vain that I rack my memory ; I find nothing in it which can compare in the smallest degree with the spectacle offered by the Chamber of Deputies. This is certainly a new thing in the world. Never has there been seen so laughable a degradation or a corruption so stupid. I defy posterity to believe the *Moniteur* of the year ; no possible official character could make even probable such baseness, such idiocy. Good God, whither are we going? What shall we find when we get to the end of this ? '

And, a month later, he adds :—

One is getting tired of this atmosphere, and, to borrow an expression from the Bishop of Hermopolis, *I am not one of those* who are the least bored by it ; I should like something else just as well. But patience ; the something else will come, and that only too soon. Everything is preparing for a change of scene, and, for myself, I feel the approach of the catastrophe of this terrible drama, when I hear a deputy, an honest man . . . confiding to the Chamber that, after having struggled for twenty years against the Revolution, he will vote for a law which sanctions the most horrible crimes of that Revolution. . . . Besides, everywhere there is uneasiness, disgust, contempt, indignation. The general discontent is growing from day to day; minds are becoming embittered, brains are getting excited ; I foresee a storm in the future. Oh! I should be happy could I find, far from Europe, in a peaceable country, a little solitude in a mild climate . . . secure from the revolutions which menace the world.

It is an interesting fact that this time of agitation and uncertainty should have witnessed the production of his greatest work of devotion; indeed, he afterwards, according to one account, considered it the greatest of his writings. I have already spoken of the *Guide Spirituel*, which was, in reality, an edition of Blosius; but besides this, the world owes to the pen of the Abbé de Lamennais the *Guide de la Jeunesse*, the *Journée du Chrétien*, and the *Bibliothèque des Dames Chrétiennes*. At the period we have reached, he brought to a conclusion his translation of the immortal work of Thomas à Kempis, and of this it is not too much to say that it was in every respect worthy of the original. Many of my readers, no doubt, will be familiar with every page, with every line of this little book, but, for the benefit of those who are not so fortunate, I shall here transcribe a few passages taken at random from the reflections added by the translator at the end of each chapter :—

The world says to the ambitious : The desire for greatness disturbs you, agitates you; rise up, push yourself into prominence. It says to the miser: Greed of gain devours you; save, heap up unceasingly. It says to the man of the world, tormented with desire: Make yourself drunk with all the pleasures. In fine, it says to every passion: Gratify yourself, and you will have peace. A lying promise this! Care, sadness, anxiety, disgust, remorse, such is the peace of the world.

Come up to this grave, look at these whitened disjointed bones; they are all that is left of a man whom perhaps you knew, and who thought no more of death a few years ago than you think of it to-day. In fact, had he not to busy himself about his fortune . . . about the future of his family. So he occupied himself with these things up to the last. Well, come now, go into that house. Thoughtless heirs are using the wealth which he had put together, and they are trying to add to it, but there is no thought of the dead. Yet something of him remains, and it is not in that tomb.

If we must often suffer through our brother, so are we not less a cause of suffering to him; and that is why the Apostle says: *Bear ye one another's burdens.* . . . But I hear you say, there are things which are hard and difficult to bear. Well, your merits will be the greater for it. It is for this that grace is given to you, that you may be able to do what would be impossible to nature alone.

You shall be happy when men shall curse you, and shall revile you, and shall say all manner of evil against you: rejoice then, and be glad, for great is your reward in heaven. In spite of this saying, how often are we not troubled by the words of men and by their judgments? We cannot bear criticism; we wish, at any price, to be praised, to be esteemed. Blinded by a vain phantom of reputation, we forget God and His teaching, and the happiness which He promises to the humble. Strange result of pride, ever gnawing at the inmost recesses of our miserable hearts! What matters it that you are outraged, abased, calumniated?

Whence comes it that this arouses in you these bitter feelings, this lively resentment? Perchance you fear lest you may have too many means of expiation, too much reason to hope for mercy. You have been wrongfully accused! Would you prefer that there should be truth in what is alleged against you? If you have not been guilty of the fault which has been put down to you, how many others are there not of which you are guilty, and of which no one speaks? Examine your conscience: you will hear there a severer voice than those which come from without. These will one day cease, but that will be heard before the Throne of the Judge in whose presence you will one day appear, far from the noise of the world, in the silence of eternity. Think of this, and you will care but little for what men may say of you.

CHAPTER IV

POPE OR KING

As the year 1825 draws to its close, the correspondence shows signs of increasing bitterness against those in power, and the idea of active resistance becomes more and more clearly defined. On December 2, he asks Berryer to come and see him, and he adds: 'We shall speak together of liberty of the press, liberty of opinion, and of all the liberties which abound in France. These people who, on every possible occasion, appeal to reason against us, who accuse us of destroying it, can find nothing better, if we open our mouths to reason with them, than to drag us before the tribunals. What odious hypocrisy! ... Shall no voice be raised to point out the inconsistency of it.' Again, on the 14th of the same month: 'Since persecution is the order of the day, we must speak out as befits the persecuted, with the boldness of faith which laughs *at those who can only kill the body*. We must have that courage which truth alone can give. And besides, humanly speaking, the more you dare, the less they dare against you.'

And on the 22nd: 'We must fight on, whatever may be the result! If our banner is not unfurled on the summit of a regenerated society, it will float over the ruins of the world.'

The position seemed hopeless. Those from whom better things might have been expected, the Chateaubriands and the Bonalds, had gone over to the enemy. The whole burden of the struggle was thrown upon the shoulders of Féli de Lamennais. He accepted the responsibility, and in March 1826 he opened the campaign with his pamphlet, *La Religion considérée dans ses Rapports avec l'Ordre Politique et Civil*, in which he uncompromisingly set forth the Ultramontane position.

The Abbé Jean felt his spirits rise at the prospect of a contest in which the faith would be championed by his brother. On February 9 he wrote to M. Querret: 'Prepare your ears for a fine row. If he does not go to prison this time, he must despair of ever going there.' Not so Féli. To him the matter was much more serious, more far-reaching in its consequences. A new Nuncio, Mgr. Lambruschini, had arrived in Paris, and it was hoped by many that he might succeed in doing something towards improving the relations between France and the Holy See. Lamennais thought otherwise. On March 18, shortly after the appearance of his pamphlet, he wrote to the Comte de Senfft :—

> You are right in expecting some good from the mission of Mgr. L., but I think you are too hopeful. . . . His influence over the Government will be nil. . . . And, even if they were to listen to him, they would not put back the future a single moment. That future lies altogether in the

moral state of the peoples, which is but the natural development of doctrines handed down to us from the past. Government, to save itself, must change its very essence, and this is impossible. . . . What is radically vicious never reforms itself. I do not speak here of the forms of government, a question which absorbs men's minds to-day, perhaps because it is the most fruitless. Society is dying, and they are disputing about the clothes with which to cover it, so clear is it that the disease is in its clothes; the wise men are never tired of telling us this, from one end of Europe to the other. My friend, why should we deceive ourselves? We stand on the threshold of a gigantic revolution, which will end in the death or in the regeneration of the peoples, but which will last, whatever happens, so long as there remain any particles of the great corpse whose dissolution began in 1789.

The Gallican party in the French Church was composed, for the most part, as has already been stated, of the older clergy, who remembered the persecutions of the Revolution, and who were content at any price to bask in the sunshine of royal favour. These were blind to the danger of allying religion to an effete and artificially maintained monarchy, which owed its existence to the national disgrace of 1815, but they were fully alive to the fact that if public opinion were allowed to grow along the lines laid down by the Abbé de Lamennais, the security of their position would be considerably impaired. The Gallican articles of 1682, which limited the prerogatives of Rome and exaggerated those of the bishops and of the State, were considered part of the law of the land. Hence it followed that a priest who openly attacked them was guilty of treason against the constitution. This gave an opening to those who were most severely handled in the pamphlet *La Religion considérée dans ses Rapports avec l'Ordre Politique et Civil*, and the author was summoned to appear in the police courts on April 20.

It was while waiting for this event, to which I shall presently return, that Lamennais became the recipient of an interesting letter :—

Friday, March 31.

Monsieur,—I have just been to your house, as I wished to propose to you personally, and with the frankness which is as agreeable to your character as it is to mine, that you should be present the day after to-morrow, Sunday, at noon, for the opening of my course of lectures on positive philosophy, the programme of which I enclose.

If you come I shall feel the value of such a mark of esteem and of interest; if not, I shall understand your motives, without your taking the trouble to say anything about it; and I can assure you beforehand that my sympathy of mind and of heart will in no way be altered by the fact. I may add as a piece of news that the audience will be a distinguished one. MM. von Humboldt and de Blainville will be there, perhaps with some other men of learning; the rest will be composed of eight or ten young men of my choice.

I wished, also, Monsieur, in coming to see you, to thank you as I ought for the way in which you spoke of me in the last number of the *Mémorial Catholique*. I hope I shall soon have an opportunity of giving public expression to the feeling with which I am inspired by the strange methods which mark the intellectual warfare of our time. I shall seize it with the greater eagerness that I have just heard of the great favour with which the ministry seems bent on honouring you. Please accept, in advance, my sincere congratulations.

Adieu, Monsieur, I hope in any case that it will not be long before I have the pleasure of seeing you.

Votre dévoué,

AUGUSTE COMTE.

Lamennais answered on the following day:—

I am as flattered, Monsieur, as I am touched by your invitation. I should accept it with eagerness were I not just on the point of leaving for the country, where I shall spend a fortnight or so in preparing a little writing, forced on me by the prosecution which the ministry is getting up against me. You may rest assured that I shall not speak of myself, but of things in general; doctrines are what interest me. How I congratulate myself, Monsieur, on having made your acquaintance, and how honoured I feel by your attachment and by your esteem, I need not tell you. I experienced this before I had the honour of knowing you personally, and the feeling has since increased. I shall seize the first opportunity, on my return from the country, to pay you a visit and to draw closer and closer, by a sympathetic interchange of thought and of affection, that bond of friendship which is so very dear to me.

Votre dévoué,

F. DE LAMENNAIS.

It is a curious fact that an acquaintance, so evidently characterised by the deepest respect and sympathy on both sides, should have been passed over by the biographers of Lamennais. Indeed, the knowledge that we possess on this matter comes to us from the disciples of the great philosopher, who, like M. Lonchampt and Dr. Robinet have described the life of their founder, or from M. Pierre Lafitte, the friend and, in the opinion of some, the successor of Auguste Comte in his work. That the institutor of Positivism looked on it as of considerable importance may be seen from the fact that he often alludes to it in his letters; that he drew from it his reasons for hoping for an alliance between Catholicism and Positivism, a scheme dear to his last days, and that he mentioned it in his will.

And yet it is in its influence on Lamennais that this relationship is chiefly interesting. When he returned from Rome in the autumn of 1824, he was, as we have seen, practically turned out of the Grand Almonry, owing to the prejudices aroused by his Ultramontanism. He then retired to La Chênaie, but he did not thereby cut himself off from the world. He was constantly engaged in writing articles for the *Mémorial Catholique*, which was practically the organ of his party. This necessitated his keeping in touch with contemporary thought, and he was bound to read anything of importance which might appear. Thus, in November 1825, we find him speaking of 'A new journal, bad in every respect,' which 'calls on men to unite together for the destruction of *all that remains of vague and mystical ideas*, and predicts that we shall be governed by *scientific and industrial authorities*.' Such was his first impression; but he seems little by little to have become fascinated by the audacity and originality of the views set forth by some of the writers. This journal was the *Producteur*.

On December 22, he writes:—'If you read the papers which pride themselves on doctrine, the *Globe*, the *Producteur*, &c., you will find in them other indications, more marked and more certain, of a universal revolution. I am becoming every day more and more convinced that it is absolutely inevitable.'

From an article by M. Lafitte, in the *Revue Occidentale* for September 1880, it appears that Comte wrote an essay entitled *Considérations sur les Sciences et les Savants*, which was published in the *Producteur* in November 1825, and that a review of it appeared in the *Mémorial Catholique* in January 1826, under the heading *A New School of Philosophy*. It was signed *X.*, but the letter already quoted would seem to point to the fact that Lamennais was the author. M. Lafitte gives two extracts from it.

Speaking of new systems, the writer says :—

> Amongst them, the *Ecole Industrielle*, of which the *Producteur* is the organ, is worthy of notice. Although it has for its special object the application of the physical sciences to the arts and to commerce, it also puts forward its theory of the foundation of social order. It is with this aspect of it that we are here concerned. The first beginnings of the system have been set forth in some articles entitled *Considérations Philosophiques sur les Sciences et les Savants*, and in others on the *Spiritual Power*; M. Auguste Comte is the author. We can see in them evidences of a mind very superior to the prejudices which characterise your common philosopher. The *ensemble* of the ideas is very remarkable. M. Auguste Comte does not present himself, like the editors of the *Globe*, with a doctrine to discover, he comes to us with one fully formed, which he promises to expound in its consecutive parts, though he has already attempted to connect these together. Hoping, then, for a further development of his theory, we must content ourselves with quoting from these articles a few reflections on the question of the day: the Spiritual Power.

'There follow,' says M. Lafitte, 'two long quotations, very characteristic and very well chosen, pointing out the necessity of the advent of a spiritual power capable of ensuring the preponderance of a general system of morals.' Then the writer concludes:—

After these remarkable thoughts, we cannot but be astounded at the author's hoping to be able *to create a new spiritual power*. What form can it take in his system? The agreement of the learned? Let us suppose, for the sake of argument, that there is such an agreement, the *esprit critique*, the critical spirit, as M. Comte calls it, remains with all its consequences; the independence of each individual reason, which, as he admits, necessarily dissolves intellectual unity, produces anarchy in minds and makes it impossible to establish anything, is still there in its entirety; for how can the reason of some men constitute a power to which the reason of other men must submit? We shall await an explanation from M. Comte before entering more fully into the subject.

In an article in the January number of the *Revue Occidentale*, 1886, besides the two letters quoted above, M. Lafitte gives us some further details, including a communication from M. Menjaud to Comte, in which he says:—'I have given your note to M. de Lamennais, whom I saw myself yesterday evening. He has read all your articles, and has lent me the *Producteur* that I may read the last.' It is dated February 27, 1826, and probably indicates the time at which the two men first met.

We have seen how Lamennais was invited to be present at the opening of the course of lectures on Positive Philosophy, and how he was forced to decline, owing to the position in which he was placed at the moment. But there were other reasons why it was impossible for him to take advantage of the opportunity which thus presented itself to him. Comte broke down from overwork, and was kept out of the arena for some time by a fit of insanity. Yet, even in regard to this he remained a philosopher, and he afterwards alluded to it as a confirmation of his fundamental idea, *the law of the three states.* According to this law, man, individually and collectively, passes through three stages in the course of his mental and social evolution. These may be roughly termed the theological, the metaphysical, the positive, and the development takes place in all the sciences, one after another, in an order which he expressed by a classification. This classification was based on the principle that the simpler and more abstract sciences come first, and the more complex and less abstract come later in order of time : thus, mathematics came first and were followed by *astronomy*; then came *physics,* succeeded by biology; and the whole series was finally concluded by a science or sciences dealing with society, religion, morals, &c. In this system the most fully evolved man reached the positive stage in the latest of the sciences, while a less advanced order of intellect only reached one of the earlier sciences, or, in whatever science he had got to, remained in one of the more primitive states of mental development, as, for instance, the metaphysical or theological. Now, from his personal experience in passing through what he called his *cerebral crisis,* Comte concluded that a brain which became subject to any kind of deterioration would go back over some of the ground which had previously been covered in the course of its evolution, and that this would take place in proportion to the deterioration.

As a matter of fact, something of this kind happened to him in 1826. He had reached the positive stage in what he then considered the last of the sciences, that which had for its object society. He fell ill, and, as a result, he became first metaphysical and then theological. The details of what happened are not known. All that has come down to us is the fact that Comte's relations with his wife were not of the happiest; that he felt a very natural desire to unburden his heart to some one in whom he had confidence; that he called on Lamennais, whom he found alone with the Abbé Gerbet, and that, 'without hesitating, he knelt down and disclosed to them, under the seal of the confessional, the internal drama connected with his odious marriage.' After this his Catholic friend seems to have persuaded him of the necessity of recognising the sanctity of the matrimonial tie by submitting to the rites imposed by the Christian Church, and himself to have performed the ceremony.

When the *crisis* was over, it is probable that the friendship continued, and that they came to know one another better and better as time went on. In later life Comte spoke of 'some memorable conferences which followed the decisive pamphlet in which I had publicly consecrated my life to the foundation in the West of the true spiritual power. Then the recognised leader of the Catholic party (the Abbé Lamennais) provoked three public discussions, in which, as worthy adversaries, without any vain hope of mutual conversion, we spontaneously arrived at the idea of a religious alliance.'

We have practically no information of what took place at these conferences; one thing only is certain, that Lamennais was profoundly influenced by many things in the positivist philosophy, and possibly also he was nettled by Comte's idea that Catholicism should represent a simple protest of the past against modern anarchy, leaving to the new system the task of organising society under the direction of a transformed and renovated spiritual power. Bearing this in mind, we shall understand the changes which now began to work themselves out in his point of view.

As has already been stated, the publication of the pamphlet, *La Religion considérée dans ses Rapports avec l'Ordre Politique et Civil*, led to its author being summoned to appear in the police courts on April 20 to answer certain charges which would be brought against him. At the trial he was accused 'of effacing the boundaries which separate the spiritual from the temporal power, of proclaiming the supremacy and infallibility of the Pope, of recognising in the Sovereign Pontiff the right of deposing princes and of releasing peoples from the oath of fidelity.' The charge was not denied. Berryer, who appeared for the defence, pleaded the absolute incompetence of a civil court to decide on a question distinctly spiritual in its nature. The law declared that the Catholic religion was the religion of the State; it was for competent authorities to say what that religion was. When he had concluded, Lamennais rose and said:—

Gentlemen, I have nothing to add to the speech which you have just heard, but I should like to say a few words on the dogmatic questions which are touched upon in my work. Though the Court has no jurisdiction in these matters, nevertheless, as they have served as the pretext for this trial, I owe it to my conscience and to the sacred character of my office to declare before the tribunal that I remain firmly attached to the principles set forth in my pamphlet: that is to say, the invariable teaching of the head of the Church; that his faith is my faith, his doctrine my doctrine, and that to my last breath I shall continue to profess and to defend it.

On the following day the accused was condemned to a fine of 36 francs. The sum was merely nominal, but the principle was of immense importance. Three days later Féli described this judgment in a letter to Mme. de Senfft :—

The public is unanimous on its astounding absurdity. It flies in the face, not only of common sense, but of every opinion. . . . I owe it to the Church to fight the matter out to the bitter end, whatever may be the result. God gives me grace to fear nothing. . . . I have given notice of a new work. . . . The bishops, on their side, are busy with their pens; they are writing declarations of doctrine, which are demanded of them in the name of the king. . . . The thing could not be better done in England. If you know any of these amiable prelates, be so good as to remind them that there is in the world a person who is called Pope, to whom, since the time of St. Peter, custom has attributed some authority in the Catholic Church. You may surprise them, perhaps, but assuredly you will be doing them a good turn.

The spring and summer of 1826 were passed in a state of violent agitation and uncertainty. Living between Paris and Versailles, he was able the more easily to observe what went on at the centre of national life, and it is from this period that we must date the final disappearance of an early ideal.

It will be remembered that at the time of his ordination he had looked upon the Jesuits as an order from which was likely to come the salvation of Israel; he had even been on the point of taking steps towards committing himself irrevocably to them. Since then an opinion had gradually been forming itself in his mind, fostered, perhaps, partly by the opposition of leading members of the order to the doctrine of the *Essai*, that they did not understand the times, and, further, that they were incapable of doing so. He saw, or thought he saw, in them the beginnings of that crystallisation which had appeared in, and then destroyed, so many of the great institutions thrown up in the course of the evolution of humanity and of the Church. To him the bold progressiveness which had marked their passage through the sixteenth, seventeenth, and eighteenth centuries had imperceptibly shrunk into a systematic policy of timid compromisings with the powers of the moment, irrespective of their possible or probable duration. Thus he wrote in July 1826 to M. de Senfft:—

The J. . . ., always the same, speak to every man in his own tongue. To them, all the world is wrong, but, at the same time, it is right. You say you would not sign the four Articles? Nor they either, assuredly; only yesterday, Father such an one said that he would rather lose his right hand. 'But would you sign them?' 'Ah! that is another thing.' Then there are some of the Fathers who think that we enter too warmly into the question. It is certainly possible to give strong reasons on either side, it is a great mistake to imagine that the Society has any opinion in the matter. This policy would be amusing if it were less distressing.

Thus, to whichever side he turned for support, his appeal was met by indifference or by open hostility. Those to whom the mission of regenerating society had been handed down by the past, seemed unwilling to commit themselves to a bold and resolute policy.

Broken in mind and body by the weight of the responsibility which was thrown upon him, his health gave way, and he was ordered to spend a month at a watering place in the Pyrenees.

It was while there that he was seen, for the first time, by Forgues, then a boy of thirteen. The latter was staying at St. Sauveur, with his mother, who received a letter from the Baron de Vitrolles, recommending to her his illustrious friend. The boy was sent with a letter to Lamennais. On hearing the name he turned over in his childish mind all that he had heard of the great writer. He pictured to himself one of those Fathers of the Church whom he had seen in frescoes, or on stained glass windows—

with keys and book, or with a symbolic sword, flowing robes, brilliantly coloured or dark, and with a long streaming beard. . . . The disillusion was complete. . . . I was shown into a little room at the back of one of those houses, built against the rocks, which form the only street in the village. . . . In the semi-darkness of the place I could just distinguish two men—one of them, thin and sorry-looking, with his head lowered on his breast, was reclining on a large straw arm-chair; the other, standing beside him, his head raised, his shoulders drawn back, and with keenness in his glance, with a Southern face, dark and full, rounded and firm in its outline, but without any very marked character: one of those which would have looked as natural under the *képi* of the soldier as under the tonsure of the priest.

The first was Lamennais; the second his travelling companion, his *garde-malade*, the Abbé de Salinis.

Both of them received me, told me that they would go in person to thank my mother, and invited me to come and see them often, morning or evening—in fact, whenever I wished. Thus I found myself, child as I was, at once, without being able to appreciate the value of it, admitted to an intimacy which the greatest men would have envied me.

I amused myself (if I may be pardoned the expression) by comparing the two abbés. They took me with them in their walks, which were never long. . . . Lamennais, soon becoming tired, would often ask us to stop near some clump of trees. We sat down on the grass. Sometimes the Abbé de Salinis would leave us; and then, either having nothing to say to me or to save his feeble breath, he drew from his pocket his copy of the 'Imitation of Jesus Christ' in Latin, and got me to translate to him aloud, here and there interrupting my crude word for word rendering of it by commentaries full of unction and of grace.

The Abbé de Salinis came back. He encouraged Lamennais to use his returning strength. Slowly, very slowly, we walked along the banks of the river, crossed over by the rickety foot-bridge, and climbed up on the other side into the delightful meadows. It was there (I remember it as if it had been yesterday) that one day we spent a whole hour in throwing stones into a narrow opening between the walls of a little sheepfold. The question was, who could get the greatest number of pebbles into this improvised target. The Abbé de Salinis won easily, but I think Lamennais was even less successful than I was.

At this time there was at St. Sauveur a young Royalist writer, A. Bazin de Raucou. He always came with us in our evening walks, but rarely in the morning ones. I can see him still, tall, refined, handsome. . . . I remember one detail in those brilliant conversations in which I had ended by taking a lively interest. I had admitted, not without blushing, that I had read 'Gil Blas' more than once. . . . Bazin, rigorous as the *Quotidienne*, for which he wrote, blamed the tolerance which had allowed such a poisonous book to come into my hands. It was Lamennais who took, not my part, but that of my excellent mother. 'Bah!' he said, 'the important point is that the child should read, and that he should like reading. The choice of books may come later.'

It is not improbable that, as he slowly recovered his strength at St. Sauveur, Féli may have discussed with the Abbé de Salinis the future prospects of the Ultramontane party in France. Forgues was too young to understand such things, and he did not realise that M. Bazin, who is mentioned here, was fighting in the ranks of the opposing school of thought, whose principal organ was the *Quotidienne*. It is possible that these daily walks, in company with the Gallican writer, may have intensified the desire for decisive action in the two priests, leading them, when alone, to talk over matters and to develop plans for future organisation. Indeed, the idea had already been suggested. In January 1825 the Abbé Gerbet had written to M. de Salinis :—

M. de Lamennais, thinking over the project of an association of ecclesiastics, of which he has often spoken to you, has come to the conclusion that we might begin by living together, say four or five of us, with the object of studying and writing. The character of such a community would soon attract public attention. We could then increase our numbers, by calling in, from to time, a few young men.

In October 1826, Lamennais returned to Paris with his companions. The ground seems to have already been prepared for the carrying out of the scheme, for, on the seventh of that month, Gerbet had written to M. de Senfft to inform him of the approaching return of the travellers, and he had added:—' M. Féli will find his room ready for him. I am moving to-day into our new house. M. Féli's room looks out into the garden . . . and is out of reach of the noise of the *Rue d'Enfer*. The Abbé Rohrbacher is coming to live with us.'

We are, then, not altogether unprepared for a scene described by Mgr. Ricard in his volume on the founder of the Mennaisian School. Whatever be its historic value it is sufficiently characteristic in all its details to be worthy of insertion here.

Two young priests, both of them chaplains of the *Collège Henri IV.*, were conversing sadly one evening in December 1826, in a little sitting room where they were in the habit of conferring together on the difficulties of their ministry. . . .

The one, vigorous, ardent, martial in his bearing, with eyes which were lighted up from time to time by sudden flashes of eagerness, was the Abbé de Salinis. The other, more reserved in his manner, almost timid, more at home as a listener than in speaking, was the Abbé Gerbet.

But it was the Abbé Gerbet who had opened the conversation on that evening by a melancholy description of the disappointments of the day.

M. de Salinis interrupted him. Boiling over with youthful enthusiasm, he laid bare his convictions on the possibility of successful action in favour of Catholicism.

'France,' he said, ' is tired of incredulity, and, above all, of that brutal incredulity which tramples on the most intimate feelings of the human soul, naturally Christian. . . . It aspires to a positive belief which, without shocking the mind, may satisfy the needs of the heart; in a word,' cried the young chaplain, 'France desires a rational belief! There lies our hope,' he concluded, ' but there also lies the danger.'

' To realise the one and to neutralise the other, the work of the Catholic Apostolate should tend to a double result: to keep up and develop the desire for faith; to demonstrate, in every possible way, that the only rational faith is in the Apostles' Creed, explained and developed by the Church.'

At this point the conversation of the young priests was interrupted by the entry of a third party . . . who was received by the two chaplains with visible respect. He had heard the last words, and he said :—

' You wish to prove to the age that Catholicism is the only rational religion; that is well, but it is not enough. You must show it that if it does not accept the Catholic creed, it excludes itself from the society of reasonable beings; the common consent of all ages and of all peoples ; in a word, that it is mad ;' . . . and he continued with warmth : 'The longer I live the more certain I become that I can force these good people, so confident in their incredulity, to say their *Credo* to the last syllable, or to admit by their silence (for I shall forbid them to open their mouths) that they cannot say, *I am!* . . . To work then, and we shall bend this nineteenth century under the yoke of Catholicism.'

The gentle Abbé Gerbet, he who was to be the Melancthon of the new Luther, replied timidly :—

'Master, do you not fear that you may irritate reason, instead of subduing it, by so absolute a proceeding? Would it not be better gradually to reconcile the human soul to religion by pointing out the intimate harmonies which exist between its dogmas, its precepts, its institutions, and the deepest needs of humanity? Is it possible to resist, for example, that demonstration which reveals in the Eucharist the most abundant source of social and moral life—in a word, the great lever which raises man to heaven? And what is said of the Eucharist can be said of all the sacraments, the channels through which true life flows out and spreads itself over the human race.'

'Well!' said the previous speaker, 'this point of view completes mine: I do not exclude it.'

Then he seemed to reflect, and looking at the two young priests as if he would read their inmost souls, he added: 'But, since we are agreed on the possibility of exercising an extended influence over our poor diseased society, why should we not unite our efforts? A single man has but one voice, feeble enough at best; but an association!'

Thus was founded the famous Mennaisian School. A little band of resolute men had taken upon themselves the apparently hopeless task of regenerating a society in whose throat the death-rattle was already making itself heard, and of forcing it, whether it would or no, to return to life and health. What great things lay hidden in these small beginnings we shall presently see, but, meanwhile, we must return to the personal doings of him who was the soul of the undertaking.

Lamennais spent the first months of the year 1827 in Paris, but the state of his health seems to have caused considerable anxiety to his friends, so much so, that the Abbé Jean came to the capital in

April for the purpose of accompanying him to La Chênaie, where it was thought that he would obtain that absolute repose which was so necessary to him. The two brothers made the journey in short stages, and reached their Breton home towards the end of the month. As soon as he had settled down, Féli seems to have tried to occupy his mind with the study of Italian, but he found it impossible entirely to banish from it all thought of the great scheme which he had set on foot. On May 2 he wrote to Mme. de Senfft:—

I have for some time been persuaded that a general revolution is inevitable, and that all the efforts of right thinking men should be directed to the future. It is necessary to lay in advance the foundations of a new society; the old one is rotten, it is dead, and it cannot be raised again. It is mere folly to put one's trust in Governments which are no longer governments, and which can no more become so. Our work lies in the creation of peoples; that will always be possible till the time appointed by God for the end of things. The Church has a great mission before it, which it will fulfil; but the hour is not yet come, though it cannot be far off.

The hour was not yet come. Jean returned to his work, and Féli's right-hand man, the Abbé Gerbet, came to La Chênaie in July. On the 18th of that month he wrote to M. de Senfft apologising for the fact that his host had not answered the last letter which he had received from Italy. He said: 'M. Féli is in bed, recovering from an attack of fever, which lasted for eighteen hours. The first symptoms of it appeared last Sunday. He is now better, but he is still too weak to write.'

Gerbet was mistaken; this was but the beginning of a very serious illness, which, after a duration of several weeks, reduced the sufferer to such a state of feebleness that he stood for a moment as it were on the brink of the grave. On July 29 the Abbé had once more to write to M. de Senfft:—

In my letter of last week I told you of the illness of M. Féli, and, at the same time when I wrote, his state was not such that I should have felt justified in alarming you. But since then there has been a bilious fever with spasms, at first interrupted, then continuous faintings, and now a terrible weakness. M. Blaize came in the first days of the illness, and M. Jean has just arrived. We are in consternation. I should be glad to be able to think that our affection magnified in our eyes the danger of his state; but I cannot. If I have waited so long before writing to you, it is because I have been hoping, from day to day, for some improvement of which I could tell you. But do not think that all hope is lost; no, no. I had faith in what remained for him to do, for the accomplishment of his mission, and I have not lost this faith. . . . I shudder at the thought of the shock this letter will cause you.

In the first days of August Féli partially recovered, but there was a relapse towards the middle of the month, which once more threw his friends into consternation. It was not till September 8, when the danger was past, that Gerbet summoned up courage to describe in detail the whole course of the illness to M. de Senfft. On that day he wrote:—

I cannot tell you how much he has suffered from his frightful spasms, nor with what patience, nor yet what I experienced myself when, on two separate occasions, he fainted in my arms. I thought he was dead.

sad memories; I pass to those which are more consoling, but which are connected with the most terrible moments.

He had asked at an early stage for the last sacraments, and, the day on which he received them, was very beautiful in his strong faith and his humble resignation. . . . Face to face with death . . . he said to me from time to time things which broke my heart, but which at the same time comforted me.

'*Of what use*,' he said, '*are honours, riches, reputation, when one has come to this?*' I answered that he had never cared much for them. '*My friend*,' he said, '*I should like to go away: I have had enough of the earth.*' I remember that one night, when he was a little better, to divert him I told him that it was a beautiful night, and that the moonlight was splendid; he tried to raise himself that he might see it through the window, and he answered, falling back again: '*For my peace, God grant that it may be the last.*' When his dear brother arrived (it was he who gave him the last sacraments) he said to him, after some moments' conversation, '*I leave you the finest thing in the world—the truth to defend.*' At another time, I asked him whether he would like anything to drink; his ideas were becoming confused, he did not understand my question, but, interpreting it in a manner analogous to his habitual thoughts, he answered, '*What can one desire but that the will of God should be done.*' This brings me to the most cruel moments. Alas! after the postscript of my sad letter of July 27-28, which must have reassured you a little. What a day we passed on the 27th! The heat was stifling; from six to ten o'clock we believed him to be in his agony. His poor brother begged me to renew the absolution of the dying.

At eleven he began to get better. . . .

This chapter may fittingly be concluded with some extracts from a letter written by Féli himself to Madame de Senfft, on September 25, the first day on which he was allowed to put pen to paper.

I

So I am back again in the world. I had touched the port, but a powerful hand thrusts me forth once more into the middle of the waves, *iterum jactatus in alto*. Alas! I had had enough of the earth and should not have been sorry to leave it.

The first symptom of my illness was a bilious fever; but as soon as this attack had subsided, another, the nervous character of which I soon recognised, began to show signs of its presence. I told the doctor of it, and expressed my opinion that it was here that the principal evil lay hidden; he paid no attention, and I became rapidly worse. My brother and my brother-in-law had been sent for and they were with me. I received, while still conscious, the last sacraments. God gave me strength, and I did not suffer for a moment from regret or anxiety, though I knew and fully realised the precariousness of my state. As it became hour by hour more alarming, they called in another doctor from Dinan, and fortunately he judged it prudent, from what had been told him, to bring the instruments necessary for an operation, the slightest delay in the performance of which would infallibly have caused my death. God so willed it that he did not deceive himself for a moment as to the nature of the illness or the treatment required; the least hesitation would have rendered all remedies useless. As it was, the evil made frightful progress. On Sunday, July 29, I was at death's door. Pulse and respiration had ceased for some seconds, and the doctor waited only for the moment when I should pass away. Nevertheless, wishing to neglect no possible means, he asked for some ammonia; they looked about and discovered some in my cupboard; he succeeded in bringing about a slight beating of the heart—it was the beginning of my return to life. The danger continued for some days, but it ceased altogether on the Feast of St. Peter's Chains. My convalescence has been long and painful, interrupted by spasms, suspended by a relapse caused by the almost sudden death of a favourite servant to whose bedside I was called, in the middle of the night, that I might hastily hear his confession. At this moment I am totally wanting in strength, but that is a matter of time. . . . I should certainly like to pay you a visit, and to repose myself in the soft sunshine of your friendship, but just now I cannot think of travelling; I could not bear it. And besides, I must employ, in defence of religion, the time which God has left me, perhaps only for that. . . . Good-bye, good-bye, I must end this for my poor head is tired.

CHAPTER V

THE REVOLUTION OF JULY 1830

LAMENNAIS was profoundly impressed by the fact of his illness and of his recovery. He was convinced that he had been dragged back into life only that he might become the instrument of Providence in the carrying out of its designs in the world.

'Persuaded,' he said, in a letter of October 2, 1827, 'persuaded that in snatching me from the arms of death, where I had already as it were fallen asleep, She only wished to give me time to recall to society the duties which it has forgotten, I shall hold it a crime and a direct turning away from what God demands of me, if for my personal satisfaction, or even for that of my dearest friends, I were to interrupt for a single moment the work which lies before me.'

From the closing months of 1827 to the final catastrophe of July 1830, his ideas tend gradually to assume a more definite shape. Hitherto we have seen him looking indeed to the future, partly in fear, partly in aspiration, expecting a revolution, a universal upheaving of some kind, but vague and intangible—a great and terrible movement, which will lead society through a period of anarchy to the final triumph of the Catholic Church. He now begins to see his way more clearly amid the tangled mass of facts constituting the groundwork of social science, and, above all, he is beginning to see that there is such a science, a point which, as I have shown in a former chapter, he did not clearly realise, though he suggested it in the last volumes of the *Essai sur l'Indifférence*. Thus in a letter of November 1, to Mme. de Senfft, he speaks of 'a work on Society,' in which 'the questions which I have already dealt with will be set forth from a new and a broader standpoint.'

And in another, on the 30th of the same month, to M. Berryer:—'The men who appear to lead have almost always less part in the progress of events than is generally supposed; they are themselves carried along, and the real force which moulds the future lies in ideas universally prevalent, *whose action can be calculated, as in the material world that of physical forces.*' In this it is not difficult to see the result of his connection with Auguste Comte.

But there were other circumstances tending to a modification of his point of view, which, if less profound in their bearing on the growth of his mind, were more immediate in *their effects*. He was beginning to interest himself in the internal affairs of the other countries of Europe.

By the end of the year 1827 he had come to a thorough knowledge of the Italian language, and this made it possible for him to read many things calculated to arouse his sympathy for the way in which things were progressing in that country. Nothing could have been more congenial to his habitual way of thinking than the idea of a nation owing its independence and its liberties to the leadership of the Sovereign Pontiff, which formed the basis of much that contributed to the patriotic enthusiasm of the Italian people. We are not, then, surprised to find him in November 1827, writing to the Comtesse Louise de Senfft to ask her to send him the novel of Manzoni, which he has seen reviewed, or to learn that he afterwards became an enthusiastic admirer of the author of the *Promessi sposi*.

Nor did he confine himself to one aspect only of the writings of that brilliant but unfortunate nation.

In December 1827 he wrote to Mme. de Senfft :—

I have not read *Foscarini*—who is the author? Italian literature is tending to take in the north a direction which may put new life into it. The south is still languishing, but the movement will spread, and if, instead of making use of it, they try to put it down by force, it will become, above all things, hostile and dangerous. What astonishes me more than anything is the fact that governments seem everywhere incapable of understanding their true interests. I took it into my head to read *Jacopo Ortiz*, the author of which has just died near London. It is a mere copy of Werther, a kind of thing which I do not like, and which essentially belongs to a system of destructive ideas. Monti preferred the *Purgatorio* to the two other parts of the great poem of Dante. The last stanzas of the *Paradiso* seem to me superior; they enrapture me. I advise you to read Petrarch—he is sometimes obscure, artificial, and strained; but, taking it all round, his poetry is marvellously beautiful and pregnant with feeling. I have just begun Villani. He reminds me of the simplicity of our old memoirs, but he has not their grace, their artlessness or their charm. It is a curious fact that Italian prose should never have been able, in any work, to stamp itself with an original or distinctive character. Machiavelli himself is dull, with neither eloquence nor strength nor imagination in his style. In quite another sphere, F. Liguori, so esteemed for his Tuscan elegance, is still more feeble; he bores me to death. Speaking of the prose writers, I was forgetting Boccaccio, but I hardly like to mention him, and besides, his merit lies more in purity of expression and in a kind of simplicity in his dialogues—a simplicity, it is true, crude and vulgar—than in any of the higher qualities.

Passing from Italy to countries nearer to his northern home, Lamennais was especially impressed by the position of two of them, Ireland and Belgium. Rumours which reached him from the first strengthened in his mind the idea of united Catholic action, and he dreamt of the *rôle* of an O'Connell. In February 1829 he wrote to Mme. de Senfft:—'We have nothing to hope for here till energy is aroused among Catholics. Before that happens ideas must be revolutionised, which will take time. In Ireland the Catholics have got themselves a hearing.' In the same letter he quotes a note on the Belgians, who had raised the standard of active resistance to the Government of the Netherlands, which had attempted to interfere in the internal affairs of the Church:—
'Belgium is saved. The Government has been so terrified by the general movement [of the people] that the . . . new bishops have been nominated as they desired. A short time ago the hereditary prince told the Comte de Merode that he quite recognised the injustice of the treatment which had been meted

out to the Catholics, and that if he came to the throne they should have nothing to complain of in him.' In another letter of about the same date he says:—'Belgian Catholics are far in advance of us . . . for with them the principles of Christianity have not been obscured by Gallicanism; they realise the necessity of curing themselves of that terrible disease called Royalism, which, little by little, has destroyed all the forces of society.'

Thus he followed, step by step, the progress of the Revolution which was to end in the total independence of the most Catholic country in the modern world. Nor did he stop here. Raising his eyes and prophetically sweeping the horizon of European politics, he saw everywhere the same signs of approaching dissolution. On July 7, 1830, within a few days of the final catastrophe, he wrote to the Marquis de Coriolis:—'A great commotion seems to me to be inevitable, and in this France will not be alone; the whole South of Europe has its eyes fixed on her; twenty millions of men—in Italy, in Spain, in Portugal—will suddenly rise at the first cry of liberty which goes forth from her.'

But how were matters progressing in that country which was to give the signal for a general rising?

Lamennais recovered from his illness in September 1827, just in time to witness the last agony of the Villèle Ministry, which had been in office since the accession of Charles X. in 1824. Of the importance of that Ministry it is sufficient to say that it found the Bourbon monarchy strong and comparatively popular, and that it left it irretrievably ruined. In the closing months of 1827 the Government found itself in steady opposition to the majority of the Chamber. Had M. de Villèle consulted his dignity rather than his desire to retain office, he would have resigned, leaving to his opponents the task of dealing with a crisis for which they were in part responsible. But he thought otherwise, and so gave to the world the contemptible spectacle of a minister clinging convulsively to a position which he felt to be slipping away from him. This was too much for the gravity of Lamennais. On December 21 he wrote to Berryer:—

> Do you not think, my dear friend, that if one were as anxious to save one's soul as that man is to remain a minister it would be as if one were already in heaven? But such energy is only for hell—hell in this world or hell in the next. For I do not think that there can be down there, in the empire of shades, any prison equal to those official residences so desired and so sought after, at the gates of which stand and watch the ghosts whom Æneas saw at the entrance of the kingdom of darkness. Why then, Mr. President, do you require so much pressing? Come, now, a little reason . . . but, instead of listening, there he sits counting: one vote, two votes, ten votes, fifty votes! A minority of fifty! The pen falls from his hand, his head is weighed down; he is absorbed by some great thought. Then he begins once more to count; his face expands; he has discovered a new combination, a law of attraction, hitherto unknown, which will cause the legislative bodies (they are not celestial bodies) to gravitate round their centre, which is himself. It is done; the ministerial universe will go on. On the first day he is hopeful; on the second day he is hopeful; but on the third—good-bye to the law, good-bye to attraction, good-bye to the universe, good-bye to everything! And he says: 'At

least understand that after me there will be no more sun. I warn you, at most the moon will remain to you.' This is met by a chorus of voices: 'Long live the moon! We love the moon! We want the moon! Give us the moon!' And I think that, willing or no, the sun will have to give place, which would be very sad if we were not already in midwinter.'

And the Abbé de Lamennais had reason to welcome the approaching fall of this ministry. The situation was curiously complicated, and at first sight the position of the Ultramontane priest seems somewhat paradoxical. The Government had been defeated by the Liberal majority, which had set before itself as an ideal the establishing on a permanent footing of those revolutionary institutions which he hated and looked on as supremely anti-Christian. One of the causes, if not the principal cause, of the unpopularity of M. de Villèle was the fact that he had attempted to shield the Church from the ecclesiastical proposals of the Liberals. Under him the office of Minister of Public Worship had been held by Frayssinous, Bishop of Hermopolis, who, before the appearance of the *Essai sur l'Indifférence*, had, from his *Conférences*, been looked upon as the most successful contemporary defender of the Catholic faith. To the ordinary observer, then, it might easily have seemed that the interests of religion were intimately bound up with those of the existing *régime*, and that the blow which destroyed the ministry was principally and fundamentally aimed at Catholicism itself. Indeed, Lamennais thoroughly realised the truth of this opinion, but he did not stop here. Searching into the deeper meaning of events, he asked himself the question: 'Why should these things be?' And the answer came to him, wafted on the breath of all the ages of humanity: ' It is because the Church, in its official representatives, has renounced its birthright.' For what was called religion was a mockery, a mere parody of religion, a State organisation of opinion in the highest matters calculated to sustain the puffed and swollen pride of a bastard monarchy which hoped to maintain itself by sacrificing all else to the Revolution. What wonder, then, if the people looked on Catholicism simply as the keystone of a gigantic conspiracy against their moral as well as against their material advancement, and if they had grown to hate it! To Lamennais such hatred was preferable to the indifference against which he had protested in the early years of the Restoration; nor was it without its doctrinal basis. The Governments which had succeeded one another since 1815 had imitated their predecessors in insisting on the acceptance by the clergy of the Gallican Articles of 1682, which declared that the decisions of the Pope were subject to ratification by a general council or the tacit acceptance of the universal Church, thus making it possible for the bishops of any nation, by a simple protest, to practically nullify them, and which further laid down the principle that Papal utterances were, in the publishing of them, subject to the jurisdiction of the civil power. Lamennais had, as we have seen, in 1826, boldly proclaimed the opposite theory, and had even maintained the right of the Sovereign Pontiff to release subjects from the oath of fidelity. Connecting this with his previous statement, that Catholicism was but the summing up of the unanimous voice of the peoples, and with the fact that, through his relations with Comte and the increase of experience, he had come to a clearer understanding of that element of movement, of evolution, which he had not fully realised in his earlier work, it is not difficult to see by what process of reasoning, without any fundamental change in his point of view, he began to perceive that there was no very great gulf of separation between himself and the Liberal party. The deposing power of the Pope and the deposing power of the people were but two expressions for the same thing, with this difference, that while the first was orderly, and might be looked on as a guarantee of co-operation with the general progress of human affairs, the second contained within itself dangerous germs of an all-destroying anarchy, and was only justified by the fact that the other had been denied and made impossible of application by those in power.

This much being said, we may return to our narrative.

It was in vain that M. de Villèle strained every nerve to get himself maintained in office. The position was untenable, and in January 1828 he resigned. This event was followed by the formation of the Martignac Ministry, which held office till August 1829.

During the first weeks of the new administration, Frayssinous continued to hold the portfolio for ecclesiastical affairs, but, in March, he had to give way before the hostility of the opposition to everything which recalled the days of M. de Villèle. Lamennais mentions the fact, in a letter to Mme. de Senfft, dated March 10, 1828 :—' As I prophesied . . . Frayssinous is withdrawing after having brought France to the verge of schism. The party is singing the praises of his successor.'

That successor was Feutrier, Bishop of Beauvais, and it is not too much to say that from the narrow, immediate point of view, his policy weighed more heavily on the Ultramontane position than that of his predecessor. The new Government, owing its existence to the decisive victory of the Liberals at the end of 1827, was bound to make concessions. From this state of things resulted the two famous Ordinances of June 1828: the first, depriving the Jesuits of the right of directing or teaching in colleges; the second, limiting the number of seminaries and regulating many things in their internal discipline.

It was expected that the bishops, who had almost unanimously accepted the Gallican propositions, would not offer any considerable opposition, but, in this the framers of the decrees were disappointed. On July 14 the Abbé Jean was able to write to M. de Senfft :—

No doubt the Church will be subjected to fresh trials: they will be painful and bloody, but we shall be victorious;

a violent crisis is the only thing that can save us. *Portæ inferi non prævalebunt.* Let us have confidence and courage. Is it not a grand thing to see the French episcopate, which we thought so feeble, rising as one man in the hour of danger, turning towards Rome and saying with the prophet, *Levavi oculos meos in montes unde veniet auxilium mihi?*

And this opposition made it practically impossible to carry out the measures forced on the Government by the Chamber. For it was necessary, at any rate in dealing with the seminaries, to get authentic reports from the bishops on those already existing in their several dioceses, and these were in many cases refused. One of the answers received by the Bishop of Beauvais was especially characteristic. He had sent an official communication, amongst others, to Clermont-Tonnerre, Archbishop of Toulouse, inviting him to send in the required information. The only reply he received was the following:—

MONSEIGNEUR,—The motto of my family, which was given to it in 1120 by Callistus II., is this: *Etiamsi omnes, ego non.* It is also that of my conscience.

I have the honour to be, with the respectful consideration due to a minister of the King,

A.J. CARDINAL ARCHBISHOP OF TOULOUSE.

The position of the ministry was embarrassing. Placed between the possibility of schism, and the practical certainty of revolution, one course only was open to them, and Chateaubriand was directed to work the matter at Rome. As a result, on September 25, a circular was sent by Cardinal de Latil to all the bishops.

MONSEIGNEUR,—The King having deigned to communicate to me the *answers of Rome* relative to the ordinances of June 16, and having invited me to impart them to you, I have the honour to inform you that His Holiness, convinced of the absolute devotion of the French Bishops to His Majesty, as he is of their love of peace and of all other true interests of our holy religion, has answered that *the Bishops should confide in the wisdom of the King in the carrying out of the ordinances and should continue in agreement with the throne.*

It was natural enough that some doubt should have been thrown on the strict authenticity of this laconic communication, but as Rome, on being appealed to, judged it prudent to maintain silence, the document acquired the desired authority.

So the Government was saved. The *sop* of ecclesiastical independence had been thrown to the *Cerberus* of the Revolution.

The movement of 1789 had been directed primarily against the clergy and the nobility—so appear to have reasoned the friends of the Restoration; if monarchy had fallen in '92, it was only a natural result of its having identified itself with these fallen institutions; but the Revolution itself was not, in principle, directed against the Monarchical system. The fact that the contrary had appeared to be the case was due to a mere accident, tragic enough, no doubt, but still not irremediable. To prevent future mistakes it was necessary for Royalists to convince the Revolution of their goodwill. The nobles had already been deprived of power and influence, but the clergy, though severely hit, still showed signs of life, and might some day become embarrassing. It was not denied that the monarchy was Catholic, or that its representative was the *Most Christian King*, nor, again, that religious authority was necessary to keep alive the idea of the sanctity of the State establishment. But a sacrifice had to be made, a Jonah had to be thrown over as a peace-offering to the angry deep. M. de Coriolis showed that he understood the situation when he said that a particular speech from the throne could be summed up in the words: 'I love papa, the good God: I love mama, the Revolution.'

As I have said, the successful carrying through of this masterly stroke of policy was somewhat impaired by the resistance of the bishops, who could not be got to see the matter in a proper light. But now Rome had spoken, and so even the most uncompromising Ultramontane must be satisfied. Thus, all difficulties were removed, and the Government was free to deal with Liberalism, unembarrassed by the possibility of a flank attack from the clerical side.

At least, so men thought, but they had forgotten the *solitary of La Chênaie*.

Matters went on smoothly enough during the three months following the circular of Cardinal de Latil, and the ministers were beginning to congratulate themselves on the success of their manœuvre, when suddenly, in February 1829, a book appeared, which at once changed the whole aspect of affairs. It was called, *Des progrès de la Révolution et de la Guerre contre l'Eglise.*

In this work Lamennais boldly separated the cause of Catholicism from that of the Monarchy and, incidentally, from that of the Jesuits, who had been most severely dealt with in the ordinances of June. But, in doing this, he in no way identified himself with the revolutionary movement. Royalty, it is true, had abandoned the Church to its fate, so now Catholics must leave the monarch and his supporters to fight their own battles; but they could look back in fond remembrance to 'the time when Providence recalled from exile the family of our ancient kings.' So, too, the Jesuits were incapable of dealing with modern society, and it would be fatal to the Catholic cause if it were thought that theirs was essentially bound up with it; but it should not be forgotten that the attack on them was in some measure inspired by hostility to religion, and therefore Christians should have nothing to do with it.

Turning, in the opening pages of his book, to the actual situation, he briefly states the object of the task which he has undertaken: 'We demand for the Catholic Church the liberty promised by the Charter to all religions; the liberty which is enjoyed by Protestants and Jews, and which would be guaranteed to the followers of Mahomet or of Buddha if any of them existed in France. . . . We demand liberty of conscience, liberty of the press, liberty of education—in a word, what the Belgians have demanded of a persecuting Government.'

Having thus brought home to his readers the very practical and immediate bearing of his work, the author plunges into an historical analysis of the relations between Church and State, and he concludes that Christianity brought liberty into the world with the creation of an *independent spiritual power*; that Louis XIV. proclaimed despotism, and brought society back to the point at which Christianity found it: whence the Revolution. But Christianity has thoroughly saturated the population of Catholic countries: *Mens agitat molem,* and it is this which has produced the war between the people and those in authority.

Must we, then, ally ourselves with the Revolution? By no means. Liberalism, in deifying individualism, must eventually find itself placed between despotism (Hobbes) and anarchy; for it is impossible, on its accepted principles, to decide what form of Government is legitimate. In a word: 'To ally ourselves to liberalism, while it remains under the influence of the theories which now characterise it, would be to ally ourselves to anarchy itself—that is to say, to an opinion which has no power but to destroy. . . . While, to identify ourselves with authority, in the form it has assumed under the influence of godless maxims, which free it from every rule and all dependence, would be to lean on that which is falling, on a thing which, henceforward, no mortal power can save, and to alienate the people from religion by sacrificing, to a few men hopelessly blinded, their holiest rights and their legitimate future.'

Therefore priests and laymen should work to make the Church an independent force, resting on its own traditions, which, trusting in its own strength, can quietly await the catastrophe, and then, seizing its opportunity, step in and save the world. 'Whatever men may do, there are two needs which demand satisfaction, and which are inherent in human nature: the need of common doctrines, which form the society of minds, and the need for each mind of developing its particular activity.'

But this book will be better understood through the events which followed its publication than by a detailed analysis of the contents of its pages. Before turning, however, to the consideration of these, there is one fact of considerable interest and importance which must not be passed over.

M. Lafitte has pointed out in the earlier of the articles quoted above, that Lamennais here commits himself to Comte's classification of the sciences, which he arranges in the following order: 'Mathematics, astronomy, physics, chemistry, physiology . . . which he justifies on the principle of the *preponderance of reason* and the *growth of complication*.' It will be observed that there is one notable exception, *sociology*. This may perhaps be accounted for on the ground that he had not yet sufficiently made up his mind to feel justified in committing himself thus far in public, or by a desire to avoid shocking the preconceived opinions of the majority of his readers; for he had already, as we have seen, expressed himself in a letter as holding the opinion that society could become the subject of a science when he spoke of '*ideas, universally prevalent, whose action can be calculated, as in the material world that of physical forces.'*

It is needless to say that this declaration of war from the pen of the Abbé de Lamennais fell like a thunderbolt on the ministerial and politico-ecclesiastical world. The state of things was described in a letter to the author by M. Waille, the editor of the *Mémorial Catholique* :—

It is difficult to describe, Monsieur l'Abbé, the effect produced by your last work. The diplomatic body combining together to demand, of all the Courts, the provocation of its condemnation at Rome ; the bishops hastening to Paris, as if their dioceses were on fire ; the Archbishop of Paris fulminating, the others getting ready to do so ; the terror of the Nuncio himself ; the humiliation and irritation of the Jesuits and their friends, who, out of spite, have renounced what they hitherto admitted of the doctrine of *general consent*, &c., &c. . . . Nevertheless the revolution continues on its way ; the Capuchins are being turned out of Marseilles, in the Chamber a motion has been brought in to banish those congregations of men which have up to now been considered as authorised by the law. They are thinking of ordering the J[esuits] to leave the kingdom. Mgr. Feutrier *permits* the bishops to pray for the Pope. Shall I go on with this enumeration of insults—on the one hand, persecution, on the other, servility ?

We can imagine the effect of such news on the vivid imagination of Féli de Lamennais. His combative feelings were thoroughly aroused when he heard that the Archbishop of Paris had issued a pastoral letter against him, for this event followed almost immediately on another, with which he had become acquainted through the newspapers, the death of Leo XII.

It was while he was still in a state of violent agitation, caused by this double blow, that he wrote to Madame de Senfft on February 28, 1829 :—' Yes, the death of Leo XII. is a great calamity; I deeply feel his loss. However, permit me to say it, I cannot regret the happiness and peace I should, without doubt, have found with him. . . . It has been God's will that I should remain here; I become every day more and more convinced of it. To work, to defend the Truth . . . to suffer for it, such is my lot. . . . The Archbishop of Paris has just attacked me in a pastoral; he would not have dared to do it had the Pope still been living. No doubt other bishops will follow the example of this Court prelate, and not one of them will say anything on the other side; so I shall speak myself.'

This resolution was followed by the writing of two letters in reply to the archbishop, and on April 28 he described the result to M. de Senfft: 'As you have seen, I have cut matters short with the Archbishop of Paris. He admitted—and I believe him— that he "had not read my book." They say that his only object in publishing the pastoral was to get the *cordon bleu* at Pentecost.'

In the same letter there is an explanation on the Jesuits, who were naturally very indignant at his contemptuous treatment of them, and one of whom had written to M. de Senfft, laying stress on the fact that Pius VII. had seen fit to restore the order without changing anything in its constitutions, but saying nothing of the contrary action of Clement XIV., who had suppressed it in the eighteenth century. M. de Senfft had forwarded this letter to Lamennais, who was himself in correspondence with a member of the order, and who now enclosed a note which he asked his Austrian friend to forward, when read, to his Jesuit correspondent, and he added :—

Thirty or forty pages would have been necessary for the clear expression of my meaning. The more I think of it, the more strongly I become convinced that, without great changes in the spirit and in the organisation of the order, it is impossible for it to live; within half a century it will be once more suppressed by the Holy See. I do not deny that it was impiety which overthrew it the first time; but it was not impiety alone, for this would have been powerless had it not been supported by a very wide-spread opinion which has grown up again during the last fourteen years, and is increasing every day. When the J . . . fell, Europe was tired of them. Those who wish truly to serve them should recognise this, and try to get them to see it themselves; blind enthusiasm can but hasten their destruction. Their true friends are those who tell them the truth. May they acknowledge this, and frankly admit that there is much in them which might be reformed, and that on such a reform, now more necessary and more pressing than ever, depends their existence in the future! They are, nearly all of them, so convinced of the perfection of their institution, that it seems like a sort of fascination. For my part, I know nothing perfect in this kind but the Church. All else is man, and participates in his infirmity.

In France the opposition to the work among the official classes and their supporters was almost universal. M. Roussel speaks of a bishop who wrote a private letter condemning the book, but who, on his opinion being made public, took the trouble to read it, and was sorry for what he had said.

But news from other countries was more consoling to the author. In July he received a letter from Belgium, in which the writer said:—

> Last winter I resisted the temptation of writing to you. ... But an opportunity now offers itself; the Sovereign Pontiff, the Congregation of the *Index*, has just given a fitting answer to the French Government. Allow me to offer you my sincerest congratulations; it is a triumph for all who share your opinions. For my part I must thank you personally. I owe to your work repose of mind and peace of conscience. A Catholic, strong in faith, I was a Liberal in politics, while nearly all the Catholics I knew spoke of the interests of throne and altar as inseparable, and I saw that incredulity was almost always bound up with Liberalism. The contradiction was for me the source of painful questionings and lively misgivings in my confessions, and yet I could not bring myself to look on the peoples as mere flocks legitimately given over as a prey to the crook of an incapable shepherd, or to the knife of a butcher. Your book, sir, appeared, and was, for me, as a great light which suddenly lit up those dark places where I had been groping for so long. I saw the truth, and I threw myself eagerly on the treasure so long desired. I seized it; I made it mine, and since then, Papist, Ultramontane, I have found the calm tranquillity which I had lost. For this, sir, accept my sincerest thanks. Your book has caused a great sensation in this country; three editions have been sold out; our old Flemish blood was stirred as we recognised the principles which guided our fathers in their long struggle against despotism.

Indeed, the assurances which he received from different quarters were sufficient to convince the author that the shaft had struck home, and he could afford to laugh at the hostile attitude of those against whom he had directed it. On the other hand, his new departure necessarily involved a political separation from many of those who had been his closest allies in the past, but who were not absolutely dominated, as he was, by the religious principle.

M. de Vitrolles, for instance, looked on the book as indicating a complete change of opinion. In May he wrote to Lamennais :—

Was it not you who told me that a man was what society had made him; that he owed to it everything, even his thought, his speech? . . . Do you then mean, by the 'development of the principle of liberty,' the restricting as much as possible of this sacrifice of natural independence. Do you think that, with us, too much weight is given to the social side of things? Diminish, if you can, the religious and the political yoke, and you will soon have made an end of France and of society itself. You are impressed by the abuses of authority: what would you think of those of the opposite principle? What sort of men has your imagination created—disinterested, devoid of passion? . . . You see, I do not understand you . . . and this poor despotism, in which I should have liked to take refuge had anyone been able to establish it . . . My friend, you wander alone with your pure and noble imagination. Your thought is of a very high order, but it is in the clouds, and far from our poor planet, whose form and whose methods you will not change. Who has pointed out more forcibly than you have that it is impossible, with impunity, to separate oneself from ideas received and accepted by the generality of mankind? . . . My dear man, you are alone, you will be understood by no one. This comes of living for years together a solitary at La Chênaie! The world uses up mental energy; it holds all at a level, low enough in the scale of ideas; but solitude leads us, little by little, to an eccentricity which in its turn has its disadvantages and its dangers.

Thus Lamennais was misunderstood even by his most intimate friends. There is evidence in his correspondence of considerable irritation and resentment at the way in which his suggestions were received by many from whom he had expected sympathy and support; but fortunately there was other work before him, which prevented him from dwelling too exclusively on matters unpalatable to one of his nervous and impressionable temperament.

Mention has already been made of his agreement with the Abbés Gerbet and de Salinis to found a school for the defence of the Catholic faith, and the explaining of it to the modern world. For the carrying out of their plan something of the nature of a religious order was necessary, and in this the organising powers of the Abbé Jean were not to be despised.

This indefatigable priest had hitherto, as we have seen, devoted the greater part of his energies to the foundation and development of his *Brothers of Christian Instruction*; he was in 1827 called upon to take part in a work which was more far-reaching in its object. One of the first steps in the carrying out of the scheme has been picturesquely described by an eye-witness, M. Houet, the late Superior of the Oratory of Rennes.

Forty years ago, at Vitré, in 1827, I was concluding my studies at the seminary of that town. One day an ecclesiastic, small, thin, with a sunburnt complexion, quick of eye, with forehead broad and high, already deeply furrowed, appeared in the refectory. His unwonted presence drew the attention of masters and pupils, but especially of the former, who seemed as surprised as they were honoured by such a visit. This priest was the brother of the celebrated author of the 'Essay on Indifference,' then at the height of his glory. A man of action, he had recently founded a society of priests for the needs of the diocese. He had a private interview with the principal professor of the establishment, and some months afterwards that professor with two of his pupils joined the congregation of M. de Lamennais. I was one of those pupils.

Thus was formed, as a national institution, the celebrated Society of St. Peter, destined to become a centre of Ultramontane and Mennaisian propaganda.

While the Abbé Jean was using his influence with the seminaries, Gerbet and Féli himself exerted themselves by correspondence to the gaining of recruits to the movement. Their efforts were successful, and a band of devoted disciples gathered round the master.

The main body of the community was established at Malestroit, where aspirants to the priesthood were prepared for the moral and intellectual struggle which was before them by men like the Abbés Rohrbacher and Blanc. But the chief interest centres at La Chênaie, where Lamennais, who had been elected Superior-General, gathered round himself a few young men whose rarer qualities pointed to a brilliant future.

It would be difficult to imagine anything more fascinating than that life of piety, study and recreation which marked these days of quiet preparation in the little house surrounded by woods in the wilds of Brittany. It has been described for us by the immortal pen of Maurice de Guérin, who joined the community at a later date.

In December 1832 he wrote to his father :—

I left Paris . . . on Wednesday. . . . I had met there M. Jean de L., the brother of M. Féli, and hoped I should have been able to travel with him, but he advised me to go alone, as his business would detain him indefinitely in Paris. . . . I arrived at Rennes on Friday evening, and was put up at a house of the missionaries, founded by M. Jean; next day I got as far as Dinan with the post—that is to say, within two leagues of La Chênaie. There I was fortunate enough to meet one of my fellow disciples, and we went on together.

M. Féli received me like a good father, and I embraced him with the affection of a child, and with an emotion which you can understand. MM. Gerbet and . . . also received me kindly. Next day I began a little retreat of three days which has just come to an end. I sorely needed this lustral water. Our mode of life is very pleasant. We get up at five (I am sure that they will laugh at my laziness when they find it out); then there is prayer, with meditation or reading; dinner at twelve; supper at eight, and at nine or ten, bed. Such is our day. Our recreations are spent in walks in the garden or the woods, stick in hand. . . . There is another new-comer besides myself. . . . We shall be four in all, and I do not think the house could hold much more.

We are surrounded . . . and, as it were, stifled by the woods; the unevennesses of the ground are so slight that it is almost a plain, so that it is a rare thing to come on a good view, and when we do so, we see only that immense uniformity which characterises the surface of forests. . . . To the west of the house is a pond shut in between two woods which border it with overhanging trees. They say that in summer it is charming. . . . The house itself is crowned with a sharply angular roof which covers the attics. It is white . . . and can be seen through the woods. The chapel is in front, at the bottom of the garden; it is quite small and simple, and suitable to the solitude of the place. There is a low Mass there on Sundays and feast days, as the parish is a long way off. The garden is vast, well kept, and cut through by sandy walks, some of them bordered by evergreens. Half of it goes round the house to the left, and is separated from the other half by a large terrace planted with lime trees. . . . On the north side, corresponding to this garden, is a yard surrounded by farm buildings, whence one can hear the crowing of the cocks and the quacking of the ducks, which we can see from time to time. . . .

So far I have heard nothing of my work; M. Féli has put off speaking to me of it till after my retreat, which comes to an end to-day. I had forgotten to tell you that he is my disentangler, my plucker out, the holder of my secrets. It is such a short time since I arrived that my details have necessarily been of the external, general kind; as we get on they will become more subtle, more personal, more interesting. My interviews with M. Féli have not been long, on account of the meditation involved in my retreat. To-morrow we are to have a serious talk. Do you know what was the subject of our first conversation? 'What sort of weather have you usually in your part of the country?' was the first question; and then he asked me about my travelling companions, my age, the high tide at St. Malo, Calderon, how to catch oysters, Catholic poetry, Hugo, the principal kinds of fish to be found on the coast of Brittany. . . . The great man is small, slender, pale, with grey eyes, an oblong head, a nose broad and long, a forehead deeply furrowed with lines which come down between the eyebrows to the root of the nose; dressed from head to foot in coarse grey cloth. He walks up and down his room at such a pace as to tire my young legs, and when we go out for a stroll, he walks on in front, wearing on his head an old battered straw hat.

A few days later he wrote to his sister, Eugénie de Guérin :—

I am getting used to the desert . . . my habits are conforming themselves to my new life, and my eyes are already accustomed to the thorny moors and the dull brown of the forests. There must be in me a considerable fund of sympathy that I should have been able so quickly to get to like these uncouth steppes, and the dark belt of woods which surrounds us. La Chênaie is truly a hermitage in the midst of solitude, and one can say, without exaggeration, that one hears there only the sighing of the wind in the branches of the trees, and that nothing is seen to pass but the clouds. Often, in spite of habit, we wonder at our profound isolation, and ask ourselves how such silence can be. In this way work becomes a need, an absolute necessity. Thought cannot gambol in this uninviting country, it is forced to stay at home and to turn in upon itself, for contact with the outer world would wound it.

All this means that I have got to work, and that the work is serious and without interruption. M. Féli has set me to do modern languages, beginning with Italian, and Catholic philosophy, with the history of philosophy. I am glad of an opportunity of learning modern languages; they are an important vehicle of the sciences. Of dead languages I am learning only Greek. I know a little already, which will help me over the first difficulties. You see that I am in the first beginnings of an immense work . . . but we have so great a general at our head that I feel full of confidence, and as it were certain of victory.

There are now four of us young men. Each of us has a

bedroom, but as there is a dearth of fire-places, we meet together for work in a common room, round a good fire. I have, without much difficulty, got accustomed to getting up at five o'clock; I even find that I sleep the better for it. I love our little chapel at the bottom of the garden. We go there the first thing in the morning to serve or to hear Mass. Then comes breakfast, with butter and bread, which we toast to make it more palatable; butter always plays an important part in our meals. Dinner is solid, with coffee and liqueurs when there are visitors, and it is seasoned by a running fire of anecdotes and witticisms, most of which come from M. Féli. Some of his sayings are charming, and he is continually going off into flights at once lively, pointed, and brilliant. In this way he finds an outlet for his genius when he is not at work; he ceases to be sublime and becomes delightful. M. Gerbet is also pretty good at telling stories, but he is usually more serious than M. Féli. . . .

I have seen M. Féli in the sitting room. . . . [He] lets you say your rosary without interrupting you; then, when you have said 'I have done,' he begins to speak words grave, deep, luminous, full of unction. His moral conversation, like his books of devotion, is filled with Holy Scripture, marvellously interwoven with his language. It lends to it a peculiar sweetness. He loves us as a father, and addresses each of us as '*My son*.' Yesterday, when the last of us arrived, he seemed deeply touched. 'Our little family is increasing,' he said to me, and he embraced me tenderly. We learn more from conversation than from books. In a few words he suggests points of view which are invaluable in their bearing on different branches of knowledge. Everything that falls from him elevates and warms the soul; one feels the presence of genius.

Such was the impression made on Maurice de Guérin by the daily routine at La Chênaie, such were his thoughts on the central figure of that small community. It would be impossible to imagine anything more vivid than the picture which is conveyed to us by these simple descriptions. We can almost see the various actors as each pursues his allotted course. We feel that we are in the presence of a deep reality when he describes to us a scene in the woods which surrounded La Chênaie :—

A strong north wind rolled over the forest—the trees were bent and writhed furiously at every blast. We saw through the branches black fantastic masses of cloud flying along, and seeming to touch the tops of the trees. From time to time, breaking through some momentary opening in the great sombre veil, a ray of sun flashed like lightning into the bosom of the forest. These fitful streams of light gave to the depths, so majestic in their shadow, an appearance of something wild and strange, like a smile on the lips of the dead.

But, as we turn over the pages of the *Journal* or of the correspondence, we become gradually aware of the fact that we are not in presence of nature alone. Maurice may love to wander in the woods, or to loiter on some mossy bank, soothed into dreamy reverie by the soft murmurings from the teeming incidents of forest life, but we feel that in his solitude he is never alone, that he is always, in thought at least, under the influence of a powerful personality : for had he not owned himself a disciple of the Abbé Félicité de Lamennais?

And, as it was with Guérin, so it was with those who went before him. For we must remember that the young poet did not join the community till 1832, at a time when many things had happened of which, as yet, nothing has been said, and when one at least of his most intimate followers was about to separate himself for ever from the master, on the horizon of whose career the dark clouds of gloomy tragedy were already beginning to gather.

At the period we have reached none of these things had come to pass, and the future seemed pregnant with great things to the first band of neophytes who ranged themselves under the banner of the solitary of La Chênaie.

It is a curious fact, characteristic of the vivid contrasts so often seen in the course of his stormy career, that at this moment, as we stand as it were trembling on the threshold of a movement which will lead us we know not whither, the great genius in whose mind the thing is being evolved suddenly lets fall from his pen a work which breathes, above all things, a spirit of tender pathos and deep sympathy with his fellow-men, very far removed from what the outward arrangement of events might have led us to expect.

In January 1828 he had lost his father, M. de Lamennais, and in the summer of 1829 death had snatched away from him his uncle Des Saudrais, who had done so much for him in his childhood and in the days of his first waking into consciousness in the world of literature. About this last he had written: 'I have just lost my poor uncle, who has been to us a second father. The two brothers on the same day married two sisters; they are together now. So . . . all things pass away, so all things die! Beati mortui qui in Domino moriuntur!'

And thus it happened that on November 1 of this year 1829, depressed in mind and worn out in body, he had retired to his room, not perhaps without having reminded his young disciples of the sorrowful commemoration ordained by the Church to take place on the following day. The scene has been graphically described by his nephew Blaize:—

It was in 1829, on the evening of the Feast of All Saints. We were all together in the drawing-room of that old granite house teeming with so many memories. M. Lorin, the maternal ancestor of M. de Lamennais, painted in his judge's robes, looked down at us gravely and kindly. Madame Lorin, dressed in yellow damask sprinkled with little flowers, and in a velvet cloak trimmed with fur, her hands in her muff, softly smiled at us. But time had passed over those dear faces, and had left but a shade of sadness. My grandfather and my grandmother Lamennais, many of their children and their grandchildren, my great uncle Des Saudrais and his devoted wife, had lived in this house, and had found in it a little rest and happiness. On such a day they too had thought of their dead, and hoped for them the joys of heaven. The autumn wind was carrying along in clouds the yellowed leaves from the old oaks which had seen so many generations pass away, and causing to vibrate the rows of slender needled twigs on the branches of the pines, which rose like black phantoms in the darkness. How many loved voices mingling with the rumours of the night cried to us from the tomb 'Remember!' . . .

M. de Lamennais came into the room and read to us his *Hymn of the Dead*:—

Ils ont aussi passé sur cette terre, ils ont descendu le fleuve du temps ; on entendit leurs voix sur ses bords, et puis on n'entendit plus rien. Où sont-ils ? Qui nous le dira ? Heureux les morts qui meurent dans le Seigneur.

Pendant qu'ils passaient, mille ombres vaines se présentèrent à leurs regards : le monde que le Christ a maudit leur montra ses grandeurs, ses richesses, ses voluptés ; ils le virent, et soudain ils ne virent plus que l'éternité. Où sont-ils ? Qui nous le dira ? Heureux les morts qui meurent dans le Seigneur.

Semblable à un rayon d'en haut, une croix dans le lointain apparaissait pour guider leur course ; mais tous ne la regardaient pas. Où sont-ils ? Qui nous le dira ? Heureux les morts qui meurent dans le Seigneur.

Il y en avait qui disaient : Qu'est-ce que ces flots qui nous emportent ? Y a-t-il quelque chose après ce voyage rapide ? Nous ne le savons pas, nul ne le sait. Et comme ils disaient cela, les rives s'évanouissaient. Où sont-ils ? Qui nous le dira ? Heureux les morts qui meurent dans le Seigneur.

Il y en avait aussi qui semblaient dans un recueillement profond écouter une parole secrète, et puis, l'œil fixé sur le couchant, tout à coup ils chantaient une aurore invisible et un jour qui ne finit jamais. Où sont-ils ? Qui nous le dira ? Heureux les morts qui meurent dans le Seigneur.

Entraîné pêle-mêle, jeunes et vieux, tous disparaissaient, tels que le vaisseau que chasse la tempête. On compterait plutôt les sables de la mer que le nombre de ceux qui se hâtaient de passer. Où sont-ils ? Qui nous le dira ? Heureux les morts qui meurent dans le Seigneur.

Ceux qui les virent ont raconté qu'une grande tristesse était dans leur cœur : l'angoisse soulevait leur poitrine, et, comme fatigués du travail de vivre, levant les yeux au ciel, ils pleuraient. Où sont-ils ? Qui nous le dira ? Heureux les morts qui meurent dans le Seigneur.

Des lieux inconnus où le fleuve se perd, deux voix s'élèvent incessamment.

L'une dit : Du fond de l'abîme j'ai crié vers vous, Seigneur : Seigneur, écoutez mes gémissements, prêtez l'oreille à ma prière. Si vous scrutez nos iniquités, qui soutiendra votre regard ? Mais près de vous est la miséricorde et une rédemption immense.

Et l'autre: Nous vous louons, ô Dieu ! nous vous bénissons : Saint, saint, saint est le Seigneur Dieu des Armées ! La terre et les cieux sont remplis de votre gloire.

Et nous aussi, nous irons là d'où partent ces plaintes ou ces chants de triomphe. Où serons-nous ? Qui nous le dira ? Heureux les morts qui meurent dans le Seigneur.[1]

But the influence of the powerful personality of Félicité de Lamennais was not felt by those alone who had the privilege of living with him at La Chênaie. For many years a young Burgundian priest had been following his career. Intending, on the threshold of active life, to dedicate himself to the

---

[1] They also have passed over the earth, they have gone down the river of time ; their voices were heard for a moment on the banks, and then they were heard no more. Where are they ? Who can tell us ? Happy are the dead who die in the Lord.

While they passed, thousands of shadowy phantoms beset them: the world which Christ had cursed showed them its wealth, its pleasures, its power; they saw it, and suddenly they saw only eternity. Where are they ? Who can tell us ? Happy are the dead who die in the Lord.

As a ray from on high, appeared a cross far off to guide them on their way ; but all did not turn to it. Where are they ? Who can tell us ? Happy are the dead who die in the Lord.

There were some who said: What are these floods which hurry us along ? Is there anything after this rapid journey ? We do not know— no man knows. And as they spoke the banks disappeared. Where are they ? Who can tell us ? Happy are the dead who die in the Lord.

There were some again who seemed, wrapped in thought, to listen to a secret word, and then looking towards the West all at once they began to sing of an invisible dawn, and of a day which never ends. Where are they ? Who can tell us ? Happy are the dead who die in the Lord.

Drawn along pell-mell, young and old, all disappeared even as a vessel driven before a storm. It would be easier to count the sand of the sea than the number of those who were hurrying by. Where are they ? Who can tell us ? Happy are the dead who die in the Lord.

Those who saw them have said that a great sadness was in their hearts ; agony stirred their breasts, and, as if tired of the work of life, raising their eyes to heaven, they wept. Where are they ? Who can tell us ? Happy are the dead who die in the Lord.

legal profession, this young man had studied law at the *Faculté of Dijon.* There he had lost his faith, and become a confirmed Liberal. The later development of his mind had brought him back to the bosom of the Catholic Church, and had determined his vocation to the priesthood. But his Liberalism remained, and with it a desire to found or take part in some movement for the breaking down of that barrier of ecclesiastical officialism which stood in the way of the spiritual regeneration of the age in which he lived.

He had heard much of the sayings and doings of the Abbé de Lamennais, but, on the whole, the impression they produced in his mind was unfavourable. To him the tendency of the great Catholic writer was, on the one hand, towards that political despotism which he hated, and, on the other, to the undermining of those safeguards to liberty which were contained, in germ at least, in the teaching of the Church.

A story is quoted by Mgr. Ricard which aptly illustrates his first judgment of Lamennais, and the way in which his opinion came to be altered.

> From the unknown places where the river is lost two voices are continually rising.
>
> One says: Out of the deep I have cried to thee, O Lord; Lord, hear my groanings, give ear unto my prayer. If Thou takest count of our sins, who can bear it? But with Thee is mercy and boundless redemption.
>
> And the other: We praise Thee, O God! We bless Thee: Holy, holy, holy is the Lord God of hosts! Earth and the heavens are filled with Thy glory.
>
> And we also shall go there whence come these cries of sorrow or songs of triumph. Where shall we be? Who can tell us? Happy are the dead who die in the Lord.

In 1826 he said of him: *To be alone in the world would be for him an infallible proof that he was right.*

This was reported to Féli, who answered by sending him his works, which he read or re-read till he was won over to the cause. And his adherence was a matter of no slight importance to the founders of the Mennaisian School, for the young critic's name was Henri Lacordaire.

As early as the spring of 1823 he had seen the celebrated author, whose 'Essay on Indifference' had then just raised him to the front rank in literature, at the same time making him the centre of a violent controversy. Young Lacordaire had expected something striking, something visibly great, and he was disappointed. 'He is a little, dried-up man,' he wrote, 'with a thin, yellow face, simple in manners, abrupt in speech, and full of his book. Nothing reveals his genius. If you were to set M. de Lamennais down in a gathering of ecclesiastics, with his brown overcoat, his short breeches, and black silk stockings, he would be taken for a parish sexton.'

But all this was changed when, in the early months of 1830, he set out for La Chênaie. As he approached the house he was overcome by a sudden feeling of awe. 'Arrived at Dinan,' he wrote, 'I plunged alone, by obscure footpaths, into the woods. After asking my way once or twice, I suddenly found myself before a house, dark and solitary, whose mysterious celebrity was disturbed by no sound. It was La Chênaie.' And he went in.

Lamennais greeted him warmly, rising and shaking his hand; he then sat down again and continued the conversation which had been momentarily interrupted by the new arrival.

As usually happened on such occasions, the master spoke while the disciples hung on his words. Lacordaire, himself a thinker, and, above all things, a talker, seems to have felt an instinctive objection to this state of things, and even to have been somewhat shocked at some of the opinions expressed, as notably a philosophic exposition of the doctrine of the Trinity which seemed to him heretical. But it was too late, and he soon found himself absolutely subdued by the extraordinary fascination of the place and of the man.

Meanwhile, political events were hurrying on, and, it is needless to say, that Lamennais followed them closely. In the opening months of 1830 we find him, in his correspondence, treating with scathing sarcasm the steps by which M. de Polignac was slowly but surely leading the monarchy to its doom. On March 9, for instance, he wrote to Mme. Louise de Senfft:—

While we are on the subject of fools and knaves, let us speak of the ministers and the Chamber. . . . They will find it difficult to live together. The question is whether the deputies are to dismiss the ministers or the ministers the deputies, for it seems certain that one or the other must go; and, as there is resistance on both sides, M. de Polignac holding on, and identifying himself with royalty, it is possible that the struggle may become so intense as to bring on what is vulgarly called a revolution. Certainly it is hard enough to see a way out of the difficulty, a fact which has led M. Cottu to call loudly for a dictatorship, which means some big devil of a man who comes, caring neither for laws nor for constitutions, and throws a bucket of water over the combatants.

And so he continues, in his letters, to delight and sometimes to shock his friends by the mocking irony of his descriptions of the dying monarchy, till suddenly he is brought to a stand by the occurrence of the event which he has been predicting, but which, from its precipitancy, seems to take him by surprise.

The Revolution of July 1830 accomplished its object with comparatively little loss of life or property. The king was allowed to escape, and order was almost immediately restored in the capital. But we can imagine the mingled feelings aroused in the mind of anyone who, like Lamennais, living in a distant province, and in one of the wildest districts of that province, heard the news from Paris chiefly through the medium of vague rumours of street fighting and general disorder. The accounts which reached him seem to have somewhat frightened him, and this gives a dramatic force to a letter which he wrote on August 6 to M. de Coriolis, while standing, as it were, in uncertainty, hesitating, with his hand on the door which leads to the unknown:—

Men are seeking one another, my dear friend, and meeting as soldiers after a battle. Ah! You are alive! Are you not wounded? Have you heard anything of such an one, or of so and so? I, for example, should like to ask you about our Florentine friend, for I have heard nothing of him, nor of B——. Here, thank God, everything has gone off quietly, and, but for the colour of the flag, one would not notice any change. God grant that this state of things may continue! The vanquished have in every way deserved their defeat, and that defeat is beyond hope of recovery. It is desirable that this opinion become universally prevalent, for false hopes might do infinite harm. The time has come when each man must seek his safety in the safety of all—that is to say, in a general system of liberty. Liberty is the right and possibility of defending oneself against any arbitrary and oppressive will. It is to be hoped that this principle may prevail in the Government which they are going to give us, otherwise we shall fall into the power of a despotism which will be the more violent that real strength will be wanting to it. It is evident that the victors are already divided amongst themselves: some of them, in their heart of hearts, wish for the Republic pure and simple; others would like to see something like the despotism of Bonaparte. If these last were to succeed in winning some important points, war would begin to-morrow, and events would naturally move on, as formerly happened in England, to persecution, perhaps to proscription. Who ever can see into the future should then hope that the struggle between these two parties may be made impossible by a system of institutions, which makes of the parody of a king, who is to be given to the nation, a simple manikin. If this is done, all those, whoever they may be, who have interests in common, can and ought, if they have a grain of courage or of intelligence, to organise themselves in singleness of purpose, publicly and legally, for the defence of their interests. But if this is to be done, people must not isolate themselves, shut themselves up, so to speak, or make it a matter of stupid, fatal honour to be nothing and to take part in nothing. The strong man, the man who does not allow himself to be overcome by illusions, never abandons himself; he turns his back on the past and walks with raised head towards the future, that he may take his place there. God grant that this may be understood.

On the same day, but probably at a later hour, when the situation had more clearly defined itself in his mind, he wrote to Mme. de Senfft:—' The Duke of Orleans is to receive the crown; it will weigh heavily on his head. The greater number would prefer a Republic frankly proclaimed, and *I agree with them.*'

CHAPTER VI

THE 'AVENIR'

THEY will not hear you! And who would dare not to hear you? After all, if it happened that they turned a deaf ear to your petitions, that they met with refusal your just demands, the law has provided for such a denial of justice, as it has provided for public safety and the maintenance of order, by creating the National Guard. It calls on you to enlist in it; it confides to you the defence of your own rights. If you are ever robbed of them . . . you will have only yourselves to blame.

These are memorable words, and pregnant with revolutionary meaning, yet my readers will be surprised to hear that they were not uttered in the tribune of the *National Convention*, and that they were not spoken by any of the orators who took part in the eventful struggles of '93 and '94. They merely appeared one morning in October 1830 in the pages of an ecclesiastical paper, and in an article by a priest who had hitherto been chiefly known for his reactionary sympathies. And this fact is not without a certain interest, for the paper was called the *Avenir*, and the writer was Félicité de Lamennais.

Adequately to appreciate the contemporary influence of an undertaking which was unique in the history of journalism is, when we are separated by considerably more than half a century from the events which called for it, and the points of view which gave practical value to it, well nigh impossible. To pore over the numbers of a daily paper, when they have been collected, and perhaps grown mouldy on the shelves of a library, is not the same thing as to find them singly on one's breakfast table in the morning, and to look forward with eager curiosity and lively, perhaps passionate, interest to the perusal of their contents. And yet, even at this distance of time, it is not without a thrill of emotion that we rise from a survey, however hasty, of the collected volumes of the *Avenir*. We feel as we turn over these half-forgotten pages that we are in the presence of an enthusiasm which is not of our time, and of a boldness of human appreciation and sympathy which few to-day would be willing to concede to the average productions of the ecclesiastical mind; for the *Avenir* was founded at a time which, if it seemed pregnant with great things in the future, was no less fraught with infinite danger to an institution which, like the Catholic Church, though capable of indefinite expansion and adaptability, had its roots in the past, and spoke not only to the present, whether in time or place, but to every country and to every age.

The leaders of the movement thoroughly realised this, and there is hardly a line of their writings which does not bear traces of that principle so boldly set forth in the pages of the great fundamental work of their master, *Homo sum, humani nihil a me alienum puto.* This it was which inspired them, both in the choice of their motto, *God and Liberty*, and in the carrying out of every step in the undertaking.

The first number appeared on October 16, and it opened with a masterly article from the pen of Lamennais himself; but it was not till the following day that the paper gave an indication of its real scope, and began to show itself in its true colours. In that issue, the editors frankly committed themselves to a demand for a considerable extension of the suffrage and frequent elections, as well as for liberty, of speech, teaching, and opinion. All these and the first of them in a more advanced form, became typical of the policy of the journal. Everything else flowed from them as a development called for in the practical working of the scheme.

But this serious attitude was varied by occasional sallies of a lighter sort, in which they bespattered their more servile Catholic friends with unsparing ridicule, and endeavoured to cause them to writhe into activity under the well-directed lashings of a scathing irony :—

Everything points to the fact [said a writer in the issue of October 17] that religion should desire freedom. But no doubt it will continue to stand at the palace gates. One day the prince as he goes by will notice it, and will say, 'God be praised! there is still a remnant of faith in my people.' Religion will bow respectfully, for the second Majesty has deigned to speak before the first. The prince will open his purse, but, remembering that etiquette forbids him to give alms directly to God, he will raise his voice and say, 'My Lord Cardinal, you are my almoner.' Religion will bow still more reverently; it will return to its deserted basilicas, accompanied by the indifference of the people, but with the smile and with the gold of Cæsar.

Then they assumed a more threatening attitude. There is a refreshing boldness in an article by Lamennais which appeared on October 18 :—

Truth [he says] is all-powerful. The only thing which stands in its way is the support which material force is trying to lend to it; the very appearance of constraint in the essentially free domain of conscience and of reason, the brutal violence which does not respect the sanctuary of the soul, into which God alone has a right to enter. No man owes any account of his faith to human power, and the contrary maxim, directly opposed to Catholicism, whose foundations it undermines, has, whenever it has appeared in the world, been fruitful in blood-stained strife, calamities, and crimes without number; it has wrung from hell its Henry VIII.s and its Dukes of Alba. But will the State try to use this principle against the Church? No power to-day is strong enough to attempt such a thing with any hope of success. Such an undertaking would bring down upon it the immense body of the Catholics and all those who, without belonging to that body, sincerely wish for liberty. The time for violence has passed away; there are rights which henceforward cannot be attacked with impunity; whoever dares to touch them will be crushed by them.

Then, turning to his Catholic readers, he exhorts them to remember the dignity of their profession, and points out the disastrous consequences of the establishment of the Church :—

Understand what follows inevitably from the state of bondage in which she is held; calculate, if you can, the future results of the prolongation of a state of things which has already been so fruitful in evil : religion administered as are the customs or the octroi, the priesthood degraded, discipline ruined, teaching oppressed. . . .

And he concluded with a touching appeal to the French clergy :—

Ministers of One who was born in a manger and who died upon a cross, return to your primitive state, steep yourselves voluntarily in poverty and suffering, and the word of a poor and suffering God will become fruitful on your lips. Without any other support than that divine word, go forth as the twelve fishermen into the midst of the peoples and begin once more the conquest of the world. Christianity is about to enter on another era of triumph and of glory. Messengers of hope, see on the horizon the precursory signs of the rising of the star, and send forth, over the ruins of empires and the remains of all that is subject to the law of death, the song of life.

And so things went on. Hardly a day went by without some fresh indication that the movement would lead to something beyond mere words, something gratifying to the true friends of religion and of liberty, goading to the half-hearted and dangerous to those in power. 'It is time,' said the editors on one occasion, 'it is time that twenty millions of Frenchmen should cease to be oppressed by a system of jealous watchfulness. . . . If the idea has come into anyone's head, he will soon learn that it is not easy to impose fetters upon us ; he will learn what we are and what we can do.' And again : 'We will render to Cæsar the things that are Cæsar's, provided that we are allowed to render freely to God the things that are God's.'

This being their general attitude, we are not surprised to find that when the Government, taking advantage of the wave of anti-clericalism which had had so much to do with the revolution of July, proposed to cut down the salaries of the clergy, the writers in the *Avenir* were in no way dismayed. A Protestant paper had committed itself to praise of the Government, and had triumphantly welcomed this striking sign of the approaching doom of the Catholic Church in France. This nettled the editors of the Catholic paper, who reminded their Protestant contemporary that they had already demanded the absolute suppression of the *budget du clergé*, and they even went so far as to suggest that the principles of the Reformation should be supported by the State, as they would, from the circumstances of their origin, be well suited to that mode of treatment.

Nor does it offer matter for surprise that, within a fortnight of its foundation, the fame of the *Avenir* should have crossed the borders of France, and should even have reached the ears of a young French Catholic who, burning with an unsatisfied love for religion and liberty, had gone on a pilgrimage to Ireland to visit the hero of *Catholic emancipation*.

Charles de Montalembert was disappointed by his personal interview with the great Irish leader, who does not seem to have taken him seriously, thinking, no doubt, that he was merely a young French nobleman come to Ireland on a tour of pleasure, and who, instead of taking him into his study to talk over the destinies of nations and of religion, showed him into a room full of young people, who were occupied in killing time with frivolous amusements. But this humiliating reception in no way weakened the fascination which drew him both to the cause and to the man.

We can imagine, then, the enthusiasm with which he read the first numbers of the *Avenir*, which convinced him that there was a possibility of something similar in his own country. He wrote at once to Lamennais, asking to be allowed to take part in his labours, and his offer was promptly accepted.

Montalembert joined the staff of the *Avenir* at a time when the progress of the struggle was beginning to produce its natural effect on the writers, and his co-operation, on the whole, had a softening influence on them. There is in everything that comes from his pen an appearance of quiet conviction and of lofty, chivalrous sentiment which in the others, not excluding Lacordaire, is thrown into the background by the practical, combative, and almost revolutionary tone they have been forced to assume. An instance of this may be seen in an article of his, which traverses ground already gone over by Lamennais. The latter, in the first number, had boldly proclaimed the necessity of an absolute break with the past, and we already know, from his correspondence, how little sympathy he had with that past. 'The vanquished have, in every way, deserved their defeat, &c.' This, no doubt, was in agreement with the general policy of the *Avenir*, to which Montalembert had given his adherence; but with him this turning away from the past was robbed of much of its bitterness through his avowed sympathy with those who disagreed with him. The contrast is abundantly evident in a passage from an article which appeared on March 6, 1831, quoted by Madame Craven. It is entitled, *A ceux qui aiment ce qui fut*. He says :—

> Living apart from public life, from the struggles which have absorbed your lives, from the affections which have gained possession of your souls, we do not pledge ourselves to you as participating in your political beliefs. But we say it in all simplicity and in good faith. If you realised the depth of our respect for unfortunate loves, of our veneration for the enduring enthusiasm of your fidelity, and, above all, of our sympathy for the faith which is common to all of us, you would regret the disagreement which separates us; you would recognise in us the children of the same Father, Christians who groan at the thought of not being able to unite with other Christians in all their thoughts, and who desire to join all together in a unity which is higher than that which can be dissolved by the accidents of the world.
>
> We do not feel this sympathy for the disappointment of courtiers, the spite of officials, the mortifications of self-love or of ambition. . . . But we feel it deeply, intensely, for the disinterested longings of those provincial royalists, of those rural populations, who have never seen the Court. . . .
>
> Dominated by a thought which is higher than thrones, looking towards a future which God permits us partially to see, we do not partake of their sorrow, but we are touched by it; we do not live in their hopes, their memories, but we bow ourselves reverently before their devotion. For where devotion is, there is faith; and where faith is, there is the breath of God.

This, I think, will be sufficient to give my readers some idea of the new-comer; and it is not without reason that I have turned aside to introduce him, for in the short and brilliant though stormy career of the *Avenir*, amidst many names which call for our respect and sympathy, such as those of Gerbet and De Coux, there are three which stand prominent, they are: Lamennais, Lacordaire, and Montalembert.

The first object of the paper, as seen in the correspondence of Lamennais, and as we might surmise from the letter quoted at the end of the last chapter, was simply to defend Catholic interests in the prevailing anarchy and uncertainty of opinion. But as time went on the editors found themselves driven to a more aggressive attitude, and forced to ally themselves with interests which, though fundamentally in agreement with them, and cordially uniting with them in their hatred of the attempted reaction connected with the pseudo-royalistic *régime* of Louis Philippe, were still, superficially at least, not essentially Catholic.

The general lines of this policy were laid down by Lamennais in an article published on October 30, 1830. After speaking generally of the supposed difficulties of such an alliance, he illustrates the possibility of it by a very pregnant simile. He says:—

Imagine to yourselves a house occupied in its different stories by a Jew, a Mussulman, a Protestant, a Catholic; certainly their beliefs, and the duties which result from them, are too much in opposition to allow of the possibility of their forming a real society. But let them be possessed by a fear that a band of fanatics may come to burn that house, whose roof protects them all, or, on the triumph of different parties, to cut the throat of any of them, or to persecute them, whether as Jew, Mussulman, Protestant, or Catholic, the common danger will unite them, and, unless they themselves are blinded by a ferocious fanaticism, they will not hesitate to agree together for their mutual defence, an agreement which will create relations of kindness between them, which will facilitate and place on a calmer and more edifying footing purely doctrinal discussions on the points which separate them. In any case they will have lived, and they will have lived in peace.

Then, after alluding to the successful struggle of the Belgians under similar conditions, he says: 'And we also, whoever we may be, Catholics or Protestants, Republicans or Monarchists, heavy chains, which we had a right to believe put off for ever, still weigh upon us; we must break them.' We have a common interest. 'Let us then agree on a plan of action, let us organise ourselves; may the Chamber be deluged with petitions, heavy with hundreds of thousands of signatures; may all our voices form but one voice; may that voice, powerful, unanimous, rise as the roar of the sea when, hurling its waves against it, it strikes and overturns the insolent barrier which stands in its way.'

What is it that gives strength to our enemies? Our divisions. 'We have not wished to be free together, so we have all become slaves. May we profit by this lesson. Let us not forget that fetters travel, and that the man who forces them on others sooner or later wears them himself. Frenchmen, believe me, we should look on one another as brothers; let us not envy one another our part in that blessing, which is the more pleasing, the more abundant for each that it is possessed by the greater number, in that right which is our common inheritance, and without which there is none other upon the earth—liberty.' Then follows a terrible picture: 'See there near you those beings who cannot be named, those haggard features, that sinister eye; the spectre of '93 rises before you all bloody! You shudder, but why? What have you to fear if you are united?' And he concludes: 'What matter opinions at the foot of the scaffold? . . . Be men, and while timidity moves along bleating out its silly lamentations, hold out one hand to your brother, and lay the other on your sword.'

There is no mistaking the bearing of these words; they point to the intention of forcing matters to a crisis, and then of fighting out the question at issue to the bitter end, disdaining none of those methods which experience had shown to be necessary in times of revolution. It was not long before they began to bear fruit.

Towards the end of November, that is to say, within six weeks of its foundation, the *Avenir* felt itself strong enough to face the consequences of a direct attack on the Government. On November 29 appeared an article by Lacordaire. It was headed simply: 'Aux évêques de France': To the bishops of France.

In a penetrating analysis of the existing ecclesiastical arrangements he forces his readers to admit that State appointed bishops are not to be trusted, and that the system is utterly rotten in its most essential details :—

The episcopate which must result from it is self-condemned. Whether it wills it or no, it is bound to be unfaithful to religion. . . . The necessary plaything of the thousand changes which transfer power from hand to hand, it will mark in our ranks every shade of ministerial and anti-Catholic opinion, before which majorities grovel in turn, as their own work. . . . After having dishonoured us in the mind of the peoples, they will one day give us over, feeble and divided, into the hands of those in power, who will look upon it as a favour to give us life in exchange for our conscience.

He, then, in the deep fervour of conviction, and with that burning eloquence which was natural to him, conjures the bishops to remember the dignity of their calling and not to abandon the flocks entrusted to them, and he concludes :—

In any case we shall not betray ourselves. . . . We now make this protest; we confide it to the memory of all those Frenchmen in whom there is still a remnant of faith and of shame; to our brothers in the United States, in Ireland, and in Belgium; to all those who are in labour for the liberty of the world wherever they may be; we will carry it, barefooted if need be, to the city of the Apostles, to the steps of the confessional of St. Peter ; and we shall see who will stand in the way of the pilgrims of God and of liberty.

So open a defiance of the existing regulations could not be tolerated by a Government which was trying to get itself recognised by public opinion, and the number was seized by the police. But the editors of the *Avenir* had no intention of allowing the matter to rest before they had forced the ministers to throw off the mask under which they were attempting to hide from France and from the world their counter-revolutionary designs. On the following day they published an article by Lamennais which, in the uncompromising directness of its attack, surpassed everything which had as yet proceeded from his pen. It was headed *Oppression des Catholiques, &c.*, and it contains nothing in the least calculated to soften or modify the tone suggested by its title; nor does it leave any loophole or means of evasion to those against whom it was written. Going at once, heedless of custom or convention, to the point at issue, the writer says: 'Catholics, only yesterday, over the ruins of a monarchy overthrown by the people, they made to you before heaven promises of liberty. How have they kept them? Hardly had the words been uttered which proclaimed your freedom, when they hastened to draw tighter your chains.'

He then describes the forms of petty tyranny exercised by the Government: the drawing up by the Administration of prayers to be used for the State; the forbidding of the use of the cross in open-air missions; the enforced admission of the bodies of excommunicated persons into churches for the performance of the funeral ceremonies, &c.

If you were in France but a feeble minority, we should say to you . . . go, quit this land of tyranny. . . . Go to live among those peoples who are called barbarous; they will not come to break down the doors of the temple where you celebrate the holy mysteries, or to throw a corpse at the foot of your altars. . . .

Catholics, that is what we should say to you if your numbers were small; but you are twenty-five millions of men. Twenty-five millions of men do not, should not allow themselves to be dictated to. You have rights, recognised rights. . . . Of what use are timid complainings? Groan less and know how to will. . . . What is wanting in you but agreement . . . whence is born vigorous and continued action? They rely too much on your patience. Drag your oppressors before the tribunals; let the Chambers resound with your demands. They will have to hear you. Speak boldly and without fear. Why should you fear deputies, who can do nothing but by you? They are your servants, nothing more; they represent France, and you are, the Charter bears witness to it, *the majority of Frenchmen.*

Here a question presents itself: Who is the possessor of authority in France? A sovereign given to us by the revolution of July. By what title does he reign? In virtue of the national choice, under the guarantee of oaths, in which he undertook to respect the rights of all of us, to maintain religious liberty, and to allow freedom in matters of education. This is what he promised four months ago. Are four months then sufficient for the dissolving of such oaths? If they have not ceased to be binding, whence comes the persecution which is directed against us? Either those in authority cannot, or they will not in what concerns us, be faithful to their promises. If they cannot, what is this mockery of a sovereignty, this miserable phantom of a government? And what is there between it and us? It is, so far as we are concerned, as if it were not, and it remains for us, ignoring it, to protect ourselves.

If they will not, they have broken the contract which bound us to them, they have torn up their title deed; for we consider ourselves bound to submit to them, and to support them, on the express condition that they, on their side, hold to their engagements to us: *sinon, non.*

Having thus thrown to the winds the dearest

traditions of the Gallican clergy on the position of sovereigns in the divine economy, he sums up the charges to which the Government of Louis Philippe has laid itself open, after which he continues, pointedly distinguishing between the cause of Catholicism and that of the State-made bishops :—

> As for us, simple priests and simple laymen, let us fight unceasingly for our freedom, let us not suffer that any man dare to exclude us from the common right. We will show them that we are Frenchmen, by a determined defence of what no man may take from us without violating the law of the land. Let us say to the sovereign : We shall obey you so long as you yourself obey that law which makes you what you are, and without which you are nothing. Let us say to our brothers, whatever may be their opinions, their beliefs : Our interests are common, our cause is yours, as yours would be ours if your rights were threatened. What matter our bygone contentions, our mutual wrongs ? We were all of us, by different roads, seeking what we have now happily found. Henceforth there can be but one longing, which should blot out all painful memories, one word which should unite us : *Liberty* !

It is hardly necessary to state that this number too found its way into the offices of the police, and might have been lost to the public had not circumstances been too strong for the Government. In fact, everything seemed to show that the editors of the *Avenir* were determined to bring matters to a crisis. On November 18 an article had appeared in a Dutch paper, ' De Ultramontaan,' suggesting that there should be a correspondence between Catholic papers all over Europe, with the *Avenir* as a centre ; and this was published in the French journal, with dangerous hints at a Catholic association, to be formed with the express purpose of exposing the petty tyrannies of provincial administrations to public view; a terrible prospect to the advisers of a sovereign who was trying quietly, by the accumulation of local precedents, to work himself into the position from which his unfortunate predecessor had been ousted. Then there were rumours of schools to be opened in defiance of the law, and which would exercise their functions in spite of the State monopoly. Everything seemed to point to the fact that unless something were done this turbulent representative of an untamed and irreconcilable Catholic party would get out of hand and place the Government in a very embarrassing position.

Nor was this all. Shortly after the seizure of the number containing the second article an event took place which proved that the appeal to the friends of liberty had not been altogether in vain. The occasion was a trial in which Lacordaire happened to be involved. The point for decision turned on the question whether the chaplains of colleges were to be considered as public officials. The representative of the Crown maintained the affirmative, and he got on smoothly enough till, in the course of his argument, he began to develop the proposition that chaplains had a public character, since they were the representatives of a foreign sovereign. This was too much for Lacordaire, who sprang to his feet with the exclamation, 'No, sir! . . . We are the ministers of One who is a foreigner nowhere—of God.' Upon which, we are told, the Court shook with applause, and a workman was seen making his way over seats and heads till he got up to the interrupter, whose hand he seized, while he said, 'M. le Curé, my pals there have sent me to ask you your name.'

It was impossible to say where this kind of thing might end. That the Church might become popular at the expense of the Monarchy had by no means entered into the calculations of the wire-pullers of the Louis Philippian *régime*, and now such a consummation began to seem, not only capable of realisation, but probable—nay, even pressing and imminent. Energetic action was necessary if the evil was to be stifled in its first beginnings, and thus the Executive found itself compelled to take the fatal step of instituting a prosecution against the *Avenir*.

This step once taken, the Government necessarily entered on a downward path. Whatever might be the result, they were bound to lose. If they succeeded in gaining the legal point, they would stand unmasked before the whole of France, and they might apply to themselves a phrase of Danton's: 'Lafayette, reduced to a single face, can no longer be dangerous.' If they lost it, their credit would be gone and their enemies victorious. The blind folly of their proceedings will be more fully evident when we remember that the events here described took place within four months of the upheaval to which Louis Philippe owed his throne and Charles X. his exile. That the legal victory might have been theirs is abundantly evident from the correspondence of

Lamennais, but it is equally clear from the same source that the accused looked upon this as of comparatively minor importance. On January 14 Féli wrote to Madame de Senfft :—

> I am very unwell, and am crushed by the amount of work I have to get through. Next week I must go to Paris . . . to prepare for our trial, which is to come on on the 29th. Trial by jury, especially in those cases which are connected with politics, being the most uncertain thing in the world, it is very possible that my next may be dated from Sainte Pélagie. But what matters it? God is there as elsewhere, perhaps more than elsewhere; and there as elsewhere it is possible to defend the cause of Catholicism and of liberty. . . . Every day new streams of light are flowing over the future of the world! What matters it that so many men, the voluntary slaves of self-love and of their prejudices, persist in closing their eyes and standing in the way of Providence? Is the light less brilliant for it, or its action less powerful? While they are saying *No*, the Divine fiat goes forth over the world, sifting the germs of a new order, and the work of Heaven is accomplished.

In the same letter he ironically alludes to the fact that foreign sovereigns were beginning to take measures against the *Avenir*. M. de Senfft represented Austria at Turin :—

> I think you will be able to receive the *Avenir*, and that the prohibition will not affect you; for though no one will doubt that the king has a legitimate and unquestioned authority over the minds of his subjects, though he has the inalienable right to think for them and to judge for them, you are not one of his subjects.

This, then, was the temper in which, as representing the *Avenir*, and as the writers of the incriminated articles, Lamennais and Lacordaire appeared to stand their trial on January 31, 1831. The former, who was not an orator, was defended by M. Janvier, while Lacordaire appeared in his own behalf. From the first it was evident that the weight of opinion was on the side of the accused. Even the public prosecutor turned aside to apologise for the position in which he stood, and did involuntary homage to the illustrious upholder of the principles of liberty. M. Janvier, as was natural, gave a *résumé* of the life and work of the great writer, pointing to the fact that the cause which they all had at heart had found a representative of whom Frenchmen might well be proud. But the palm of oratory was carried off by Lacordaire, who, in a magnificent defence, analysed the anti-social policy of the ministry, and expounded to his hearers the noble ideal which had inspired the founders of the *Avenir*. He began by describing the fascination which had drawn him into the present struggle, and, with a profound bow to his leader, he said :—

I had seen him but twice in my life, and then only for a few moments, but I did not wish to leave France without meeting him face to face, without asking him for his benediction on a young man, torn by an instinct of those sorrows which were consuming his invincible genius. I saw him, I paid my homage to that man, at once great and simple, under his modest ancestral roof; he has allowed me to call myself his friend.

Much as I might feel tempted to do so, I am unable, consistently with the scope of this work, to insert, or even largely to quote from, this monument of eloquence from the inspired lips of the Abbé Lacordaire. Suffice it to say that the audience was spell-bound as he ran over the various counts of his charge against the ministry. We can imagine the scene. A young priest, fired by the memories of those days when he had sat as a law student with many who were now listening to him. We can understand his desire to show them, that though he had renounced their profession, he was in no way inferior to them; and, above all, the warmth and vigour breathed over him by the consciousness that he appeared, not merely as a professional pleader, but as the champion of a cause which he believed to be just, which was, in every sense of the word, his own. Nor is it difficult to put ourselves in the place of his audience. We can picture to ourselves the emotion with which they listened to his vivid descriptions, his scathing analysis of the motives which lay behind the actions of the Government, forcing them to realise the pettiness of those motives compared with the ideal set forth in the pages of the *Avenir*. Such, for instance, is a passage in which he quotes La Bruyère, who ironically describes a state of things not unlike that which was aimed at by the ministers of Louis Philippe :—

The great ones of the nation meet together every day at a certain hour in a temple which they call a church. At the end of this temple is an altar, consecrated to their God, at which a priest is celebrating mysteries which they call sacred, holy, awful. The great ones form a vast circle at the foot of this altar, and appear standing with their backs to the priest and the holy mysteries, but with their faces turned towards their king, who is seen kneeling on a kind of raised daïs. To him they yearn with all their minds and all their hearts. One cannot but see in this a touching picture of the principle of subordination, for the people appear to adore their prince, and the prince to adore God.

It is hardly necessary to say that the result of the proceedings was awaited with the deepest anxiety throughout the country, and when the news went forth that the *Avenir* had been acquitted, it was received with universal acclamation, for Frenchmen of every shade of religious or philosophical opinion had by this time become convinced that the cause at stake was not merely that of Catholicism, but of liberty itself, in one of its most fundamental principles—the freedom of the press.

Lamennais had now won for himself a great name in France; the eyes of all were turned to him as the embodiment of a future pregnant with great things, seen as yet only dimly and in the far distance, yet absolutely inevitable. And it is probably to his short residence in Paris at this time that we owe a characteristic incident quoted in the 'British Critic' for April 1836, from Bulwer:—

I was sitting one day [said a friend of mine to me] in the bureau of the *Avenir* (a religious journal), waiting for one of the editors of that paper, when a little man came in and sat himself shiveringly down before the small fire, from which I was endeavouring, in no very happy mood, to extract some kind of consolation. Small, plain, and ill-dressed, with large green spectacles and an immense nose, timid, awkward, there was nothing at first sight very interesting either in the manner or the appearance of my acquaintance. I spoke, however. He spoke, and in speaking his air became more firm and decided—his features assumed a new cast—his eye lit up—thought, suffering, compressed passion were visible in his countenance—and his whole person swelled out, as it were, into more spiritual and imposing proportions. 'Monsieur l'Abbé!' said my friend, entering just at the moment that my eye was fixed on a print opposite. The print was that of the Abbé de la Mennais—the person I had been talking to was the Abbé de la Mennais himself!

The acquittal of the *Avenir* was fatal to the prestige of the Government. The legal claims of the authorities had been brought to a test and had been found wanting. The opportunity was not lost. On February 3 the result of the trial was announced, almost immediately the ministers realised the fact that a powerful organisation was working against them in the country.

Adequately to describe the doings of the famous *Agence Générale pour la Défense de la Liberté Religieuse* would indeed be a difficult task. Founded on the principle that where liberty is not given it must be taken, it showed itself in every way worthy of its object. Beginning with the simple idea of combination among Catholics, it speedily developed into a gigantic organisation, having its centre in Paris, and with a branch in every department and in every district. In the carrying out of this seemingly audacious and yet, as it proved, eminently practical scheme, France was divided into three parts, which were respectively given over to Lacordaire, Montalembert, and De Coux. It was impossible for the Government to pursue its policy without becoming entangled in the powerful network thus created. Like the Jacobins in the early days of the Revolution, the *Agence* had its emissaries in every hole and corner of France. It was impossible for the meanest minion of the State to speak or act without a fear that his words might be taken down and his doings reported; and if by any chance he dared in the exercise of his functions to interfere with a parish priest or missionary, to insult the symbol of Christianity, or in any way to violate the principle of religious liberty, he might be certain that his conduct would sooner or later be published abroad in Paris, and held up to the execration of that portion of the populace which the ministry most feared, and which they wished to draw into an alliance with themselves.

Even before the publication of the result of the trial, which indicated not so much the period of the foundation as of the final completion of the scheme, the *Avenir* had given more than one indication of the methods it intended to pursue. This gives peculiar interest to a passage quoted by Mgr. Ricard; it is from an article by Lamennais, which appeared in November. Addressing the clergy, he says:—

One of your brothers refused, to a man who died outside your communion, the words of comfort and the last prayers of Christians. Your brother did well; he acted as a free man, as a priest of the Lord, determined to keep his lips pure from servile benedictions. Woe to the man who blesses fraudulently, who speaks of God with a venal heart! Woe to the priest who mutters lies over a coffin; who accompanies souls to the judgment of God through fear of the living, or for a vile payment! Your brother did

well. Are we the grave-diggers of the human race? . . .
Your brother did well; but the *shadow of a proconsul* imagined
that such independence was out of place in a citizen so mean
as a Catholic priest. He ordered that the body should be
placed before the altar; was it necessary, in order to do this,
to force the doors of the temple where rests, under the protection of the laws of the fatherland, under the safeguard
of liberty, the God of all men and of the great majority of
Frenchmen ? . . . a mere sous-préfet, a salaried minion, from
the sanctuary of his abode, protected from arbitrary treatment by thirty millions of men, sent to the house of God
a corpse. This he did whilst you were sleeping, trusting
in the oath to observe the Charter of August 7, at the very
moment when they were exacting from you prayers to bless
in the person of the king the representative of the liberty of
a great nation. He did it in the face of the law, which
declares that all religions are free; but how can a form of
worship be free if its temple be not so, if they can bring
there any filth, with arms in their hands? He did it in the
teeth of the expressed will of a great part of the nation, he,
this sous-préfet. . . . Now that man is sitting by his hearth,
satisfied and pleased with himself. You would have made
him turn pale if, taking your dishonoured God, a staff in
your hand and your hat on your head, you had brought him
to some wooden hut, swearing no more to expose him to
insult in the temples of the State.

But now the position of the *Avenir* was no longer
uncertain. The Government had made its move and
had been checkmated; consequently the future was
with Lamennais and his friends.

As has already been suggested, the nearest approach to this scheme in recent French history was
the famous organisation which played such an important part in the early days of the Revolution.

The *Club Breton*, in the first beginnings of the States-General, was simply a comparatively informal association of liberal deputies, but it soon grew into that vast system of political police which issued in denunciations of the opponents of liberty to the national assemblies, or to the central Jacobin Club in Paris. So now the *Agence* began to take the form of a kind of Jacobinism of the press. As in the former case, it had its local committees and its spies, who wormed their way into all the mysteries of provincial government. No village mayor, no sous-préfet, no police agent, no one in fine who had the misfortune to wear a Government uniform, was safe from them. They did not, as in the case of the Jacobins, send their denunciations to the Chamber, or to a central club, but to the editors of the *Avenir*, who could now publish everything under the guarantee of the freedom of the press. Thus these things found their way to public opinion, and to a public opinion which was impossible at the time of the Revolution. The effect of such denunciations was, no doubt, less personally dangerous to the denounced, but it was in reality more terrible, more lasting, and it might become infinitely more powerful as an engine of political warfare. For its strength lay in this, that standing on a broad basis, the *Avenir* appealed to the great majority of Frenchmen, not as mere parts of a system driven together by fear, but as free and enlightened beings. Revolution was contemplated as a possible, and with some, a desirable outcome of the agitation; but the leaders of the movement differed from their predecessors in doing the work altogether through a leavening of opinion, and in believing that the result would be brought about by a general movement of society as a whole. This made their action infinitely more unpalatable to the friends of the past than that of the Jacobins, for if less immediate in its results, it was less likely to lead to a reaction, and it seemed probable that by secularising the monarchy and depriving it of its divine sanction it would prepare the way for its final and irrevocable overthrow.

Yet even from the practical and immediate point of view the *Agence* appears to have been often successful. Numerous are the instances in which the Government seems to have been forced to act contrary to its intentions, and to give the lie to its principles. We are told, for example, that when the military commander at Aix ordered the Capuchins to put off their distinctive dress, the *Agence* prosecuted him, and obtained his removal; and that when a bishop was nominated to the see of Beauvais, who was not considered worthy of the position, such an outcry was raised in the *Avenir* that the candidate had to be withdrawn.

Throughout the spring of 1831 the movement continued steadily to make its way in public opinion. Lacordaire had clearly laid down the principle for which they were contending, when, in the course of one of his many pleadings in the law courts, he startled his hearers by an expression which I here quote from the report in the *Avenir*.

God has become free with the liberty of a citizen; we demand for Him no other, we simply ask that He should be recognised as a citizen of France. [Some murmurs, the sense of which escaped us, reached the orator. He turned to that part of the Court whence they came, and said:] 'Gentlemen, if I recognised in the world to-day a nobler title than that of a French citizen, or a better guarantee of liberty than the right to it, I should give it to him who deigned to become the slave of men that he might win freedom for them.'

Thus stated, the issue was perfectly clear, and it was not long before an opportunity was found for putting it to the test.

In the practical working out of the system of State monopoly in education, a useful distinction was made by the authorities. Special professional, moral, or religious training was in some cases permitted, but everything which came in any way under the category of a liberal education was strictly prohibited. In practice this led to an abundance of legal casuistry and much misunderstanding. It appears, for instance, that the clergy of Lyons were in the habit of giving gratuitously to their choir boys lessons in Latin and other things, which were not considered absolutely essential to their immediate calling. They were prosecuted and forced to dismiss the children and to allow them to attend the State schools. 'Very well!' said the editors of the *Avenir*, 'you think you have only to deal with choir boys; we shall force you to fight the matter out with men.'

They determined to open a school in Paris in defiance of the regulations of the Educational Department. The business was undertaken by Lacordaire and Montalembert, who, on May 9, assembled a number of children and proceeded to exercise the functions of ordinary schoolmasters, announcing their intention of restricting themselves in nothing, and of paying no deference to the State monopoly. The police, as it was intended they should, heard of it, came to the place and ordered the children, 'in the name of the law,' to leave. 'In the name of your parents,' said Lacordaire, 'I command you to stay.' And the children, inspired probably by the prospect of a row, unanimously answered, 'We will stay.' What followed we know not, but eventually the room was cleared, the papers sealed up, the doors locked, and a prosecution was instituted against the offending schoolmasters.

This time the law was against them, but it so happened that the trial became the means of their uttering their protest before the highest tribunal in the land. Charles de Montalembert, through the death of his father, had just succeeded to the peerage, and he now claimed his right of being tried by the august assembly of which he had become a member. The claim being admitted, the privilege had to be extended to Lacordaire, as the circumstances of the case would not allow of a separate trial.

The occasion was a great one, and we can imagine that the accused were not unprepared when they appeared at the bar of the House on September 20.

The task which the procureur-général had to perform was by no means an easy one. The managers of the free school had acted in accordance with a clause of the charter which expressly proclaimed the principle of liberty of education; but no law had as yet been passed to give effect to this clause, and, consequently, it was evident that they had acted illegally. This fact formed the main basis of the prosecution; but the argument was dangerous, and might be interpreted in a manner very embarrassing to the Executive. For the procureur, besides being the representative of the established Government, owed his position to the revolution of July, and to the very irregular and certainly illegal proceedings which had followed it, in which, in his official capacity, he had played a leading part, notably in the prosecution of the leading members of the Polignac ministry, for violating a clause in the charter not yet regulated by a law. The comparison was an awkward one, and it was natural enough that the minister should not allude to it in his speech, confining himself rigidly to the legal question, in which he was undoubtedly in the right. But Lacordaire had by this time acquired considerable facility in debate; and when he rose to make his defence, he went straight to the point, which, it was hoped, would be avoided:—

My lords [he began], can I believe my eyes? I am astounded at finding myself in the place of the accused, while the procureur-général appears as a representative of the public authorities. I fail to understand how he can dare to appear against me, seeing that he himself lately, in this very hall, committed the crime of which he now accuses me. For what is this accusation which he brings against me? That I have acted on a right proclaimed in the charter but not yet regulated by a law. Only yesterday he demanded of you the heads of four ministers, in virtue of a right proclaimed in the charter but not yet regulated by law! If he could do it, so could I, with this difference, that he demanded blood, while I only wished to give free education to a few children of the people. We both of us acted with the sanction of Article 69 of the Charter. If the procureur-général is guilty, how can he accuse me? If he is innocent, again how can he accuse me?

And so he continued, following in detail the various counts of the accusation, and the arguments by which they were supported, till he succeeded in branding the *régime* of Louis Philippe as depending for its sanction on repressive laws, passed under those very forms of government whose rejection by the French people was the excuse for its own existence.

It would be impossible to imagine anything more damaging to a ministry which was trying to subsist on the fiction of Liberalism. Such a defence, worked out with all the force of professional acumen, was infinitely more calculated to lower his accusers in the eyes of the rising democracy than the burning but youthful enthusiasm of Montalembert, who wished that, if faith was to be destroyed, it should have for its tomb 'the liberty of the world!' or even his own eloquent conclusion: 'When Socrates, in that first and famous trial for freedom of teaching, was about to quit the presence of his judges, he said to them, " We are going out of this place, you to live, I to die." Not thus, my lords, do we leave you. Whatever may be your decision, we go out from here to live; for liberty and religion are immortal.'

The law was against them, and they were condemned to a fine of 100 francs, the minimum penalty. But to this they were indifferent, for they had gained a moral victory, and they went forth into the world, confident in the future. The cause they had fought for was not yet gained, but it had only to await the day when not only the *régime* of Louis Philippe, but monarchy itself, would be driven from France by the Revolution of '48.

The *Avenir* had now been in existence for almost a year. Short though the time had been, it had done an immense work. Religion, which, since the days of Bossuet, had been identified with the idea of the divine right of kings, was now freed from that encumbrance, for it had been shown that the interests of Catholicism might be very well defended by those who were utterly indifferent to the fate of monarchy, and who looked on it merely as an accident in the growth of the social organism. Nay, the editors had even gone further than this in threatening that, if the authorities stood in their way, they were ready to have a hand in their overthrow. In this sense must be understood their constant appeals to the people, their recommendations to Catholics and friends of liberty to join the National Guard which had been so powerful in the days of the Revolution, the organisation of the *Agence*, that terrible and merciless *Jacobinism of the press*. In fact, everything tends to show that they went the whole length of the democratic demands—the unrestricted freedom of education, of speech, of conscience, and of the press. In March they had published an article by Lamennais in which he pointed out that, whereas the Royalists had nothing to lose by the establishment of a *Republic*, the Republicans had very little to gain if the existing system were properly worked. The principle was already there, the final transformation was merely a matter of time. This article, too, contained a remarkable passage advocating *universal suffrage* :—

Amongst those who are independent, who enjoy in the commune the rights of citizenship, how and on what principle will you admit some to the exercise of their inalienable rights, while you exclude others? Any distinction which it may please you to make under this head will be an insult to those whom you subject to a shameful exclusion, and will rest on a basis at once arbitrary, whimsical, and absurd. For if you are asked to explain how you came to form your categories, you must answer that you acted on a presumed capacity for exercising the right. It follows from this, that you declare the majority of Frenchmen incapable of rising to the effort of intelligence which is necessary for deciding if such an inhabitant of a commune has the reputation of being a man of ability and of honour. But who is more capable of judging than they are? Get this into your heads; the man whom they choose will, in nine cases out of ten, be the one who has given the greatest guarantees as a local administrator, and, as an elector of deputies, whose mission should come from the whole nation, and consequently from the communes.

And see what a debasing solution you have found for this problem of capacity, which you yourselves admit to be a difficult one. You go to every Frenchman and you ask him, 'What do you pay in taxes?' 'I pay,' says one, '240 francs.' 'Good! you must be a man of intelligence; go and vote, we give you leave. And you, how much do you pay?' 'I only pay 239 francs 99 c.' 'That is unfortunate; but we cannot allow you to vote, for the presumption is that you are a fool.' Is not this, I ask, a bitter mockery of common sense and of justice?

Not the least important evidences of the influence of the *Avenir* are the State prosecutions in which from time to time the editors were involved. In these, as we have seen, they came off in every case victorious, at least in public opinion. On the whole, we may say that by the autumn of 1831 they had fought their way into a very great position, and had come to be recognised as the tried champions of the principle of liberty in all its forms. The representatives of the king and of the king's religion had been everywhere defeated, and men were coming to see an almost unnecessary connection between Ultramontanism and Democracy, between the Pope and the People.

Meanwhile a more powerful enemy was slowly but surely undermining their position.

Since the signing of the Concordat under the consulate, nomination to the episcopal sees had been practically in the hands of the State. Under Napoleon, as we have seen, the bishops preserved a certain amount of independence. Succeeding immediately to the prelates who owed their position to their acceptance of the civil constitution of the clergy, and forced to recognise as their colleagues a number of these who had been allowed to continue in office, they naturally looked with horror on anything which savoured of schism. Then, again,

Napoleon was a usurper, while the traditions of the episcopate were strongly Royalist; they were, therefore, naturally ready to oppose him on every possible occasion. This being so, it offers no matter for surprise that they steadily resisted him in his designs on the Church.

But the Restoration brought about a change in their attitude. As their predecessors under Louis XIV. had supported that monarch in his opposition to Rome, so in the later period these courtly prelates had been ready to resent the interference of what they considered a foreign power with the royal prerogative; hence the difficulties with which an Ultramontane like Lamennais, ardent Royalist though he had been in his earlier days, had had to contend.

After July the king was no longer legitimate, and the Catholic-royalist party, with the bishops at their head, would have liked to organise an agitation for the return of the Bourbons, or, at any rate, to have got the world to believe that the new *régime* was absolutely inconsistent with the principles of Catholicism.

What must have been their horror when they read the first numbers of the *Avenir*! How great must have been their consternation when they began to realise that all that was most energetic in French Catholicism was being dragged into a movement directed, it is true, against the government of Louis Philippe, but holding out the hand of friendship, not to the exiled Bourbons, but to the democracy! In the eyes of many such an alliance was no less than blasphemous, and we can imagine their impotent rage as they felt that their power was slipping away from them. Of what use were worn out formulas, setting forth the impiousness of rebelling against a sovereign by divine right, when those who were hourly undergoing martyrdom for the cause of Catholicism were boldly proclaiming the rights of the people, and were coupling them before all men with the name of God? Many were the pious tea-tables round which heads were shaken as the situation was gravely discussed, and a dignified protest was entered against a movement which seemed likely to lead to a state of things unique in the history of Catholicism, a division into two parties: the one composed of the bishops and the old nobility; the other, as the *Avenir* was never tired of reminding them, in respectful irony, of simple priests and simple laymen, under the leadership of a man who had deserted the cause with which he had hitherto been identified.

From the shaking of pious heads at the tea parties of devotees, to gossip and story telling, the distance is not very great, and there is evidence that the case before us was no exception to the rule. Things were gravely whispered round, and it was charitably hoped that they were not true. Sayings were repeated in slightly exaggerated form, but it was supposed that they meant nothing serious; and so on through all the carefully guarded detail of conscientious slander. However the thing may have happened, for the facts have not come down to us, it is certain that during the year 1831 Lamennais was continually being subjected to this kind of petty persecution. An instance of it may be seen in a letter which he wrote on April 16 to the Abbé Auger :—

I do not know who showed you the letter, said to be in my handwriting, in which are expressed opinions which should inspire horror in any Catholic. Just such a letter has been secretly circulated in the south of France. So far I have not been able to discover the centre of these infernal machinations; but I have already got hold of a clue, by the aid of which I hope I shall succeed in finding it out. All honest people are interested in the public exposure of the authors of these cowardly calumnies, these infamous intrigues, and I have too much confidence in your sense of justice and your good faith to doubt for a moment that you will give me all the information in your power to assist me in obtaining this end. I ask nothing of you which is not an obligation of justice, a rigorous duty, nothing which I have not the right to demand in a court of law. What I want to know above all things is the name of the person who showed you the letter in question. Under similar circumstances I should not hesitate to do for you what I now ask you to do for me, and I should believe, if I did not do it, that I was not only wanting in charity, but that I was committing a horrible act of injustice.

I have the honour to be, respectfully, Monsieur l'Abbé,
        Your very humble and very obedient servant.

Considering the irritation, which was natural under the circumstances, we cannot but be agreeably surprised when we find him on the following day, after informing a correspondent that he has given *carte blanche* to his friend the Abbé Cambalot to act for him, adding : ' I have reason to believe that a priest actually in misfortune is not altogether a stranger to the intrigues of which I complain. I do not wish to make his position worse;' and he adds that a written apology from various people concerned, to be published in the *Avenir*, will be sufficient.

This is but an isolated instance. The stories continued to be circulated during the year 1831, and the situation became intolerable, especially when it was discovered that reported expressions of opinion on the part of the Nuncio, Mgr. Lambruschini, were going round with the rest.

From what we already know of the temperament of Lamennais, we can easily imagine the galling effect of these cowardly, underhand operations. He was deeply wounded. There is evidence in his correspondence of constant trouble from that nervous illness from which he seems never to have been wholly free. But the harm done was not merely personal, it reacted on the movement which Lamennais represented. The bishops began to censure the *Avenir* in their pastoral letters, and many of them used their authority to prevent its reception by the faithful in their dioceses. This policy may have been short-sighted, but it was eminently successful. Amongst Catholics the condemnation was re-echoed by the worldly wise, the interested, and the timidly devout—all those, that is to say, the slothful serenity of whose devotional or social atmosphere had been disturbed by the somewhat acrid tones of the uncompromising journal, and who seized the opportunity which now offered itself of turning over and composing themselves to sleep through that great drama of human society, the action of which was beginning too vividly to impress them, lulled into repose of conscience and of nerves by the consoling thought that the catastrophe would not be from God, but from the devil. On the other hand, this storm of episcopal censure was not without its effect on those who, though not recognising the pre-suppositions of Catholic theology, had been drawn to the movement by the boldness of the enterprising paper. For though Catholicism as a mere protest of the past was a thing on which they could have looked with indifference, as embodying formulæ interesting from an antiquarian point of view, and as having a place in a former stage of the growth of the human organism, it was a very different matter when it presented itself speaking to the modern world in its own language, and prepared with the most powerful organisation that world had ever seen, to place itself at the head of the movement produced by the throes of struggling humanity in its effort to give birth to a future already seen, but as yet unrealised. With the opposition of the bishops, and more especially when that opposition took the form of definite ecclesiastical censure, the ideal which had at first seemed possible, and even imminent, became a mere chimera, the phantom of youthful or overwrought brains. As a result, the *Avenir* was discredited with many who would naturally have sympathised with it, though not agreeing with its fundamental doctrines.

The circulation began to fall off, and the situation became impossible.

We are not, then, surprised to find Lamennais writing in November to Madame de Senfft:—

The bishops have destroyed everything; they are forbidding people to read our journal; they are persecuting priests suspected of a leaning towards our doctrines; they are moving heaven and earth to revive Gallicanism, kindling a hatred against the Church, the consequences of which frighten me, whilst we had succeeded in bringing back, not only to the faith but to the practise of religion, many even from amongst the atheists. And what are their methods of attack? Interdicts, intrigues, underhand dealings, a frightful system of organised calumny; and this opposition has been supported by Rome. Without explaining herself . . . without wishing to pronounce a judgment we asked for humbly six months ago, she encourages and even urges on her enemies and ours. The position is untenable; we are going to abandon the *Avenir* and the *Agence*, which was working splendidly. The only barrier which stood between the Church and material force is about to fall . . . my soul is torn with grief. They repel, they trample on those who ask only one thing, that they should be allowed to sacrifice themselves, and the triumph of the Church would have been certain had they only wished it. . . . But no, her rulers have said it, it is necessary that she should die, it is necessary. . . . I cannot go on. One cannot in cold blood speak of the death of religion and of society.

Had, then, the light gone out? Had this noble ideal been dashed to the ground? I do not think so. The passage continues with a suggestion of hope. But the blow was a terrible one. On such occasions Lamennais, always irritable, was unapproachable. At this time he was living in Paris, and it is more than probable that his appearances at the offices of the *Avenir* were looked forward to with dread. Under the circumstances, to venture to advise him required a considerable amount of courage. Nevertheless, a man was found who had that courage—it was Lacordaire. With a simplicity and loyalty which do honour to his character rather than to his judgment, he suggested that the principal editors should go on a pilgrimage to Rome, personally to lay their case before the Holy See, and Lamennais, swayed, perhaps, by conflicting thoughts, and probably buoyed up by a sudden hope, answered, ' Yes, we will go to Rome.'

Then the *Avenir* came to an end.

An article was written, signed by all the editors, in which they bade farewell to their readers, announcing the approaching departure of Lamennais, Lacordaire, and Montalembert. There is a touch of sadness in their description of the short but brilliant career of the journal; there is a tone of deep humility and submission in their attitude towards Rome, but there is a ring of defiance to their Gallican opponents, to those whose dearest prejudices they trampled on in this very act of filial piety. Indeed, the friends of the Government must have realised the full weight of the blow which was aimed at them in this article of November 15, the last act in the career of the *Avenir*, the first in that long agony of the Gallican theory which was to end in the Vatican Council.

Eight centuries ago, Philip Augustus, led away by the violence of his passions, determined to repudiate a queen to whom he had always denied her conjugal rights. Ingerburg of Danemark appeared before a council, composed partly of laymen, partly of ecclesiastics, and they read to her the sentence which deprived her of her crown. The poor virgin of the north did not understand the language of the Franks. . . . But when they had explained to her by signs the destiny which was in store for her, she gave utterance three times to a cry which is of every language and in every heart: 'Rome! Rome! Rome!'

She was brought back to her prison. But her cry had crossed the mountains, and the echoes of the eternal city had repeated it. Celestin III., and after him Innocent III., then occupied the See of Peter. The divorce was declared null, the servile council censured, the kingdom placed under an interdict until Ingerburg was restored to the throne of France.

And we also give utterance to this immortal cry. The successor of Innocent III. is at the Vatican.

One word more. We said, a year ago, in an article which had the glory of bringing down upon us the first manifestations of administrative anger: *We now make this protest. . . . We will carry it, barefooted, if necessary, to the city of the Apostles, to the steps of the confessional of St. Peter, and we shall see who will stand in the way of the pilgrims of God and of liberty.*

The pilgrims are about to depart. May God protect them!

CHAPTER VII

APPEAL TO ROME. CONDEMNATION

WHEN, in the early days of the great Revolution, the tricolour flag was adopted by the victorious Liberals as a national emblem, it was prophesied that it would go the round of the world.

Under Napoleon this prediction had almost been fulfilled. It is true that this did not happen till the principles which that emblem represented had been thrown into the background, and almost totally obscured by the military organisation of the democracy; still, it was those principles which gave a sanction to the operations of the imperialised Republic flowing over the borders of France, and permeating the monarchical populations of old Europe.

In no country was this result more thoroughly realised than in Italy. Undermined by internal discord, sapped in its vital energies by the petty contentions of local States, the land of the Cæsars and of the Renaissance had become the legitimate prey of foreign enterprise—the hope of Austrian statecraft. With the invasion of the republican armies all this was changed. General Bonaparte, stirred perhaps by personal ambition, or possibly by the Italian blood which throbbed in his veins, but more probably by both of these, laid the foundations of unity and independence in the creation of the Cisalpine Republic, formed of the central States whose sovereigns he had driven out. As Emperor of the French he continued this policy, adding considerably to the original conglomeration, and transforming the whole into the Italian kingdom. Thus it happened that when he fell, in 1814, the greater part of Italy had come to be united into a single State, while those provinces which preserved a shadow of independence were governed by nominees of the Emperor, that is to say, of the French Revolution.

The series of military operations which led to the overthrow of Napoleon in 1814 has been generally considered as a *War of Liberation*, and, on the whole, the description is not utterly inapplicable to it, though there are grave reasons for questioning the motives of those principally concerned. On the other hand, thus to describe the dealings of the Powers with Italy would be to invert the meaning of terms. The net result in this case of their deliberations was to place the sovereignty in most of the States in the hands of the nominees of Austria, and to shatter the hopes of those who aspired to national unity and independence. There were, however, three important exceptions, and these in the end led to the failure of the system: they were Piedmont, the Roman State, and Naples.

The first, with some additions, was restored to the house of Savoy, the second to the Pope, while the last was continued to Napoleon's former marshal, Murat, who had bought the favour of the victors by an opportune desertion of his leader. It was in Naples that the troubles of the established order first began. It was there that the afterwards powerful secret society of the Carbonari first made its influence felt. Murat, who had learned the lesson of combining ambition with an appearance of liberalism at the Court of Napoleon, favoured the movement, and when his former master returned from Elba, he invaded the neighbouring States, calling on the Italian people to join him in a struggle for national independence. The attempt was premature, and it ended in the capture and execution of the enterprising general, and the re-establishment of the Bourbons in his kingdom; but it had the effect of spreading the idea of national unity, and of demonstrating the utility of an organisation like that of the Carbonari.

That society continued to grow till it had a branch in every part of the country; and it formed the centre of the many conspiracies and dangerous, though abortive, attempts at revolution with which the newly established Governments had constantly to deal in the period following the final overthrow of Napoleon in 1815.

Nowhere was its action more pronounced than in the States of the Church, and it is with these that we are here principally concerned. It is abundantly evident, from contemporary literature, that the Popes might at this time have succeeded in winning for themselves a great position, as the representatives of a great idea; but, unfortunately, no one capable of realising this was elected to the See of Peter. Pius VII., himself a Liberal, was ably supported by such men as Consalvi, but though he showed considerable courage in his dealings with Napoleon, he was incapable of adopting and carrying through a great scheme of policy, and when he died, in 1823, nothing had been done to convince the Italian people that the Papacy was ready to undertake the responsibility of placing itself at the head of the movement for national existence.

His successor, Leo XII., the friend of Lamennais, was mediæval in his sympathies. By nature he was by no means despotic, but his reign became the occasion of a fatal reaction, sometimes marked by frightful atrocities, as in the case of the condemnation of upwards of 500 persons at Ravenna, by the truly proconsular *Legato a latere*, Cardinal Rivarola, for different degrees of complicity in the action of secret societies. Thus it happened that the name of one of the best intentioned of Popes came to be identified in the eyes of the Italians with the revival of inquisitorial methods, the encouragement of informers, secret trials before interested tribunals, and all the abominations of which men had fondly imagined that they had finally disappeared. This period, too, was marked by odious measures, such as the depriving the Jews of their civil rights, and subjecting them once more to all the degrading regulations of the Ghetto, from which a growing humanity had freed them; and by the encouragement of societies of the nature of the *Sanfedisti*, which, from their harmless origin as religious confraternities, had come to assume a politico-ecclesiastical aspect, as organisations for the furthering of reactionary aims. This last fact became of the utmost importance in the history of the Roman States, for the Sanfedisti grew into a powerful and partially authorised system of police, which promoted the denunciation and prosecution of all who were suspected of affiliation to the Carbonari and similar societies.

The result was inevitable. Hundreds of men were condemned on evidence which was justly considered insufficient, for any evidence would be considered insufficient when it was got up by a party and examined before a secret tribunal. Consequently, when Leo XII. died, his body was accompanied to the grave by the execrations of his temporal subjects, who naturally forgot the undoubted good that he had done in the suppression of brigandage and the introduction of certain necessary reforms. Lamennais, who knew this Pope only in his pontifical capacity, expresses his indignation at this treatment in his correspondence. Perhaps, had he known the facts, he would have refrained from doing so.

In March 1829 began the short and stormy pontificate of Pius VIII. He found his own dominions in hopeless confusion, ready to revolt on the slightest provocation. Then came the revolution of July 1830, in Paris, and it was the signal for an outbreak in Poland and in Belgium, while we know, from Silvio Pellico's account, in his *Mie Prigioni*, that it was the cause of considerable trepidation to the Austrian Government, especially in its dealings with Italy. This universal ferment of the Catholic world seems to have undermined the health of the luckless pontiff, and he died on November 30, 1830.

The interregnum was taken advantage of by the Carbonari. During the sitting of the conclave, the low, sullen murmurings of approaching revolution in Rome reached the ears of the assembled cardinals. On February 2, 1831, Cardinal Capellari was dragged from the quiet seclusion of a cloister, and ascended to the chair of St. Peter as Gregory XVI. His election was immediately followed by a general conflagration. On February 4 there was a rising in Bologna, where the people imprisoned the legate, and established a provisional government, and this was followed by similar outbreaks in the neighbouring portions of the States of the Church. The new Pope, as I have said, was a monk inexperienced in the things of the world, and the position in which he found himself must have filled him with consternation. The papal troops were not to be trusted. In many cases they showed signs that they were ready to fraternise with the people. To call in the Austrians would be a dangerous step, for their recognised policy was gradually to reduce the whole of Italy to a state of dependency; and, besides, the French Government had proclaimed the principle of non-intervention in the internal affairs of other countries, and had stated its intention of supporting this principle by force of arms. This being so, Austrian intervention must inevitably be accompanied by a French invasion. But the situation got steadily worse, and everything seemed to point to an approaching dissolution of the temporal power. There was no help for it. Austria, hardly waiting for a formal invitation, sent an army into the Papal States, and so did France.

Thus the year 1831 was passed between continued fighting with the revolution and dangerous diplomatic moves. On the one hand, the Pope was trembling before the threats of a rising and angry democracy, which might possibly become victorious; and, on the other, he was wavering between the fear of Austria and uncertainty as to the intentions of France, which was nominally in sympathy with the insurgents. A compromise with the revolution was impossible; things had gone too far. There remained then only the two intervening Powers, and of these it was of the utmost importance to conciliate the French, whose active help of the Italians would be fatal to the papal cause. So great was the confusion in the council chambers of Rome, that the Sovereign Pontiff had not yet been able to issue the customary letter of greeting to the Catholic world on his election.

And so the year 1831 drew to its close, amid the clashing of arms, the underground rumours of the smouldering fires of a democratic revolution, and the hopeless flounderings of a tangled diplomacy, when suddenly the news went round that three Frenchmen had arrived in the Eternal City to ask for the blessing of the Pope on the principles of Liberty, Equality, and Fraternity, together with all the demands of a militant democracy.

. . . . .

The news of the withdrawal of the *Avenir* was received with loud expressions of indignation by the friends of liberty in France. Letters of condolence were poured in upon the editors, and the pilgrims set out on their journey accompanied by the prayers and good wishes of a crowd of sympathisers. Their passage through the departments was like a triumphal progress. At Lyons they were greeted by the workmen, who had risen against their employers and obtained the mastery of the city. Their reception at Marseilles has been graphically described by Mgr. Ricard from information obtained on the spot :—

At the Porte d'Aix the dusty diligence in which they journeyed was met by a crowd of admirers, who gave them an enthusiastic welcome, and drew them, in the midst of repeated cheering, to the modest hotel in the Rue du Petit Saint Jean, where they were to pass the night.

Next day, at a given hour, when Lamennais appeared in the church of St. Théodore to say his Mass, all the clergy of the town had assembled spontaneously . . . and the sanctuary was filled with canons and priests in their distinctive dress.

The bishop, too, Mgr. de Mazenod, was there ; he assured Lamennais of his sympathy, thus separating himself from the great majority of his colleagues, and he invited the three travellers to a magnificent reception given in their honour at his palace.

Passing into Italy by the Riviera, they were enraptured by the subtle enchantment of the scenery and the soft fragrance of the atmosphere. But Lamennais soon awoke from his dream.

Such [he tells us in his *Affaires de Rome*] is the influence over us of our earliest impressions, that even here, in the midst of these smiling and magnificent scenes, nothing seemed to me to equal those which had delighted me in my young days—the rugged, bare coasts of Brittany, its storms, its granite rocks lashed by the green waves, its crags whitened by their foam, those long, deserted strands, where nothing strikes the ear but the low moaning of the sea, the sharp cry of the sea-gull wheeling in the mist, and the sad, soft note of the swift.

As they advanced into Italy, he seems to have become more and more disenchanted: 'We saw pigeons perching on the cornices of a hall painted by Raphael, while a wild caper forced its roots between the joints of the marble, and lichen covered its green and white slabs.' Everywhere they were met by the inevitable signs of decay: 'From twelve to fifteen Franciscans wander to-day in the vast solitude of the convent of Assisi, formerly inhabited by six thousand monks.' In passing through Umbria they came upon a spectacle which suggested painful reflections: 'There, guarded by a body of papal sbirri, was a troop of poor wretches chained together, two and two. The faces of many of them bore more evident traces of suffering than of crime. They crowded round us, holding out their hands, and crying piteously for some *bajocchi per carità*. We had before us the descendants of the masters of the world.'

Then they came to the Eternal City. Very different was the impression it produced on them, but especially on the two priests, for Montalembert was too young as yet to strike out a course for himself; he was content to follow, provided he could find a leader worthy of the high aspirations which troubled his youthful imagination, and for the present he had found such a leader in Lamennais.

For some time past Lacordaire had been troubled by doubts as to the wisdom of the course he had been pursuing. As we have seen, it was not without grave misgivings that he had joined Lamennais in 1830. He had inwardly struggled against the fascination of the great writer. He had objected to his philosophy, he had been frightened at his political tendencies, and he had secretly rebelled against the absolute submission required by the master of his disciples. Nevertheless he had been drawn along, almost in spite of himself, by the subtle power of superior genius. Thus he had become a most active and enthusiastic co-operator in the work of the *Avenir* and of the *Agence*, and had fully committed himself to the principles advocated in every phase of the movement. He did not regret the fact. 'However cruel,' he wrote, 'our present situation may be, it can take nothing from the enjoyments of the year which has just drawn to its close; it will remain eternally engraven on my heart as a virgin who has passed away.' But he felt the growing influence of Lamennais, and he was frightened at it. Now that the *Avenir* was withdrawn, he was no longer buoyed up by the excitement of active work, of alternate victory and defeat. He was conscious that a mysterious power was gaining possession of him, and he felt that he was not strong enough to struggle against it.

To him, then, Rome became a means of deliverance. He was deeply impressed by the awful grandeur, by the venerable majesty of the Eternal City. Before this all else seemed to fade away—the *Avenir*, liberty, Lamennais himself became as nothing in comparison.

To the leader of the movement the matter appeared in a different light. He had already seen Rome, and it did not now burst upon him for the first time in all the grandeur of its secular majesty. For him such emotions had had their day, and his present feeling was one of bitter disappointment. Like Lacordaire, he seems to have lost some of his confidence in the policy of the *Avenir* and of the appeal to Rome, but his motives were very different from those of the young and enthusiastic priest. On January 8, shortly after their arrival in the Eternal City, he wrote to Gerbet: 'As to our doctrines, every one here . . . admits that there is nothing in them which can lead to a condemnation. We are drawing up a memoir dealing with the whole business. The matter would soon be ended were it not for political considerations. It is these unfortunate politics which are everywhere destroying religion.' And about three weeks later :—

The Pope is a good religious man, who knows nothing

of the things of the world. His real and deep piety inspires him with a passive courage—that is to say, he would suffer anything rather than violate his conscience. But at the same time it would be impossible to be more wanting in active courage. . . .

Imagine to yourself an old man surrounded by men, many of them tonsured, who manage his affairs; men to whom religion is as indifferent as it is to all the cabinets of Europe—ambitious, covetous, avaricious . . . blind and infatuated as the eunuchs of the lower empire. Such is the government of this country, such are the men who have everything in their hands, and who daily sacrifice the Church to the vilest interests and the most vainly conceived of their temporal affairs. They count the peoples for nothing, and see in the world only ten or a dozen men who have become, because they are powerful, or seem so, their true divinities. And, in spite of this, everything is sinking or passing away, everything is dying. There are a few virtuous people who see this and who groan at it; but the remedy, where is it? I cannot see it. That is why I am convinced that God will take upon Himself the saving of what men are destroying, and that something great is going to happen. In a few years, perhaps, the Church, freed by extraordinary events, will regenerate itself, and till then there is nothing to hope for. Matters are hurrying towards an immense reform . . . which will begin in the next pontificate. . . . I know of nothing more depressing than what we are here forced to look upon. Only the divine promises can make it bearable. . . . This being so, it is very doubtful whether we shall be able to go on with the *Avenir*.

It was in no very hopeful mood, then, that Lamennais set himself to work the business of the *Avenir* in Rome. Whatever may have been the facts of the case, he was fully convinced that the representatives of the Powers had been before him, and that the cause of the movement would become hopelessly entangled in the network of diplomatic intrigue which surrounded the luckless pontiff. So far as he could see, the authorities were, on the whole, favourably disposed. It was strongly hinted to him that his presence in Rome was embarrassing to the Pope; that he would do well to return to France. It was pointed out to him that the *Avenir* had been allowed to run on for more than a year without any sign of official disapprobation from the central authorities; that it was simple madness to expect the Holy See to put itself at the head of a movement which had still to win for itself a title to recognition as a legitimate outcome of the evolution of human society. That such an open mark of favour from the father of all Christians would be a flagrant violation of the rights of conscience, an act of persecution against that vast majority who still held to the old ideas.

That both Lamennais and Lacordaire realised this there can be no doubt, but it is equally evident that they differed fundamentally in the meaning which they gave to the movement in which both had played so prominent a part. To the younger man the thing they had been contending for was liberty, and, above all things, liberty in matters of religion. Years afterwards he described the scene in which he had proposed to Lamennais the pilgrimage to Rome, and he added : He should have answered :—

My dear child, you do not know what you propose. Rome is not in the habit of deciding on opinions which God has given over to the reason of man, and, above all, opinions produced by the variations of local politics. Did O'Connell go to Rome to consult the Pope? In the midst of that terrible agitation for national and religious liberty in Ireland did the Pope intervene to direct or to put a stop to it? No! Rome was silent, and O'Connell spoke for thirty years. We cannot do as he did, for we have not, as he had, a unanimous nation at our backs. . . . Time has not been with us; let it go by. Our thoughts will germinate in the minds of men . . . and one day, perhaps soon, during our lives or afterwards, we shall see our ideas rising from their ashes, schools freely opened, religious communities established in every corner of the land, and the hatred which now assails us turned into that goodwill . . . which is the true guarantee of all the liberties.

Lamennais, on the other hand, had gone further than this. In the struggle for liberty he had come to realise that there was another question of infinitely greater importance, and which seemed to demand an immediate solution. He had been forced to accept as allies that vast multitude of the toiling people, the outcasts of society, and, from recognising their sympathy with the movement of the *Avenir*, his soul had gone out to them in all the deep compassion of his yearning, imaginative nature. This idea had obtained so complete a mastery over him, that it had become an integral part of his religion. Living in the Eternal City, face to face with the mitred majesty of the successors of St. Peter, he seems to have resolved to risk everything rather than allow the Church to draw back from a position which he considered to have devolved upon it from its divine institution. He thoroughly realised the difficulty of the situation. Everything he saw in Rome tended to convince him that the authorities wished to avoid a decisive explanation. The demands of the pilgrims for an interview with the Holy Father were met by continued procrastination, and it is probable that this had a considerable influence in the working of his powerful imagination. There are evidences of this in his correspondence, but it is most clearly seen in a passage from an unfinished work, written about this time and published some years later, at the end of the *Affaires de Rome*. It is the first of those apocalyptic utterances of which more will be said hereafter :—

Centuries upon centuries had passed ; it was upon the evening of one of those long days which are the days of God ; the sun, encircled as in a winding sheet by clouds, had gone below the horizon, night was coming on ; a heavy, stifling atmosphere hung over the earth ; wearied flocks, the peoples, lay in those vast parks which are called empires, kingdoms, and from time to time strained their necks, bruised by the yoke, seeking a little air to cool their burning throats ; and these parks were guarded by armed men ; and whenever there was the least movement, one heard the clanking of chains.

And as I looked, my soul, stupefied, was troubled, and I heard a voice : 'Son of Adam, what dost thou see ? ' And, as I did not answer: 'Thou seest the peoples redeemed by Christ.'

And on the top of a steep hill I beheld an immense building, shining as with a thousand fires ; and I went up to it, and my eyes, dazzled by the reflected light of gold, of crystal, and of precious stones, perceived, sitting on thrones draped with purple, men whose heads were crowned with diadems ; and, looking towards the plain, they said : ' All that sleeps there is ours ! ' And at their feet were other men, humbly bent before them, and women, half naked ;

P

and these, their eyes fixed on the crowned men, seemed to watch for a gesture, a look; then, kneeling down, they said: 'All that sleeps there is yours!'

And sumptuous tables were got ready, spread with delicious viands and exquisite wines; and the crowned men and the bowing men, and the half naked women, sat themselves down around these tables, and the perfume of the flowers and a beautiful melody made their senses drunk, and they floated softly in a cloud of voluptuousness. From time to time was heard from without the harsh sound of clanking irons, and they laughed. . . .

Then the crowned men retired to another place, and their faces became darkened, and they began, in secret, to take council together. Suspicion, anger, hatred were in their eyes, and they smiled with their lips and embraced one another. Suddenly there was a movement among the armed men who guarded the parks, and a terrible cry went forth from the multitude, and the sky was reddened with fire, and rivers of blood flowed over the plain, and women, clasping to their breasts their little children, fled, and at every step their feet stumbled over dead bodies. Then I turned towards the crowned men, who had smiled and embraced one another. The crown had fallen from the heads of some of them; the others cried: 'It is well, our name will be for ever glorious!' And they divided amongst themselves all that had escaped from the ravages of fire and sword.

And I looked at that, and my soul, stupefied, was troubled, and I heard a voice: 'Son of Adam, what dost thou see?' And, as I did not answer: 'Thou seest the anointed of the Lord, the temporal vicars of Christ.'

And my swollen breast was heaving, and I went down into the plain and sought a refuge from the vision which pursued me; and I met some old men, clothed in priestly robes; they held in one hand a purse full of gold, and in the other the mysterious book of doctrine and of prayer, and every page of the book was marked with the seal of the crowned men; and the old men said: 'Peoples, obey the crowned men; your property, your lives are theirs; whatever they do, you must suffer it without resisting, without murmuring.' . . .

And I looked at that, and my soul, stupefied, was troubled, and I heard a voice: 'Son of Adam, what dost thou see?' And, as I did not answer: 'Thou seest the pontiffs of Christ.'

And I went into the Temple; I wandered through its long, deserted aisles; the ascending arches were lost in the darkness; a silent horror took possession of me, a cold shudder ran through me. At the end of the sanctuary, on an altar, lit by a dying lamp, I perceived, as it were, a shadow something unutterable, a divine form which seemed bent under a load of chains.

And as I looked, I trembled; my brow was damped by a cold sweat, and I heard a voice: 'Son of Adam, what dost thou see?' And, as I did not answer: 'Thou seest,' it said, 'the Christ, the Redeemer of the world.'

Then I fell upon my face upon the earth; my life in time was, as it were, suspended, and what passed in me has no name which can be uttered by human tongue.

Such an outburst leaves no doubt on the mind as to the attitude of the Abbé de Lamennais in demanding a judgment from Rome on the doctrines of the *Avenir*. But Rome seemed unwilling to commit itself. A memoir had been drawn up by Lacordaire and presented to the Holy See, in which the principles of the movement were set forth, but no intimation had reached the pilgrims that they were either condemned or approved. They had demanded an audience of the Pope, but the authorities did not seem inclined to grant it, and put the matter off from day to day. After waiting for some weeks,

Lamennais became impatient, and redoubled his efforts. As a result a partial concession was made, and an interview was promised on condition that the pilgrims should not mention the business which had brought them to Rome. I borrow the traditional account of it from Mgr. Ricard.

On March 13 the three champions of liberty were admitted to the presence of the Holy Father:—

Lamennais fell on his knees.... Gregory XVI. raised him up immediately, with a smile of kindness. He held in his hand a large snuff-box ... and, after slowly opening it, he said quietly, 'Do you take snuff?'

The Abbé took a pinch for politeness sake, inwardly cursing, and saying that he had not come to take snuff.

The Pope then took one himself, gravely sniffed it in, not without soiling the front of his cassock.

'Are you fond of art?' he said abruptly.

'At times, Holy Father.'

'At times? That is not enough.'

'I like it in its place,' said Lamennais, slightly angered ... 'but just now ... '

'You know it is what is best in Rome,' said the Pope, quickly.

'After something else,' replied Lamennais, 'and, if your Holiness will permit me ... '

The Pope interrupted him.

'Have you been to see the Church of St. Peter's Chains, Monsieur l'Abbé?'

'I have, Holy Father; and would to God it was the only church in chains in the Christian world!'

The Pope pretended not to notice the allusion.

'I suppose you saw Michael Angelo's Moses?'

'It is his masterpiece; but, for my part, with all the devotion ...'

'I think you are wrong,' said the Pope, with warmth.

'I can show you another masterpiece of Michael Angelo, which can well bear comparison with it.'

And he took from his writing-table a silver statuette.

'Do you not recognise the claw of the lion?' he added, handing it to Lamennais.

Lamennais looked at it with a far-off air, as a man preoccupied with another thought.

'Examine it carefully,' said the Pope.

Lamennais looked at it again.

'I should like to be able to make you a present of it,' continued the Pope, 'but nothing here belongs to me; I have received, and I must hand it on to my successor.'

He laid his hand on Lamennais' head.

'Farewell, Monsieur l'Abbé.'

And he gave him his benediction.

Lamennais was very angry. He had come to Rome, hoping against hope that the pilgrimage might result in winning for the Church a place in that future which seemed to him to be inevitable; and now his worst fears seemed to have been realised. Nevertheless he wrote immediately to the Abbé Jean:—

We have just come back from an audience with the Pope, who received us very kindly, and who presented each of us with a medal. He also gave me his benediction for you, and for the children who are in your schools. . . . *You will get this rather late, as I am sending it by Lacordaire, who is leaving the day after to-morrow for Paris.*

This last sentence is especially important, as it compels us considerably to modify the account which has come down to us of the separation which now took place between Lamennais and Lacordaire.

Cardinal Pacca, it is said, wrote to the pilgrims, advising them to return to France, and to trust to time to justify their ideas, and hinting that the Holy See would rather leave the matter open for the present. The letter was received by Lacordaire, who brought it to Lamennais. The latter read it and announced his intention of remaining in Rome. His young disciple was very much shocked at his attitude, and tried to turn him from his resolution, pointing out that either they should not have come to Rome, or they should have been prepared to submit to the decision of the Sovereign Pontiff, whatever it might be. The discussion ended in an open rupture, and Lacordaire decided to return alone to France. That something of this kind happened it seems impossible seriously to doubt, and if we had to rely exclusively on the later writings of Lacordaire, we might conclude that the description was in no way exaggerated. But this letter would seem to point to the fact that the quarrel was not so serious as it seemed when judged by the light of later events, or at any rate that it did not appear so to Lamennais. This view is, I think, fully confirmed by a letter which he wrote shortly afterwards to Gerbet, in which he mentions the fact that an examination of the disputed doctrines has been promised, and refers him, for further details, to Lacordaire, whom he will shortly see. Such confidence in one with whom he was in a state of open rupture would seem, to say the least of it, imprudent.

In any case, Lacordaire now returned to France,

and, as Montalembert had decided to go on a visit to Naples, Lamennais accepted an invitation from 'the excellent Father Ventura, then General of the Theatins,' to stay with him at Frascati. It was while living here, in the quiet seclusion of the cloister, that he wrote the greater part of that burning denunciation of the ills of the Church and of society, already alluded to, which did not see the light till many years afterwards, when it appeared at the end of the *Affaires de Rome*, the last act of the terrible drama which was even now being enacted.

Thus he gave vent to his feelings while waiting for a decision from Rome. But he waited in vain. He was aroused to a full realisation of the critical position in which he stood by the publication of the letter of Gregory XVI. to the Polish bishops, in which the unsuccessful patriots were condemned, and informed that the schismatic Tsar was their lawful sovereign, and that they were morally bound to submit to him. At length he resolved to return with Montalembert to France, announcing his intention of going on with the *Avenir*.

There is a note of sadness in his description of that farewell scene, when he passed out for ever through the gates of the Eternal City :—

> Our resolution once formed [he tells us in the *Affaires*], we did not take long in preparing for our journey. It was an evening in July. From the heights dominating the valley through which winds the Tiber, we looked back sadly for the last time on the Eternal City. The fiery rays of the dying sun lit up the cupola of St. Peter's, fitting image of the ancient glory of the papacy. Little by little

surrounding objects, losing their colour, were disappearing into the darkness. In the uncertain twilight we could just see, here and there as we passed along, the remains of tombs standing by the roadside. Not a breath relieved the heaviness of the atmosphere, not a blade of grass moved in the general stillness; no noise was heard, but the dry, monotonous grating of our travelling carriage as it advanced slowly over the deserted plain.

We need not dwell on the details of this journey, the story of which is beautifully set forth in the pages of the *Affaires de Rome*. Suffice it to say that the two travellers arrived at Munich in August, and were enthusiastically received by the leading citizens of that place. There they were joined by Lacordaire, who happened to arrive during their stay, so that the party presented no appearance of rupture to the outside world.

Lamennais seems to have been very favourably impressed by the attitude of those whom they met. 'Our stay here,' he wrote to Gerbet, 'will have been very useful to us; it has resulted in sure and valuable friendships.' So high, indeed, did they stand in public estimation, that they were entertained at a banquet given in their honour, at which most of the leading men in Bavaria were present, amongst others a young and rising ecclesiastic called Döllinger. These things in themselves are worthy of note, but the banquet owes its chief interest to an event which occurred in the midst of the festivities. The president had just called on the assembled guests to drink to the union of French and German Catholics. The toast was received with rounds of applause, and the noise had hardly died away when Lamennais was seen to get up and leave the room, called away by a sudden message whispered to him by one of the servants. When he got outside, a sealed packet, together with a letter, was delivered to him. This last was in the handwriting of Cardinal Pacca, and a glance at its contents revealed to him the meaning of the message. He returned to his place very much agitated, and there was an awkward silence among the guests, but he said nothing. After dinner, as soon as he found himself alone with his disciples, he told them that the *Avenir* had been condemned. He had received the encyclical *Mirari vos*.

The blow must have been a terrible one. He had reached the age of fifty, and, with a mature mind, had formed an ideal of the true meaning of the Catholic religion. To him this ideal had become a necessary outcome of his faith. His companions were younger men, and had joined the movement as already existing, rather than as being the only possible expression of their aspirations. To Lamennais it was everything, the slow creation of the long years of a painful, struggling life. We have seen that he had given to it a deeper meaning than they had. He had realised that beyond the mere visible expressions of social organisation lay the democracy which had been slowly evolved under the influence of the Christian ideal. He had faced the problem forced on him by this fact, and he had thought that the Church might place itself at the head of this power of the future, and might thus win for itself a place in the modern world; and now all his hopes were shattered, and his whole life must have appeared to him empty and meaningless. Had he been carried away by a sudden impulse of anger we could hardly have blamed him, for the groundwork of self-restraint might well have seemed to have been snatched away from him. It is only when we have grasped this fact that we can realise the almost superhuman heroism of his advice to his trembling and perplexed disciples: 'We must not hesitate to submit.'

And when they got back to Paris he drew up a formula of submission, which was signed by all of them:—

The undersigned, editors of the *Avenir*, members of the *Agence pour la Défense de la Liberté Religieuse*, being now in Paris, convinced by the encyclical letter of the sovereign pontiff, Gregory XVI., of August 15, 1832, that it is impossible for them to proceed further without placing themselves in opposition to the expressed will of him whom God has charged with the government of His Church, believe that it is their duty as Catholics to make this declaration, that, respectfully submitting themselves to the supreme authority of the Vicar of Jesus Christ, they quit the arena in which for the last two years they have loyally struggled. They hereby call upon their colleagues to give a similar example of Christian submission.

Consequently—

1. The *Avenir*, provisionally suspended since November 15, is now finally withdrawn.

2. The *Agence Générale pour la Défense de la Liberté Religieuse* is hereby dissolved. All business already begun will be brought to a close, and its accounts liquidated, with the shortest possible delay.

CHAPTER VIII

THE VOICE OF THE PEOPLE

Thus, after giving himself absolutely to the cause which he believed to be just, after an almost superhuman struggle, in which he had staked health, ease, reputation, and peace of mind, he found himself disowned by that power in whose interest he had sacrificed everything. The blow was one which might well have shattered the faith of a colder and less sensitive nature. But Lamennais, appearances notwithstanding, was not devoid of that element of stability which moulds the characters of the great teachers of humanity. He resisted the impulse of the moment, and submitted to what he considered a dictate of the universal reason. I cannot insist too strongly on the heroism of an act which would have been impossible had it not sprung from the deepest conviction. But the strain was beyond the power of human endurance. He tried to persuade himself that he was free from future obligation to a society determined to destroy itself, that his public career was ended, and that he might now rest from his labours, trusting only that God would save His Church from the general destruction. But he did not succeed in this. Now, as formerly, his genius refused to be tamed, and rebelled against a decree of perpetual inaction :—

I remember [says Ste-Beuve] that when the Abbé Lacordaire returned from Rome with M. de Lamennais, I went to call on them at their rooms in the Rue de Vaugirard. I met M. de Lamennais in a room on the ground floor, and he spoke to me about what had happened in Rome, and of the Pope, in a way which startled me, considering that he openly made his submission. He spoke of the Pope as one of those men who are destined to bring about great and desperate remedies. But when I went upstairs and saw Lacordaire I was struck by the contrast; he spoke reservedly, and with submission, of the misfortune which had happened to them, and I remember, amongst other things, that he made use of the simile of a 'seed, which, even if fertile, must be kept back in its growth, that it may sleep for a whole winter under the ground.' . . . Comparing these things, I concluded that the relations between the first floor and the *rez-de-chaussée* were not very cordial.

And so we are not surprised to find that the correspondence almost immediately begins to show signs of the decisive struggle which now raged in his inmost soul, rending him, and gradually obliterating the old landmarks :—

Quos vult perdere, Jupiter dementat [he wrote to M. de Coriolis on September 15, 1832]. These words are terribly true, and every moment now brings them home to us. Emperors, Tsars, absolute monarchs, constitutional kings, see how they hurry along, they seem to be pressed for time. . . . Ah! what a magnificent procession! Stand aside a little, please, that I may see it pass. Farewell, good people! Pleasant journey!—since you are contented, so am I. After all, I think you are right; henceforward, what can you do with the people, and of what use can you be to them? Your mutual relations are becoming rather strained; you massacre them, and they cut off your heads. This sort of thing becomes rather tiresome in the long run; go away, and take your heads with you! It is much the wisest course. Do not listen to those bad people who tell you that an imperial, royal, princely or a ducal head is valuable only for what rests on it, and not for what is in it. That the contents are not worth much, I admit; but the other is worth still less just now. *Andate dunque, andate, e buon viaggio.*

We shudder as we turn from the quiet irony of this letter to the fierce passion which compelled him to write, some weeks later, to Madame de Senfft :—

Catholicism was my life, because it is that of humanity; I wished to defend it, I wished to raise it from the depths into which it was sinking deeper every day; nothing was easier. The bishops found that it did not suit them. Rome remained; I went there, and I beheld the foulest cesspool which has ever sullied the eyes of man. The vast drain of the Tarquins would be too narrow to give passage to so much uncleanness. There, there is no god but interest. There they would sell the peoples, they would sell the human race, they would sell the three Persons of the Holy Trinity, separately or in one lot, for a piece of land, or for a few piastres. I saw that, and I said to myself, 'This evil is beyond the power of man,' and I turned away my eyes in horror and in fear. Do not lose yourself in the sterile and ridiculous speculations of the politics of the hour. The thing that is being prepared is not one of those changes which are ended by compromises, and which treaties can regulate, but a total overthrow of the world, a complete and universal transformation of society. Good-bye to the past, good-bye for ever; nothing of it will remain. The day of justice is come, a terrible day, in which it will be rendered to every man according to his works, but a day of glory for God, who will take once more into His hand the reins of the world—a day of hope for the human race, which, under the guidance of the one true King, will set out once more towards new and greater destinies.

These facts being noted, we can appreciate the terrible drama which is about to be enacted before us. The central figure, the hero of countless battlings with himself and with the world, has now arrived at an age when most men begin to look back fondly to work done, and to dwell complacently on a life which has not been wholly useless.

We have followed him, step by step, from his unknown childhood in the wilds of Brittany; we have struggled with him; we have felt ourselves moved to deep sympathy in the uncertain moments of his career. And now that he has reached the highest point, has won his way to a position among the world's great men, we are perplexed. Oppressed by a vague feeling of uneasiness, we know not what to make of it. We see him standing, uncertain, crushed by a load of disappointment, utterly despondent. We try to understand him, we wish that, penetrating into the inmost recesses of his wounded soul, we could force it to yield up its secret, and once more sympathise with him, perhaps console him, but we cannot. He is an enigma, as impenetrable as the rocks on his native shore.

Wandering in thought over the ruins of his past, his mind may have been disturbed by the faint memory of a far off scene, on the storm lashed ramparts of St. Malo, when there stood on those walls, holding the hand of his companion, a little boy of eight years old. His thin, pale face was turned towards the sea as he watched with deep, sad eyes the fierce battlings of wind and wave, and listened to the angry roaring of the waters. He looked and listened, and, in his childlike mind, he seemed to ponder some thought beyond his years ; then, turning scornfully towards the groups of men and women standing round, he said to his companion : 'Ils regardent ce que je regarde, mais ils ne voient pas ce que je vois.' Perhaps, too, he had begun to realise that that scene was a picture of his own life.

And to his contemporaries he was as enigmatical as he is to us. The news of the condemnation was received by the Gallican party with a shout of applause, and it was confidently expected that the blow would be fatal, not only to the Liberal but to the Ultramontane movement. We can imagine their surprise and consternation when they heard that Lamennais had submitted without the smallest hesitation. They had charitably supposed, I do not say hoped, that he would, in the heat of the moment, be betrayed into some act of resistance, if not of open rebellion. They had realised that the slightest indication of this would be sufficient to destroy the movement he represented, which was based on the most thorough recognition of the prerogatives of the Holy See. Lamennais, by his attitude, had completely defeated them ; the Ultramontane position seemed stronger than ever, and even in those matters which had been dealt with in the encyclical, Royalism could hardly hope for anything but hatred from those whose condemnation it had brought about.

Then began an agitation almost unexampled in the history of human folly. That vast crowd of empty-headed devotees which formed the moral basis of the ecclesiastico-political establishment, seeing nothing of the heroism of the attitude of the Ultramontane leader, conscious only that their formidable opponent was still staggering under the blow which had been dealt to him, and that the opportunity was favourable, brought to bear on him all the arts of pious mediocrity, and strove to drive him to rebellion by the never ending insinuations of conscientious slander. Like gnats around the helpless form of a wounded lion, they swarmed about him, maddening him with their incessant buzzings, causing his sensitive skin to writhe in impotent irritation from the injected poison of innumerable though tiny stings; and they were urged to this, as M. Roussel says, by a double motive—'that he was a lion, and that he was wounded.'

Lamennais describes this in his *Affaires de Rome* :—

> Hardly had our declaration been published, when sayings, expressive of mistrust and anger, began to be whispered about. It was not complete enough, explicit enough, it was too like the *respectful silence* of the Jansenists. Intrigues were set on foot, calumny was quietly sown, timorous souls were disturbed by those charitable insinuations, always uttered in a sorrowful tone, 'which one does not want to believe, which one does not believe; and yet, so many people repeat them!'

Then came direct provocations, insults, public misrepresentations. They hoped in this way to draw us into discussions as delicate as they were dangerous in our position. We saw the trap and avoided it by keeping silence. Their anger was redoubled. They had not expected such moderation, and—why should I not say it?—a patience which seemed like contempt.

Under the circumstances only one course was possible. The *Avenir* had been condemned, because society was not yet ready for the ideas which it represented. It remained, then, to educate the rising generation, to prepare his young disciples to take their place in that future which was slowly but surely being matured. With this object, Lamennais returned to La Chênaie, and there, with Gerbet and Lacordaire, he awaited the arrival of his young neophytes. But, even in this small beginning, the signs of approaching trouble were not altogether absent, and the three friends must have been oppressed by a vague feeling of sadness and uncertainty as they strolled together through the shady walks, or sat of an evening in the drawing-room of that house, the walls of which, mysterious in their solitude, gave back the echo of the winds, which sighed around in the leafy stillness of the forest; for Lamennais had now begun to realise that a rupture between himself and Lacordaire was inevitable, and it was clear to all who were intimate with him that the fatal day was not far off.

They avoided an explanation for the present, and, as the pupils arrived, they were received by the three friends, who seemed to them absolutely at one in the objects which they had in view. But such reticence only added to the awkwardness of the situation :—

The house [says Lacordaire, in one of his later writings] resumed its accustomed aspect, a blending of solitude with animation; but if the woods were the same in their silence and their storms; if the Breton sky was unchanged, it was not so with the heart of the master. The wound was still open, and the dagger was daily turned in it by the hand which might have snatched it out and put in its place the balm of God. Terrible clouds passed and repassed over that forehead from which peace had departed. Broken and menacing words came from those lips which had formerly poured forth the sweetness of the Gospel; it sometimes seemed to me that Saul was before me, but none of us had the harp of David to calm these sudden outbursts. . . . Terror and the gloomiest forebodings slowly took possession of my wounded soul.

Such a state of things could not last.

Maurice de Guérin arrived in December 1832, and he immediately wrote to his father, describing the almost paternal affection of M. Féli, and the kind welcome he had received from MM. Gerbet and Lacordaire. It is evident that he sees no sign of the fatal discord which divides the nucleus of the little community. And yet shortly afterwards he had to write to his sister: 'M. Lacordaire left us two days after my arrival; pressing business called him to Paris.' Little did he think, when he wrote these words, that the two friends were now parted for ever.

The incident which led to this took place one day at the mid-day meal. The conversation had unfortunately been turned to political questions, and

Lamennais, as usual, taking the lead, was soon lost in a kind of running commentary on the parties which divided France. In the course of this, he spoke sarcastically of the exiled royal family. Lacordaire was shocked, and apparently an unpleasant discussion ensued, for after luncheon the young priest retired to his room, where he wrote a long letter to his leader, which he addressed, and laid on the table. He then put together his things and went away without a word to anyone. His soul was filled with sadness as he walked through those solitary woods teeming with so many memories. 'From a certain spot,' he says, ' I saw him through the trees surrounded by his young disciples. I stood still, and looked for the last time on that unhappy great man. And then I went on, not knowing whither I was going. . . . Everything seemed to be crumbling away around me.'

Later in the day the letter was brought to Lamennais, and when he read it he realised that the blow which had been impending for so long had fallen, that the greatest of his disciples had left him :—

This afternoon [said the writer] I am leaving La Chênaie. Honour compels me to it, for I am convinced that henceforth my life must be useless to you on account of the difference in our opinions on the Church and society. . . .

I believe that neither during my life, nor for a long time after it, can the Republic be established in France or in any other country in Europe, and I cannot adhere to a system which takes for granted a contrary conviction.

. . . .

Only in heaven will you know how I have suffered during the last year at the very thought of causing you pain.

In all my hesitations, my difficulties, my contradictions, I have thought only of you; and however hard my life may be, no regret will ever equal those that I have felt. I leave you now at peace with the Church, greater in public estimation than you have ever been, so far above your enemies that they are as nothing in comparison. . . .

I do not know as yet what will become of me. . . . Wherever I am, you shall have proof of the respect and attachment which I shall always have for you, the expression of which I beg you to accept, for it comes from a broken heart.

Deeply as he felt it, Lamennais concealed this sad event from his young companions, and the inmates of La Chênaie gradually settled down to their work, not however without some misgivings as to the attitude of the master. François Dubreil de Marzan, for instance, had written in September to M. Houet:—

Only this evening I received the sad news of the dissolution of the *Agence* and the final discontinuance of the *Avenir*; with it I may almost say that I received the dissolution of my hopes, forgive the expression. I who owed my life to these doctrines, which I thought were those of salvation, must we abandon them? If so, what are we to believe? What does all this mean? Is it chaos, is night coming on, or is the darkness which was already there becoming deeper? . . . In heaven's name write me something, give me some words of hope if you can. . . . Tell me how we stand. Oh! in heaven's name a word from you . . . you will take a heavy load from my heart! But I was forgetting—you promised to come and see me; such a visit would be a godsend to me just now. I want some one who can say to me, *All is not lost! There is still hope.* But I shudder when I think that you may not be able to come; at least write to me, not to lose my faith. . . .

And so he continues, pouring out his sorrows and his difficulties to his sympathetic friend, in a letter the language of which, broken and confused, is an evidence of the depth of feeling which inspired it.

Then there were petty persecutions, hints that the members of the little community were not sincere in their submission to the encyclical, or assertions that such submission meant more than they intended it to mean. Houet himself was attacked, and even the careful Rohrbacher did not escape suspicion, and had to write a formal retractation. But this kind of thing did not prevent them from carrying out the objects which they had set before themselves, and La Chênaie soon resumed its activity as the headquarters of the Order of St. Peter.

I have already alluded in a former chapter to the mode of life which characterised this hermitage on the borders of the forest of Coetquen, as set forth in the writings of Maurice de Guérin. We are now in a position to appreciate the pathetic meaning which lies hidden under the apparent artlessness of his style. The tender, almost paternal reception given to each of the young students on their arrival, the evident emotion with which the master noticed the increase of his 'little family,' made a profound impression on Guérin. He realised that to place himself under the direction of the *solitary of La Chênaie*, was to involve himself in the uncertain though brilliant fortunes of a man whose every action was being watched just then with breathless interest by a crowd of sympathisers in every part of the civilised world. Hitherto he had known Lamennais only by reputation, and his mind was filled with a mysterious awe of him :—

For the last three weeks [he wrote on Christmas-day, 1832] I have been living the life of a recluse, but a voluntary one, finding in the desert what is not often seen there . . . the most lovable society and the sincerest friendship. There are four of us here fleeing the world and seeking with the Master rest and light. . . . When first I came into the presence of M. Féli (for so we call him in our family circle) I was seized with that mysterious trembling which always results from the contact with divine things and great men, but this soon gave place to confidence and sympathy, and I felt that our imagination gives us a very false idea of great souls when it represents them as inaccessible and in some sort to be dreaded by the vulgar ; far from it. Glory seen close at hand is kind and simple as a child, and no one is easier to get on with than a great man. M. Féli forced me, so to speak, to forget his fame in his paternal kindness and the tender familiarity of his conversation. His whole genius gives utterance to itself in sympathy.

Never, perhaps, in the history of religious institutions has there been got together a body of men so varied in their genius and in their aspirations as those who now gathered round the man in whom was centred all that was best in the thought of his time. For besides the constant residents, such as Gerbet, who afterwards became Bishop of Perpignan, Maurice de Guérin and others, men of the calibre of the Abbés Blanc and Rohrbacher, Cambalot, Montalembert, Salinis, St. Beuve, and many others, drew their inspiration from La Chênaie, and visited it from time to time.

But it is to the younger element that this period owes its chief fascination. Nothing could be more beautiful in this respect than the inspired utterances of poetic natures like Maurice de Guérin and François Dubreil de Marzan. This last had set before himself, as the object of his unceasing endeavour, the conversion of a young friend of his, Hippolyte de la Morvonnais, and the letter in which he described his success to M. Houet bears evident traces of the tender feeling which had supported him in the work.

After speaking of the solitary life he is leading, he says :—

I must remind you that my hermitage is not far from another, in which is living a friend who is very dear to me, *very* dear, for my life is fused in his, for my soul *est souvent toute parfumée de la bonne odeur de la sienne.* I spoke to you of him last year. . . .

Now this friend who, even then, was very dear to me, has now become even more so. . . . You know how he stood at that time. Though filled with love, he had not that faith which leads to action. . . . What drew him towards Catholicism was the sight of faith and liberty going hand in hand, the unity of the two forces in humanity which had seemed the most opposed. But . . . when he saw the leaders of the Church drawn up in line with the kings of Europe, making common cause with them, and ever ready to serve under them, he had great difficulty in getting over the obstacle ; in a word, he believed absolutely in the Catholicism of M. de Lamennais and not at all in that of the encyclical.

. . . I had to explain to him the doctrine of the infallibility of the Church, which I myself had only just begun to understand, and then I brought him twice to La Chênaie during the pilgrimages which I made to that place this winter. These pilgrimages were like those of Israel, going to consult the Lord in Shilo. He came back . . . calm and strong; his faith increased every day. This sympathetic soul was in need of all the love which is to be found in the Catholic communion. His happy admission into the great Christian family was fixed for Holy Week; and, on Easter morning, at La Chênaie, after our retreat, I trembled with joy at seeing him seated beside me at the Holy Feast . . . in that chapel which you know so well.

This it was which inspired Ste-Beuve with a beautiful passage in his *Notice sur Maurice de Guérin*, which, despite its historic inexactitude on an important point, is none the less not without a certain relative value :—

Let us imagine to ourselves [he says] La Chênaie, still known as a holy place, on Easter Day 1833, a glorious morning, and the touching scene which was being enacted there. He who was still the Abbé de Lamennais was saying in the chapel his pascal Mass, his last Mass (*sic*), and was giving with his hand communion to his young disciples who had remained faithful, and who believed that he also was faithful; there was Guérin, Élie de Kertanguy, François Dubreil de Marzan, a fervent young poet happy in the thought that he had brought to the Holy Table a new recruit, a friend, older than himself by ten years—Hippolyte de la Morvonnais, himself a poet. There were at that moment at La Chênaie, or about to come there, men whose society and conversation was fruitful in the purest joys: the Abbé Gerbet, a gentle soul, tender in sympathy; the Abbé Cazalés, affectionate, versed in the mysteries of the inner life. There were other names which have since won for themselves a place in the various paths of science—Eugène Boré, Frederick de la Provostaye; it was a pious and learned gathering. Who could have said then to those who grouped themselves round the master, that he whose hand had just given them communion would give it no more to anyone, would refuse it for ever to himself—that the time was not far distant when he would be able to describe himself as an *oak broken by the storm*, with this proud motto : *I break, but I do not bend?*

That this touching and beautiful description is only partially true is evident from a letter of Maurice de Guérin himself, written on May 16, 1833, to M. de Bayne :—

It is generally thought [he says] that M. Féli is a proud and irritable man. This opinion, which has prejudiced many Catholics against him, is absolutely false. It would be hard to find a man more steeped in humility and in self-renunciation. If it were otherwise, he would not understand Christianity, which is summed up in humility; and certainly his realisation of it is beyond expression. His life is a continuous devotion and sacrifice to the mission he has received. . . . This is the secret of all that he does. . . . What has been taken for personal pride is only the intrepidity of the apostle. In this sense the martyrs and the Fathers of the Church were very proud. I say this with the greater assurance, that I came here with some of that prejudice against his character which is current in the world, and that I was only undeceived when I had studied his life and seen into the inmost recesses of his soul. The task he has undertaken is so hard, and costs him so much, that it would be simple madness to cling to it as he does if glory were his only object; for, in very truth, it is a bundle of thorns which he presses against his breast.

His conversations are worth books, they are even better than books. If you have not heard them, you cannot imagine the charm of these chats, in which he gives full play to his imagination ; philosophy, politics, travels, anecdotes, epigrams, witticisms, gibes, all these are poured from his mouth in forms at once original, lively, striking, and incisive, with suggestions which are deep as well as new ; sometimes varied by similes admirable for sense and poetry, for he is essentially a poet. From the age of seven he has been in the habit of studying nature in its smallest details, and he has laid up an immense store of observation, whence he draws comparisons which give to his thoughts a great lucidity and infinite charm. In the evening after supper we go into the drawing-room. He throws himself on to a large sofa, an old thing covered with worn-out red velvet, which stands directly under the portrait of his grandmother, whose features have a certain resemblance to those of her grandson, and who seems to look down on him with pride. It is the hour for conversation. Then, if you were to come into the drawing-room, you would see over there, in a corner, a little head, nothing but a head, the rest of the body being absorbed by the sofa, with eyes shining like sapphires, pivoting about on its neck; you would hear a voice, sometimes grave, sometimes mocking, broken now and then by long bursts of harsh laughter: *c'est notre homme.* Just beyond is a pale face with broad forehead, black hair and fine eyes, bearing traces of habitual sorrow and suffering, and speaking little: it is M. Gerbet the saddest and most gentle of men.

Then follows a passage invaluable for its description of the work which was being done either at La Chênaie or in connection with it:—

The editors of the *Avenir*, dispersed by the suppression of the paper, are none the less continuing their Catholic work. M. Féli is engaged on his great book, which, I am sorry to say, will not be ready for two years. . . . M. Gerbet is going on with his lectures on the introduction to the philosophy of history, and M. de Coux with his on political economy. Montalembert is writing articles for the *Revue des Deux Mondes*, and has just published a remarkable one on *Vandalism in France*. M. Féli lately sent to the same review a paper on Micali's history of Italy. M. Rohrbacher is at Malestroit, in the Morbihan, where there is a house on the model of this; he is working on a history of the Church. Boré is studying Oriental languages in Paris. M. Dault-Duménil is writing a book on Calderon, the Catholic poet, whom he intends to drag from his concealment in Spain that he may reveal him to the age. M. Cambalot is giving himself up to preaching, while M. Jean de Lamennais is entirely occupied with the schools of his *Brothers*, which now number about twenty thousand pupils. Of M. Daguerre's doings I am ignorant; and, *if I may speak of myself in connection with these great names*, I am picking up the crumbs which fall from the table round which these learned men are sitting, for, if my mouth is small, my hunger is great, as a little girl said when she asked for an alms.

But perhaps the greatest testimony to the thoroughness of the work done at La Chênaie is to be found in the insidious reports which were circulated by those who wished to drive the leader of the movement to his ruin. Nothing, for instance, could be more suggestive than an article quoted by M. Roussel from the *Ami de la Religion* of October 15, 1833, which was originally borrowed from the *Invariable de Fribourg*. We smile as we read the description of the seminary of Saint Méen, where the teachers

> instil into their disciples the philosophic and religious doctrines of the *Avenir*, and especially the political principle of the sovereignty of the people. In literary studies, as novels are the most ordinary vehicle of liberal opinions, and contain the most pronounced expression of the doctrine of progress, the professors not only allow their pupils to read them, but take care to procure them for them, that they may be able to keep pace with the movement of the century.

And continues the writer :—

It is no doubt with the same object that several hours every day are devoted to the reading of the works of heretics and of irreligious philosophers, as well as of revolutionary papers. In the fine arts a similar liberty is allowed. In music, for example, a student may hum what airs or sing what songs he likes. In fine, except dancing and fencing, for these have not yet been included in the list of necessary accomplishments, nothing is wanting in these young Levites of progress.

Then comes the terrible accusation that, 'besides heretical and infidel works and impious newspapers, they study there Arabic, Hebrew, Syriac, Chinese, Greek, Latin, and nearly all the living languages'; and, to make matters worse, these things are spread about the country by missionaries, 'who are as anxious to gain proselytes to the party as they are to win sinners to repentance,' though this does not apply to schools of the Abbé Jean de Lamennais.

Separated as we are by a considerable period in the evolution of history from the movement against which these attacks were directed, and which thus won from its opponents an involuntary homage, it is possible for us to appreciate the full value of such testimony to the thoroughness of the work produced by the ardent apostles who followed the inspiration of the master, whether at St. Méen, at Malestroit, or at La Chênaie. But had we been living at the time when those things happened, had our lot been cast in one of those communities, and, more especially, had we been living in daily intercourse with the great genius who had founded them, we should have formed a very different opinion of the attitude of the politico-ecclesiastical world, and we should have realised the importance of an attack which took advantage of already existing suspicions, sprung from the infinitesimal but potent germs of systematic calumny.

It is impossible for us not to sympathise with the boldness of the idea which Lamennais strove to inspire in his disciples, or the steadfastness of purpose manifested in the carrying out of the undertaking. We cannot fail to recognise that, even after the condemnation of the *Avenir*, he still thought it possible that the Church might take its place in that renovated society which he saw to be inevitable, even if it did not win for itself the position of leadership in the actual transformation; but the facts which have come down to us compel us to admit that the insidious machinations of a party slowly becoming conscious of its own weakness were not altogether unsuccessful, and that they gradually convinced him of the utter ingratitude of the adherents of the Catholic religion in France—of a religion, that is to say, which owed to his own personal efforts the immense improvement which had taken place in its position, and the fact that it had almost won for itself a title to serious consideration in an age whose interests seemed entirely alien to it.

This it is which accounts for those sudden outbursts of passion, those apparently unaccountable fits of gloomy melancholy which often perplexed and saddened his disciples. M. Roussel tells me that he heard from one who lived about this time at La Chênaie, that Lamennais was in the habit of shutting himself into his room in the morning and remaining for hours together alone with his work. Sometimes, without the slightest warning, the door would open, hurried, agitated footsteps were heard in the passage leading into the garden, and, looking out, his young friends saw him rushing aimlessly towards the woods, pushing madly forward, evidently intent on losing himself in those wandering natural paths which wound their way into the tangled darkness of the forest. On such occasions they knew that interference was useless, and they waited quietly till the crisis was over. Only one man among the many who lived at La Chênaie, from time to time, had any influence over, and dared to approach, him—the Abbé Gerbet. Sometimes, too, he would frighten them by gloomy forebodings. On March 24, 1833, Guérin wrote in his journal:—

E—— came up to me very much agitated and with tears in his eyes. 'What is the matter?' I said to him. 'M. Féli frightened me.' 'How?' 'He was sitting behind the chapel, under the two Scotch firs; he took his stick, drew a coffin on the ground, and said to me: "I want to be buried there. But there must be no monument, only a mound of sods. Oh! how happy I shall be!" I thought that he was feeling ill, and that he had a presentiment of the approach of death.'

And on May 9 he interrupts himself in the middle of a fascinating description of the sylvan beauties of a summer at La Chênaie:—

But, my God, it cannot last! Yesterday M. Féli pointed out to me some leaves which were already pierced and crumpled by insects.

It rained all last night, and there is an appearance of freshness everywhere. At seven o'clock this morning I took a stroll by the pond. The trees overhanging the water were dripping into it, and each drop fell on the smooth surface with a little splash which had something plaintive about it. It was as if the trees had been weeping all night, and their last tears were thus sadly dying away.

'Do you know,' said M. Féli the other day, 'why man is the most suffering of creatures? It is because he stands with one foot in the finite and the other in the infinite, and is torn asunder, not by four horses . . . but by two worlds.'

One day, too, on hearing the clock strike, he said to us: 'If we were to say to that clock that it would be broken at a given moment, it would none the less strike its hour until that moment was come. My children, be like that clock; whatever happens, always strike your hour.'

Thus, as we linger here, gazing on the ever-varying scenes of this life of hope, of study, and of peaceful wanderings over the mossy twig-strewn carpeting of this woodland hermitage, we are prevented from sinking into luxurious apathy by the too violent contrast in the colouring of the picture which fills our imagination. For as we look in thought on this simple, touching scene, where the master and his disciples, bound together by ties of love and sympathy, prepare to set forth together to the conquest of the world, we become painfully conscious that dark threatening clouds of calumny and of hatred are gathering on the horizon, and massing themselves, preparatory to sweeping down and overshadowing the little community.

And yet it is to this period, when everything seemed to combine to drive him to his destruction, that we owe one of those inspired utterances which often unexpectedly revealed to those who did not know him the true nature of his genius. It was, I think, towards the end of the spring of 1833, when the underhand machinations of his enemies had succeeded in permeating public opinion with a vague and undefined, yet fatal, prejudice against him, and when they were about to culminate in open persecution, that he gathered his young disciples around him in the little chapel, the walls of which were soon to hear his voice no more, and delivered to them the first of a series of sixteen lectures on humility, which has been preserved for us by a loving hand:—

In bringing us [he said in his opening sentence], in bringing us to this solitude God has led us far, yes, very far, for the distance from the life of the world to the life of a retreat is immense. And now that we have set aside our occupations, that our thoughts are calm and our hearts less agitated, we may turn to God, humbly and with confidence, that He may guide us in the new way and make known to us His designs over us.

And then he asked them to follow him as he ran over the heads of his subject, striving to arouse in them contempt of the world, and a gentle appreciation of the soft joys of the spiritual life.

Let us penetrate [he said in his second lecture] into the mystery of our iniquities, and we shall understand what is the nature of sin, which sacrifices outwardly our neighbour and inwardly the gifts of grace to the egoism of our personal law, violating order itself, the order of Creation, in which everything aspires to God ; the order of redemption, which is grounded on self-sacrifice, that universal self-sacrifice which redeemed the world, and which should be reproduced and perpetuated in Christian society, making every Christian, according to the opportunities which have been given him, the redeemer of his brothers. The wisdom of the ancients gave to Satan the name of *Ahriman*, or *ruler of those who have no ruler*. It says also : The man who gives utterance to the word *Moi* is a devil. The wisdom of God says : *Vae soli* (woe to the man who is alone). This saying is pregnant with meaning, and contains in itself the whole mystery of sin.

And in another place :—

Sin being a principle of egoism and of isolation, it forces each to lose himself in his own individuality. The insatiable *moi* breathes in all that lies around it ; it swells itself, develops, grows steadily, and absorbs all that is weaker than it . . . and it can be stopped in its progress only by another tyrant equal to it or superior to it in strength. There is a struggle, bloody, pitiless, and the hideous society which is composed of these things is but a seething mass of hungry combatants who come together only to devour one another. What word can describe this crowd of clashing individualities, this frightful confusion of a selfish rabble : Hell ?

You are right. Hell is nothing else. Such is the constitution of infernal society ; only the torment of fire is wanting to it. This is the state of which sin has made us citizens. Madmen that we are, we have forsaken the mild freedom of the kingdom of God, that we might bow ourselves under a yoke which is harder and more degrading. In doing so, we have become slaves of the devil, whose nature is superior to ours . . . high and mighty lord, who flatters our desire for independence while he loads us with chains, and, whether they will or no, subdues to the discipline of his army the deserters from God.

Then, after a terrible picture of the empire of evil, after a scathing analysis of the so-called pleasures of the world, he points out to his disciples the necessity of self-mortification, of denying themselves many things innocent in themselves, that they may prepare themselves to take their part in the great struggle between the forces of God and Satan, that they may contribute to the supreme triumph of Ormuzd over Ahriman.

And finally, in the sixteenth lecture, he seems to have been carried away by a vivid realisation of the forces at work in contemporary society:—

We know very well that the world deceives us . . . if, nevertheless, by a sort of fatal infatuation, we still hanker after it . . . it is, I think, a strong proof of our degradation. Thus, from the most insignificant village mayor to Louis Philippe, from Nicolas to William of Holland, each seeks to improve his own position, and, trampling on the field or the kingdom of his neighbour, he often waters it with blood. . . . Fools! Are they the happier for it? My God! Silvio Pellico, in the dungeons of Milan, of Venice, of Spielberg, where he was a prey to frightful torments, was a happier man than the pitiless Francis on his throne. The man who is absorbed in the pursuit of the wealth or greatness of the world is like a child running after a soap bubble; the bubble attracts him by its bright colours, but, when he catches it, it bursts, and leaves in his hand only a little water, dirty enough.

We can imagine the thrill of emotion with which his disciples listened to the concluding paragraphs of this lecture; the suppressed passion which had inspired the whole, which had given rise to this violent contrast between the rampant egoism of the world and the humility of the Christian, finally burst the bonds he had imposed on it, fell upon them in all the hideous reality of its practical application, and filled them with a vague, indefinable dread of things to come.

Nor had they to wait long.

The Archbishop of Toulouse had written to Rome with the object of provoking a personal condemnation of Lamennais. In May, the answer of his Holiness was published, and it constituted the first of a series of blows which were now to be aimed at the devoted head of one of the greatest of the defenders whom the evolution of the world has given to Catholicism.

It would not be consistent with the artistic purpose of this work to quote at length from documents pregnant with all the disadvantages of ecclesiastical Latin, disadvantages which are rather increased than otherwise by translation. I shall content myself, therefore, in referring to those which are now about to be forced upon us, with stating that they are all published in the *Affaires de Rome*, only translating such passages as are absolutely necessary to the subject.

In the letter to the Archbishop of Toulouse, dated May 8, 1833, the Pope, after alluding to the encyclical *Mirari vos*, in which the *Avenir* was condemned, continues :—

> The Father of light, in whom we had placed all our hopes, gave strength and power to our voice; our encyclical

was received everywhere with joy, and with an eagerness which bore witness to religious feeling, and this has been thankfully conveyed to us by the bishops, and by the most respectable persons in every order of society. More than this: the very authors and the abettors of the projects which formed the special objects of our solicitude, and to whom we took care to forward the encyclical, publicly declared that they would at once desist from their enterprises in order that they might not oppose themselves to our will. This declaration at first inspired us with the opinion that they had sincerely accepted our judgment . . . and that they would shortly give more convincing proof of this. . . . This sweet hope had revived our soul, alarmed at the difficulty of the times. . . . *But we have been once more grieved by things which are being circulated in the general public.* We therefore raise our eyes and our hands to Jesus Christ, in humble supplication, &c.

When this letter was made public, Lamennais' soul was once more filled with bitterness; the correspondence bears witness to it, and yet, after some delay, he wrote to the Holy Father, August 4, recalling the fact of his absolute submission to the encyclical, and he added:—

Nevertheless, I see, Holy Father, with profound grief, by a letter addressed by your Holiness to the Archbishop of Toulouse, and which has been published in the newspapers, that some one has succeeded in inspiring your Holiness with suspicions of which I am the object. How this has come about . . . I do not know. What are the *things which are being circulated in the general public,* and which have *once more grieved* you? The more I question myself, the further I am from thinking of anything with which I can reproach myself. What I do know, and the fact is public property, is that the *Avenir* was withdrawn, and the *Agence Catholique* dissolved. . . . That since the day when that was done, none of us have so much as thought of undertaking anything similar, and that thus we have proved our obedience to your Holiness, not only by words, but by acts as universally visible as the sun.

But, since fresh explanations have become necessary, I now declare:—

First.—That for many reasons, but more especially because it belongs to the Head of the Church to judge of what is good and useful to it, I am resolved for the future, in my acts and my writings, entirely to avoid those matters which relate to it.

Secondly.—That no one, thank God, could be more ready to submit than I am to all decisions emanating . . . from the Holy Apostolic See in matters of faith and morals, and to such disciplinary laws as it shall promulgate under the sanction of its sovereign authority.

And he concludes by asking that if this declaration be not sufficient, ' the Holy Father may deign to let me know what terms I should make use of, that I may give him full satisfaction.'

Unfortunately, the matter did not end here. The Bishop of Rennes seems suddenly to have become aware that Lamennais was Superior-General of a large and powerful order, and he called on him to resign his position as head of the society of St. Peter. This was fatal to the community on the borders of the forest of Coetquen. Maurice de Guérin described the situation in a letter to M. de la Morvonnais:—

I have lost all hope of being able to stay on at La Chênaie. M. Féli says that the impending persecutions compel him to separate himself from all association, and consequently that we must leave. The very idea is frightful, but what can we do? I must prepare to quit La Chênaie with resignation, as I entered it with joy, and to double my sacrifice; for, after having renounced the world, I now have to renounce a solitude which has become dearer to me than the world. Such is life. It seems that we are to leave this at the beginning of next week for St. Méen, where we are to make a retreat, after which we are to shut ourselves up at Ploërmel.

This means that the position of Superior had been transferred from M. Féli to Jean de Lamennais, and we are not surprised to find that the change was not appreciated by those whose choice of a leader was thus rudely set aside:—

We were told [he wrote, on October 2, to Dubreil de Marzan] in the retreat at St. Méen that our vows implied complete and passive obedience; it seems to me, on the other hand, that here especially they might apply that admirable principle of order and liberty, of variety in unity, which, while binding us together by a common rule, leaves to each the possibility of individual development. For my part I would infinitely prefer the chances of a life of adventure to allowing myself to be thus garotted by a system. It is true that M. Jean is, like his brother, a friend of liberty, but his position forces him to be careful in his expressions. It is not from him that slavery will come, but from higher up; they are forcing him to restrain us, and you will understand that if the congregation in its infancy does not *suck the milk of liberty*, it would have been well had it never been born.

And on November 7 he wrote to Morvonnais:—

The outcry which has been raging for some time against M. Féli necessitated our departure from La Chênaie. But a harder trial awaited me. The congregation has been placed in so critical a position, the object of so much irritability and suspicion, that it has been judged prudent to refuse admittance to any more laymen, and to send away those who already belong to it. So I am thrown once more upon the world, and compelled again to undertake the difficult task of mapping out my future. All this has happened so suddenly that I have hardly had time to think, or even to find a roof to shelter me.

While the members of the community, who had hoped to make their home at La Chênaie, were being thus cruelly undeceived, Lamennais himself was being hurried step by step to the fatal issue of the struggle in which he was engaged. On August 4, as we have seen, he had written to the Pope, and about two months later an answer was published under the form of a letter to the Bishop of Rennes, dated October 5. Alluding to the passage in which Lamennais had asked, 'What are the *things which are being circulated in the general public?*' &c., he says :—

Finding ourselves deceived in the hopes inspired in us by this first act (of submission), which we had considered the forerunner of declarations which would show to the Catholic world that he holds steadfastly and firmly to that sound doctrine set forth in our letter to the bishops of the Church, we had just reason to be afflicted. For while we were invoking this result in our daily supplications, a letter by the same de Lamennais was brought to our notice, published in the newspapers [*Journal de la Haye*, February 22, 1833], which 'shows clearly that he is still imbued with those principles which he formerly professed, and which we had hoped he would himself condemn.'

He also alludes to a work by Lamennais on Poland, 'a writing full of temerity and malice,' and to 'other things of the same kind which are being circulated, which point to a systematic attempt to establish what had previously been thought of. All this, without a word of protest from Lamennais, calculated to convince us that these things have been falsely and calumniously attributed to him.

But the matter which had produced the greatest displeasure in the Pope was the clause, in the last letter to Rome, in which Lamennais had stated his intention of carefully avoiding *all questions bearing on the Church and the cause of religion*, a resolution which seemed to him to point to a difference of opinion on a doctrinal decision.

After this he recalls the request contained in the letter to which this was an answer, and adds: *Let him undertake to profess, undeviatingly and absolutely, the doctrine set forth in our encyclical.*

Needless to say the letter of Gregory XVI. to the Bishop of Rennes was received with universal acclamations by the numerous enemies of the Mennaisian School, and this tended seriously to complicate the situation. Meditating on the course he ought to pursue, Lamennais foresaw that an unconditional declaration on his part would be misunderstood, and would lead to conclusions destructive of Catholicism itself. He resolved, therefore, in drawing up his answer, to maintain the distinction between his duties as a citizen and as a Catholic. Following up this idea, on November 5 he wrote once more to the Holy Father. He now declared:—

(1) That in so far as it [the encyclical] proclaims . . . the *apostolic tradition* . . . I adhere to it, *undeviatingly and absolutely*, and I acknowledge that I am bound as a Catholic to *write or approve nothing which is contrary to it.*

(2) That in so far as it decides and regulates points of . . . ecclesiastical discipline, I must submit to it without reserve.

But in the actual state of public opinion, especially in France . . . my conscience compels me to declare that if in the religious order the Christian has only to submit and to obey, he remains, so far as the spiritual power is concerned, entirely free in his opinions, his words, his acts, in that order which is purely temporal.

He had now resolved the question to a very simple issue, and it was natural that his opponents should concentrate on this, for they saw that they had driven him to his last refuge, and that he must soon decide between the renunciation of Catholicism or of the principles which had made the acceptance of it possible to him.

Meanwhile he had moved to Paris, where his presence was necessitated by his difficulties with his publishers. While there, he went to consult the archbishop, Mgr. Quelen, who advised him to write a memoir to the Pope. He did so, but before it had reached its destination the long dreaded blow had fallen. It came in the form of an answer to his letter of November 5, written this time not by the Pope but by Cardinal Pacca. Reminding Lamennais of the fact that he had asked for a hint as to the terms in which his submission should be drawn up, he informed him that his recent letter had been utterly inadequate, and had been the cause of considerable uneasiness to his Holiness. 'I say nothing,' he says, ' of certain expressions in your last letter to the Holy Father, to which I am sure you did not intend to give the meaning which they seem to indicate; but I am bound to tell you that the explanations contained in that letter have deeply wounded the mild and tender heart of the Sovereign Pontiff, who, though moved by great love for you, cannot pass over your last declaration, and is even compelled formally to disapprove of it.' And he recommends him to send to 'our very Holy Father a declaration which is worthy of you, that is to say, so simple, absolute, and unconditional as to be thoroughly in accordance with the promise you made to him.'

Lamennais was quite aware of the fact that the Gallican party, which it had been the object of his life to destroy, desired nothing more than to see him driven to some act of open rebellion, which, by placing him in an impossible position, would demonstrate the absurdity of that Ultramontanism for the growing influence of which he was mainly responsible. He could have defeated them at once by an absolute submission, but the complicated network of circumstances which now surrounded the question made it difficult for him to do this. Lacordaire had comforted himself by the reflection that, since the opinions condemned in the encyclical were mainly concerned with matters which drew their interest from the varying circumstances of place and time, the value of the Papal decisions would be determined by the natural progress of events. But now all this was changed, at least so it appeared to Lamennais. Rome had claimed that its decisions were to be accepted as part of the *Apostolic tradition*, even in matters which he had hitherto considered as essentially different from them in their nature. And these decisions, in the language of the time, constituted so many infallible decrees; for the Vatican Council had not yet been held, and the Catholic world was still wavering between two theories, infinitely less liberal than that which has since been authoritatively proclaimed. It would be impossible to imagine a more striking illustration of the truth that definition narrows the scope of a principle, than may be seen in the contrast between the Gallicans and Ultramontanes on the one hand, and the Orthodox Catholics of to-day on the other.

Nowadays the powers of the Pope are strictly defined, and infallibility has come to mean simply protection from positive error in matters of faith and morals, under circumstances of solemnity which very rarely occur, and this protection in no way precludes the necessity of taking all possible human precautions, nor the making use of all ordinary means for arriving at truth. The old Ultramontanes, on the other hand, believed in a vague, undefined, and therefore practically unlimited, infallibility—a kind of personal inspiration constantly residing in the Pope, guiding him in every act of his pontificate, and Lamennais himself in his earlier writings had committed himself to this theory in its crudest form. Compared with this, the Gallican theory seemed to lend itself to a more liberal interpretation of theology, and certainly, if the nation and not the individual be considered as the unit of religious society, this idea is not without a certain foundation in fact. But the supporters of the Gallican hypothesis had forgotten, perhaps closed their eyes to the fact, that a bishop may be, nay, is likely, when supported by an unlimited jurisdiction, to be the greatest tyrant in the world, and his tyranny will be the more unbearable that it is above criticism and that it admits of no appeal. This remark applies with equal force to a national episcopate, which is always liable in the majority of its members to fall under the influence of a dominant idea, whether this last find expression for itself in a tsar, a king, a committee of public safety, or a national assembly.

The case before us is a striking instance of this. According to the Gallican theory, a decision of the Pope could be referred to a general council by the assembled rulers of a national church, but if no protest was raised, it took its place among the authoritative decrees officially promulgated for the acceptance of the faithful, and became an essential part of the Catholic teaching—in other words, it acquired the character of infallibility. Lamennais, as we have seen, had placed himself in opposition to the royalistico-Gallican party, and consequently to the majority of the French episcopate. On appeal to Rome he had been condemned, and the bishops had not protested. As a result, the decree was irrevocable not only on Ultramontane but on Gallican principles, and the Church seemed eternally bound to the political and social doctrines of the past.

It was obvious that if this was the true statement of the case the distinction made by Lacordaire was worthless. Lamennais saw the matter in this light, and I think that it is here that we must place the date of the final and crushing blow delivered to his faith by the cruel and ruthless campaign carried on against him by his narrow, and therefore unscrupulous, co-religionists in France. He still wavered, it is true, but his letters and writings from this period bear traces of the most frightful confusion; it is a terrible medley of violent starts in a forward direction and no less violent reactions impossible to unravel; and in the heart-rending struggle which marks the course of the next few months there is nothing to relieve the painful monotony of the approaching downfall.

It was in no very hopeful mood then that he went once more to consult the archbishop. He has described the circumstance in the *Affaires de Rome* :—

Thinking over the words of the encyclical, I could not escape from the conviction that it contained things in their nature foreign to revelation, and which could not claim the *interior, exclusive, absolute, unlimited* belief of Catholics unless there were granted to the exactor of such belief an infallibility at once *absolute* and *unlimited*, in a word, as it exists in God Himself. I merely state the reflections which occurred to my mind ; I do not attempt to justify them. . . .

After having weighed the matter over in the presence of God, I went to see Mgr. the Archbishop of Paris, and I told him that, no longer understanding anything of the principles which I had hitherto understood as forming the basis of Catholic authority, only one thing seemed to me worth striving for—peace ; that consequently I had decided to sign the declaration which was demanded of me, but that this in no way applied to my duties towards my country and humanity, the sacrifice of which no authority in the world could wring from me.

The declaration, which was drawn up in Latin, ran as follows :—

I, the undersigned, in the very form of words contained in the letter of the Sovereign Pontiff Gregory XVI. of October 5, 1833, declare that I will exclusively and absolutely profess the doctrine set forth in the encyclical letter of the same pontiff, and that I will neither write nor approve of anything contrary to it.

Paris: December 11, 1833.

Thus he had finally silenced his enemies, but in doing so he had dealt himself a blow from which he never recovered. On January 1, 1834, he wrote to Montalembert :—

I came to see in this sad business only a question of peace at any price, and I resolved to sign, not only what they demanded of me, but also anything without exception that they might suggest, even were it a declaration that the Pope is God, the great God of heaven and earth, and that he alone should be adored.

And on the 10th of the same month Guérin wrote to his sister Eugénie :—

The news which I have received from Paris tells me sad things about the state of M. Féli. To anyone who knows the extent of suffering of which a soul like his is capable, or who realises the amount of pain which has been caused him, it is astonishing that he lives, and it is no uncommon thing to hear from the mouth of his friends, and those who know him well, these mournful words : *He will not survive it for two years; they have killed him.* Yes, they have killed him. Do you realise what a terrible thing is the murder of genius, of a Catholic genius armed for the faith? Perhaps the body too will die; for often the steel which pierces the soul cuts through the mortal life, and, if this happens, two murders will weigh on certain consciences.

If he recovers he will doubtless go to America.

To go to die in America, where he will find nothing to remind him of his La Chênaie! For the great lakes will not replace the pond, nor the vast forests the plantation of beeches, nor any walk the path which we made for him by the side of the water, nor any spot, that which he had chosen for his tomb behind the little chapel. My God! My God! that he should go to America to die! And what will become of us without him? Young men whom he led through the paths of science and of art, whom he nourished with his milk, whom he warmed against his breast! My dear friend, I can but allow the tears to flow and abandon myself to grief as an orphan.

Under these circumstances it must have seemed a bitter mockery when he received a letter of congratulation from the Holy Father, and we are not surprised to find him writing in the *Affaires de Rome*: 'The archbishop pressed me to write to the Pope, thanking him for his letter to me, and I answered that silence seemed to me the more respectful course.' Shortly after this the venerable prelate once more wrote to him, to try and persuade him to alter his resolution. Lamennais answered him in a letter in which occurs a passage of surpassing interest.

After maintaining that a written communication was bound to commit him, on one side or the other, beyond his intention, he continued :—

I have already declared that henceforward I would occupy myself in no way with anything relating to the Catholic religion or the Church. What more can they ask of me? Do they wish that, cutting myself off from my country and humanity, I should remain neutral in things which interest them? But what power can dispense me from my duties to them? Whatever happens, I shall fulfil them in my own small way; and if fresh persecutions are to be the reward of my fidelity . . . God, I am sure, will give me strength to withstand them, with the constancy befitting a man full of faith in eternal justice, and little thoughtful of things which are only in time.

It was probably about this time that Frederick Ozanam and his young Catholic friends called on the archbishop, with the object of persuading him to appoint Lacordaire to preach a course of sermons to the student youth of Paris. When they came into his room they were surprised to find him alone with Lamennais. As soon as they had stated the purpose of their visit, Mgr. Quelin, looking kindly at the great writer, deplored the fact that the gift of oratory had not been vouchsafed to him, as the people would have crowded to him. To which came the sad reply: '*Pour moi, monseigneur, ma carrière est finie.*'

But the archbishop was determined to do his utmost to stave off the approaching catastrophe, and shortly afterwards he paid a personal visit to Lamennais. Unfortunately there is no certain record of the details of the interview, but the fact has come down to us that while it was in progress Ste-Beuve was on his way to pay his respects, and to offer what comfort he could to the fallen leader. Arriving at the house, he met the venerable prelate at the door, looking very much agitated. Going in, he found Lamennais in one of his terrible moods, restless and irritable, and the latter, greeting him with the words '*It is time to put an end to this,*' opened a drawer and took from it a bundle of papers, which he presented to the critic, asking him to get them published for him, and he expressed a wish that the work should be anonymous. The bundle of papers was the manuscript of the *Paroles d'un Croyant.*

Ste-Beuve undertook the business, though not without some misgivings, and it is said that a few days afterwards, on calling at the publisher's to see how the work was getting on, he was astonished to find him in a state of considerable agitation and perplexity, and the good man told him that he had just been to the workshop to see how the men were getting on, and had found the whole place in an uproar at the fragments they had read in the course of their work. He maintained that he could not possibly take the responsibility of the publication, and was with difficulty persuaded to go on with it, on condition that his own name did not appear.

Meanwhile the report had gone round that something extraordinary from the pen of Lamennais was in preparation, and the archbishop wrote to him, exhorting him to reflect before taking a step which would be irrevocable. He answered on April 29 from La Chênaie, to which he had now returned, explaining the scope of the book, and denying that it in any way infringed on his resolution to write no more on matters relating to religion, maintaining, however, that he had been forced to publish it by 'the frightful state in which I see France on the one hand and Europe on the other.' But it is not the result of a sudden fit of passsion, for 'it is a year since it was finished.' There are certain passages which might seem to trespass on the domain of theology, but, 'in speaking of Jesus Christ, I have carefully abstained from uttering a word capable of being applied to Christianity, as determined by dogmatic or positive teaching.' There are, however, in it two things which will shock many of his readers: (1) 'The indignation with which I speak of kings and their system.' (2) 'The intention which I attribute to sovereigns, while laughing at Christianity, to make use of its ministers in pursuance of their personal ends.'

Then the book appeared, and society reeled as it awoke to the fact that a terrible and unexpected blow had been dealt to it, that the first note of the approaching revolution had been sounded.

To describe such a work would be difficult, to criticise it by comparison with the ordinary standards impossible. The author begins by an invocation of the Trinity, which, in a measure, prepares us for the awful grandeur of the poem which is about to be unrolled before our eyes :—

In the name of the Father, and of the Son, and of the Holy Ghost. Amen.

Glory to God in the highest and peace on earth to men of goodwill.

He that hath ears to hear let him hear; he that hath eyes let him open them and look, for the time is near.

The Father brought forth His Son . . . His Word, and the Word was made flesh and dwelt amongst us ; He came into the world, and the world did not know Him.

The Son promised to send the Spirit, the Comforter, the Spirit who proceeds from the Father and from Him, their mutual love : He will come, and will renew the face of the earth, and it will be as a second creation.

Eighteen centuries ago the Word sowed the divine seed, and the Spirit caused it to germinate. Men have seen it flourish and have tasted of its fruit, the fruit of the Tree of Life, planted in their poor abode.

Verily I say unto you, they were filled with a great joy when they saw the light, and felt themselves penetrated with the fire of heaven.

Now the earth is dark and cold.

Our fathers saw the sun go down. When it sank below the horizon the human race was seized with trembling. Then there was in that night a something which has no name. Children of the night, the West is black, but the East is beginning to grow pale.

Listen, and tell me whence comes this rumour, confused, vague, strange, which is heard on every side.

Lay your hand upon the earth and tell me why it has trembled.

Something which we do not understand is moving in the world : it is the work of God.

Is there a man who is not waiting ? Is there a heart which does not beat ?

Son of man, go up to the heights, and tell me what thou seest.

I see on the horizon a livid cloud, and around it a red light as the reflection of a fire.

.   .   .   .

Son of man, again what dost thou see ?

I see clouds of dust far off, moving on every side, clashing, mingling, confused. They pass over States, and when they are gone I see only the plain.

I see people rising in tumult, and kings grow pale under their crown. There is war between them, war unto death.

I see one throne, two thrones broken, and the people are scattering the débris over the earth.

I see a people fighting as the Archangel Michael against Satan. Its blows are terrible, but it is naked, and its enemy is covered with strong armour.

My God! it falls; it is dead! No, it is only wounded; Mary, the Virgin Mother, covers it with her mantle, smiles on it, and withdraws it for a little time from the fight.

And so the inspired author, maddened by an overpowering sense of injustice, moved to the inmost depths of his wounded soul, seizes his reader and drags him with him, compelling him to witness the successive scenes of this dream of blood, of tyranny, and of revolution, in which there is no figure and no circumstance which has not its counterpart in reality, till at last, when both are tired, there is a pause, and the dream gives place to the soft, sad accents of a plaintive song.

When you see a man dragged to prison or to death, do not hasten to say he is a bad man, who has committed a crime against his brother.

For perhaps he is a good man who has tried to serve his brothers, and who is punished by their oppressors.

When you see a people loaded with irons and given over to the executioner, do not hasten to say that is a turbulent people seeking to trouble the peace of the earth.

For perchance it is a martyr people dying for the human race.

Eighteen centuries ago, in an eastern town, the pontiffs

and the kings of that day nailed upon a cross, after having beaten Him, a rebel, a blasphemer, as they called Him.

On the day of His death hell trembled, but there was joy in heaven.

For the blood of the just had redeemed the world.

Thus, as vision follows vision, we are, as it were, torn asunder by the violent contrasts which force themselves upon us. Sometimes we vainly struggle in the grasp of a powerful hand, as, in spite of ourselves, we are plunged into the depths of hell.

The night was dark; the starless sky weighed over the earth as a slab of black marble on a tomb.

And nothing broke the silence of that night but a strange noise, as a gentle flapping of wings, which was heard from time to time over the fields and the towns.

Then the darkness grew deeper, and there was no man who did not feel his soul shrink, as a shudder ran through him.

And in a room draped in black and lit by a red lamp, seven men clothed in purple, and with crowns on their heads, were sitting on seven seats of iron.

And in the middle of the room was a throne built of bones, and at the foot of the throne, as a stool, was an overturned crucifix, and before the throne a table of ebony, and on the table a vase full of red, foaming blood, and a human skull.

And the seven crowned men seemed thoughtful and sad. . . .

And one of them got up, staggered towards the throne, and put his feet upon the crucifix.

As he did so, his limbs trembled, and he seemed about to faint. The others looked on in silence; nor did they move, but something, I know not what, passed over their faces, a smile which is not of man. . . .

And he who seemed about to faint stretched forth his

hand, seized the vase of blood, poured some of it into the skull, and drank.

And the drink seemed to strengthen him.

And, raising his head, this cry was heard as a low rattling in his throat :—

'Cursed be Christ, who has brought liberty into the world!'

And the six other crowned men rose up all together, and all gave utterance to the same cry :—

'Cursed be Christ, who has brought liberty into the world!'

After which, when they had returned to their iron seats, the first said :—

'My brothers, what shall we do that we may destroy liberty? For where its reign begins ours ends. The cause is common to all of us: let each one propose what seems good to him.

'This is my advice. Before Christ came, who dared to oppose us? It is His religion which has destroyed us; let us abolish the religion of Christ.'

And all answered : 'That is true. Let us abolish the religion of Christ.'

Then each in turn arose and gave his opinion. One, that science and thought should be crushed out; another, that communication with foreign nations should be forbidden; another, that division and hatred should be sown among the people to prevent their uniting against the sovereign; another, that they should act on the principle that 'the executioner is the chief minister of a good prince'; another, that they should destroy the energy of their subjects by corruption, to which last all answered :—

'That is true, we must sap their energy, their strength, their courage by corruption.'

Then the seventh, after drinking, like the others, from the human skull, spoke thus, with his foot upon the crucifix :—

'Away with Christ! there must be war to the death, eternal war between Him and us.

'But how can we draw the people away from Him? To attempt it would be useless. What shall we do then? Listen! We must gain over the priests of Christ with property, honours, and power.

'And they will command the people, in Christ's name, to submit to us in everything. . . .

'And the people will believe them, and will obey for conscience sake, and our power will be greater than before.'

And all answered : 'That is true. We must win over the priests of Christ.'

Suddenly the lamp which lit the room went out, and the seven men took leave of one another in the dark.

And this saying came to a just man who, at that moment, was watching and praying before a cross : ' My day is at hand. Adore and fear nothing.'

. . . .

Through a mist, grey and heavy, I perceived, as often happens at the hour of twilight, a plain, bare, empty, cold.

From the middle of it rose a rock, from which fell, drop by drop, a brackish water, and I heard the soft, dull dripping of the falling drops, and there was no other sound.

And seven paths, after winding through the plain, came up to the rock, and near that rock, at the entrance to each, was a stone smeared over with an indescribable something, damp and green, like the slime of a reptile.

Suddenly, on one of the paths I saw a shadow moving slowly along, and when it came nearer, I realised that it was not a man, but the resemblance of a man.

And in the place where the heart should have been was a clot of blood.

And it sat down upon the stone, which was damp and

green, and its limbs trembled, and, bowing its head, it hugged itself with its arms as if to retain a remainder of warmth.

And by the six other paths, six other shades made their way to the damp green stone.

And they sat there, silent and bent, under the weight of an incomprehensible agony.

And their silence dragged on, I know not how long, for the sun never rises over that plain, and they know there neither morning nor evening; but the drops of water, in their falling, measure a time, monotonous, unbroken, dreary, eternal.

And the thing was so horrible to see, that if God had not given me strength I should not have been able to bear it.

Then one of the shades, with a convulsive shudder, raised his head, and sent forth a sound like the harsh, dry sighing of the wind as it blows through a skeleton.

And the rock sent back these words to my ear:—

'Christ has conquered, be He cursed!'

And a shiver ran through the six other shades, and, raising their heads together, they gave utterance to the same blasphemy: 'Christ has conquered, be He cursed!'

And immediately they were seized with a greater trembling, the fog grew thicker, and for a moment the water ceased to drip.

And the seven shades were bent once more under the weight of their secret agony, and there was a second silence longer than the first.

Then one of them, without rising from his stone, motionless, and leaning forward, said to the others:—

'So it has happened to you as it has to me. Have all our plans been brought to naught?'

And each in turn related how his attempt had failed.

Then the seventh shade:—

'Christ has conquered, curse Him!'

And all together made answer :—

' Christ has conquered, curse Him ! '

And I saw a hand advancing; it dipped its finger into the dark water, whose drops measured, in falling, eternal time, and it marked the foreheads of the seven shades, and it was for ever.

Yet hardly have we realised the full meaning of these terrible pictures, when the scene once more changes, and we seem to be listening to a far off echo from the Sermon on the Mount :—

When a tree stands alone, it is shaken by the winds and stripped of its leaves ; and its branches, instead of standing out, are lowered as if seeking the earth.

When a plant is alone, finding no shelter from the rays of the sun, it languishes, droops, and dies.

When man is alone, the wind of power bends him to the earth, and the greed of the great ones of the world absorbs the sap which should have nourished him.

Therefore be not like that plant or that solitary tree ; but be united one to another, and lend to one another your mutual support and protection.

So long as you are disunited, so long as each seeks only his own good, you have nothing to hope for but suffering, misfortune, and oppression.

Consider the sparrow, how feeble it is ; is there anything more helpless than the swallow ? And yet, let a bird of prey appear amongst them, and they drive it away by crowding round it, and pursuing it all together.

Learn then from the swallow and from the sparrow.

If any man separate himself from his brothers, fear follows him in his walking, sits beside him when he is at rest, and does not leave him in sleep.

If, then, any one asks you : ' How many are there of you ? ' Answer : ' We are one, for our brothers are ourselves, and we are our brothers.'

For God has created neither small nor great, nor masters, nor slaves, nor kings, nor subjects; He has made all men equal.

But amongst men, some are stronger in body, in mind, or in will, and these it is who wish to rule over others, when pride or covetousness have destroyed in them the love of their brothers.

And God knew that it would be so, and this is why He commanded men to love one another, that they might be united, and that the weak might not fall under the tyranny of the strong.

For he that is stronger than one is less strong than two, and he that is stronger than two is less strong than four; and so the weak need fear nothing when, loving one another, they are truly united.

A man was journeying through the mountains, and he came to a spot where a great rock had rolled across the path, and filled up the whole of it, so that it was impossible to pass it, either on the right hand or on the left.

Now this man, seeing that he could not continue on his journey because of the rock, tried to roll it aside, and he wearied himself, and all his efforts were vain.

Seeing this, he sat down full of sadness and said: 'What will become of me? For night will come on and will overtake me in this solitude, without food, without shelter or means of defence, at the hour when wild beasts wander abroad in search of their prey.' And as he sat, lost in thought, another traveller came up, and when he had done what the first had done . . . he, too, sat down and buried his head in his hands.

And after him came many others, and none of them could move the rock, and a great fear came upon them.

Then one of them said to the others: 'My brothers, let us pray to our Father who is in heaven; perchance He will have pity on us in our trouble.'

And they heard him, and a prayer went up from their hearts to the Father which is in heaven.

And when they had prayed, the same man said : ' My brothers, who knows whether what no one of us could do alone might not be possible to all of us together ? '

And they rose up, and all together pushed against the rock, and it gave way, and they continued their journey in peace.

The traveller is man, the journey is life, the rock is the misery which besets him.

No man, alone, can move that rock; but God has so measured the weight of it, that it cannot stand against the united efforts of those who journey together.

Thus lazily turning over the pages of such a work, we are drawn to it mainly by historic and artistic sympathy. We realise the beauty and the grandeur of it, but it is difficult for us to form any conception of its effect on the minds of contemporary readers. Almost immediately after its appearance, the Baron de Vitrolles sent to Lamennais a list of opinions which he had heard, in conversation, on a book which Royer Collard aptly described as '93 *going to its Easter Communion.*

' But how could you have allowed him to publish such a work ? '

' How could I have prevented it ? '

' It is an abominable book, every social principle is attacked in it. How violent, how brilliant it is ! '

' There is no such thing as government if the laws are insufficient to condemn the author at the assizes.'

' It is sublime, and besides, it is true. Legitimacy is an impious dogma. God is the only legitimate ruler.'

' You don't mean to tell me that the Abbé de L. M. is a religious man and a believer ; every doctrine of religion is overthrown in his work, and I have underlined three passages which prove that he is a deist . . . at least.'

'The Cabinet has just met, and two hours were given to the discussion of the advisability of prosecuting the author. Guizot was for the prosecution and M. de Riguy against it, not because he did not consider it an execrable production, but for fear of scandal, and because he thought it would lead to nothing.'

'Chateaubriand, too, said in confidence: I had imagined that in my articles I had said all that could be said . . . but now I am thrown completely into the shade.'

'But, said Castelb . . . if the Abbé de Lamennais had read the Gospel.' . . .

'What sublimity of thought, what perfection of style! . . . Language contains nothing to equal the ode, the elegy: *La mère et la fille.*'[1]

'What black fury is in the chapter on the kings! . . . that foaming blood, those skulls! . . . and the description of the seven coffins! The author has out-heroded Herod, as Hamlet says.'

'The best of it all is, that the author is now proved beyond doubt to be mad, and it is to be hoped that he will soon be shut up in the *Petites Maisons*. I should not be sorry if Chateaubriand followed him.'

'What a pity that so great a talent should have been turned away from the defence of sound doctrines, the only ones capable of saving society!'

'It is the cross surmounted by the red cap.'

'It is the Apocalypse of Satan.'

'It is Babeuf taken into the service of the prophet Ezekiel' . . .

Is this enough for you? I might, if I wished, give you four more pages of it.

The Baron de Vitrolles was a man of the world, and was capable of a thorough appreciation of the greatness of the book. Not so those of his friends

---

[1] One of the most beautiful chapters in the *Paroles*. Unfortunately the space at my disposal does not permit me to transcribe it.

who had been inspired, in the retirement of a religious life, by the gentle regretfulness of the past, so often suggested in his earlier writings. Mdlle. de Lucinière, for instance, wrote to him :—

As for me, poor woman that I am, I cannot understand how a heart such as yours could have arrived at such a hatred of authority, since *all authority comes from God.* . . . Do read your beautiful reflection on the thirteenth chapter of the third book of the 'Imitation.' Reading it yesterday I was deeply impressed by it, and could not refrain from fervently offering up for you the prayer which terminates it.

Needless to say this was a prayer for the humility necessary for perfect submission to divinely appointed authority.

But there was another matter which caused them even deeper pain. Élie de Kertanguy had opened a correspondence with the Abbé Jean de Lamennais, *à propos* of the *Paroles*. That exemplary priest seems to have gone far towards reassuring him as to the orthodoxy of the master, when suddenly he received a further communication from the young disciple, who wrote to him on June 8 :—

One thing causes me real sorrow ; M. Féli has ceased to say Mass. Not that I look on it as a crime on his part ; his position is so extraordinary ! But I cannot help regretting that he should have imposed so horrible a privation on himself. Do you think that there is anything in his predictions (on the future of the Church and society) of such a nature that M. Féli *can no longer in conscience celebrate the Holy mysteries* ?

Matters had reached this point when a fresh blow reached him in the encyclical *Singulari nos*.

After a brief recapitulation of the different stages of the official correspondence, and an allusion to the hopes inspired in him by the absolute submission of December 11, the Holy Father continues :—

But the hope which we had conceived . . . was altogether destroyed, when we heard that he had published under cover of a transparent anonymity, and caused to be spread about everywhere, a book . . . small indeed in volume, but immense in wickedness, entitled *Paroles d'un Croyant*.

And in another passage :—

It is impossible without horror to read the pages of this book, in which the author sets himself to break the bonds of fidelity and submission to princes, hurling on every side the torches of sedition and revolt, provoking the general destruction of public order, contempt of the executive, violation of the law, and tearing up by the roots the principles of religious and civil authority. After which, in a series of assertions, as unjust as they are astounding, he tries to show . . . that the authority of princes is contrary to the divine law, and even that it is the child of sin, the power of Satan himself.

Then, turning from the matter which was the immediate object of the encyclical, he concludes by a reference to another question which had hitherto been left in the background :—

Besides, it is very painful to see the extent of the folly which may lay hold of human reason, when a man allows himself to be carried away by a love of novelty, and when he takes upon himself to seek truth outside the Catholic Church, where it is to be found without any impure admixture of error.

You understand, venerable brothers, that we here speak of that fallacious system of philosophy recently invented, and of which we altogether disapprove, a system in which, drawn along by a rash, unbridled love of novelty . . . setting aside the holy apostolic traditions, &c.

This utterance was dated June 25 and published on July 15. It does not seem to have made any material difference to the position in which Lamennais now found himself. He was warned by influential friends in Rome not to take the encyclical as a dogmatic condemnation, and so late as August 2 he wrote to Mdlle. de Lucinière :—

You are wrong in supposing that the encyclical has been the cause of moral disturbance to me. On the contrary, it is my intention to begin once more to say Mass, as soon as I am assured that I shall not be hounded out of the only resting place which remains to me in the world by a public interdiction.

But that assurance never came. We can hardly restrain our tears when we read this short sad note of the Abbé Jean, written as a last attempt to save his brother. It is even more eloquent in its silence than in the thought which is expressed in it, for he, too, was made to suffer in those institutions which had been the work of a lifetime, and which now seemed likely to perish in the storm of calumny and hatred which raged around the name he bore. The letter was dated July 18, 1834 :—

I have just come from the altar. I have offered to God the sacrifice of the body and blood of His Son, and have asked Him for that resignation, that tranquillity, that humble courage of which both of us stand in need, at a time when our souls are crushed by a great sorrow. . . . Oh, my poor Féli, how I love you! JEAN.

Yes! Poor Féli! The loss of an ideal, terrible at any time, is heart-rending when a man, at the age of fifty-two, is compelled to stand by and gaze in helpless despondency on the destruction of the work of a lifetime. It is, perhaps, fortunate that history has left us no detailed account of what now occurred. The scene is too deep for words, and we welcome the kindly hand which, reaching forward, draws a veil over a sorrow that can only find expression for itself in tears.

CHAPTER IX

PHILOSOPHIC RECONSTRUCTION

On June 11, 1834, Lamennais had written to his friend M. Querret :—

> I am dying to see you, my dear friend, that we may talk together of physics and chemistry, as we agreed. My part of the work is ready; that is to say, I have just finished jotting down about eighty pages of notes on questions rising out of the fundamental problems of the science of beings. Come as soon as you can, for I must have a talk with you.

Indeed, he had now arrived at a point in the history of his life when it became necessary for him to remodel the whole system of his beliefs. This, at the age of fifty-two, was no very easy or very hopeful task, and yet he seems to have set about it with his habitual energy, determined as he was not to allow himself to be crushed under the dead weight of disappointment and misunderstanding which weighed upon him.

It will be remembered how, at the epoch of the 'Essai sur l'Indifférence,' he had laid the foundations of a scientific as opposed to a metaphysical treatment of religion; how he had pointed out that the data of certitude must be sought for, not in the analytical processes of a mind turned in upon itself, but in history, in the universal reason, in the phenomenal manifestation of human activity in all its branches.

In my second chapter I endeavoured, to the best of my ability, to set forth some of the arguments contained in the second, third, and fourth volumes of the Essay, and at the end of that chapter I hinted that the weak point in the system lay in the fact that the author had not sufficiently realised the full meaning of the doctrine of social evolution, and had laid too much stress on the outward expressions or manifestations, and not enough on the inward workings, of the social organism. In other words, he had but inadequately grasped the fact of its organic character, and consequently the fabric, the building of which had cost him so much time and trouble, was bound to crumble away as soon as that fact was evolved in the ordinary progress of scientific thought.

At a subsequent period in his career this solvent appeared in the form of Comte's law of the three States, a law which I have already explained, and which, in principle at least, has received the sanction of one of its discoverer's most inveterate opponents, Professor Huxley. For that brilliant writer, in his essay on the *Origin of Species*, in the 'Lay Sermons,' page 245, lucidly expressed it when he said that:—

> The hypothesis of special creation is not only a mere specious mask for our ignorance; its existence in biology marks the youth and imperfection of the science. For what is the history of every science but the history of the elimination of the notion of creative or other interferences, with the natural order of the phenomena, which are the subject matter of that science? When astronomy was young the

morning stars sang together for joy, and the planets were guided in their courses by celestial hands. Now the harmony of the stars has resolved itself into gravitation, according to the inverse squares of the distances, and the orbits of the planets are deducible from the laws of the forces, which allow a schoolboy's stone to break a window. The lightning was the angel of the Lord, but it has pleased Providence, in these modern times, that science should make it the humble messenger of man, and we know that every flash that shimmers about the horizon on a summer's evening is determined by ascertainable conditions, and that its direction and brightness might, if our knowledge of these were great enough, have been calculated.

Indeed, this law, in a general sense, might be summed up in the proposition that there is a moving and ascertainable scale in the ordering of all forms of physical knowledge, in accordance with which, religion offers a solution of succeeding series or combinations of facts, pending their eventual explanation by science. And I need hardly point out, in the present attitude of the thinking world, that such an interpretation of the laws of progressive thought in no way interferes with the dicta of theology, considered as an authoritative system, though it interferes very much with the arguments for the validity of such a system, or with what has been termed natural religion. Had the author of the 'Essay on Indifference' arrived at a thorough understanding of this fact, he would have seen that it added considerably to the cogency of his argument, for while, on the one hand, a tradition which was merely handed down from the earliest times might be looked on as representing provisional or nursery doctrine, doomed to disappearance under the influence of the law of the three States, it would have been far otherwise could it have been shown that certain doctrines were the legitimate, the only possible development from the primitive ideas, and that their evolution bore a direct and necessary relation to the evolution of humanity.

It is true that such a demonstration could in no way justify us in assuming the truth of the doctrines themselves, for they in their turn might be provisional. But, could it be shown that they had been actually and consistently developed under the sanction of a visible organisation, claiming to act as a criterion, very much as do the manifestations of force in geology, biology, or any other science, it would go far towards proving the validity of that claim. And I think that the argument would become absolutely conclusive if it could be shown that the questions, the solution of which that authority had set before itself, must be eternally present to the human mind as a blessing or a curse, according to the point of view from which they are approached; the individual, which leads to mental anarchy, futile self-sufficiency, petty arrogance, morbid mysticism, faddism, and God knows what besides; or the collective standpoint, which, laying hold of this otherwise most pernicious tendency in human nature, tames it, socialises it, and makes possible its healthy and progressive co-operation with the demands of the ever-evolving social organism.

In other words, though the doctrines could not possibly claim our acceptance on their own authority, we cannot help accepting them, if it can be shown that they result from a criterion as sure, as imperative, as anything in nature.

Now I think that this is abundantly demonstrated in the case of the Catholic Church, and I hope some day to enter more fully into the matter. But for the present we must content ourselves with the consideration of it in its relation to Lamennais. He had undoubtedly been the first to suggest such a treatment of religion, and we cannot blame him if he could not see to the end of the principle he advocated, and if the further development of it was left to the great genius who founded the Religion of Humanity; yet even here there is one point in which he is superior to Comte, for that writer thought it possible that the evolution of thought might eventually lead to the complete disappearance of the supernatural element in religion, whereas Lamennais was never able to rid himself of an idea, beautifully expressed in a work which appeared at a date somewhat posterior, it is true, to that at which we have now arrived, but which was probably written in great part at this time, the *Discussions critiques et Pensées diverses* (1841), in which, after describing the untold possibilities in scientific discovery which presented themselves to the men of his day, he adds: 'Then they will once more become conscious of their ignorance. The human mind will have moved on, immense dominions will have been added to its conquests; but from the frontiers of its empire it will see a new horizon, a horizon leading off into endless space; as before, the infinite will be before it. Wearied by its labours, it will rest awhile; it will plunge once more into the mystery which surrounds it, and a new era of faith will begin.'

These things being so, I think we may safely assume that had Lamennais approached the subject in his later days, when his thoughts were matured and his ideas corrected by a wider experience and deeper learning, he would have done much to counteract the shortcomings of the 'Essay on Indifference.' For he had the inestimable advantage of being a Catholic, an adherent of the only system of religion capable of the treatment here indicated; and there is abundant evidence that the progress of his mind was leading him to some such conclusion.

We have seen how, during the years which immediately followed the appearance of his great Catholic work, his mind began to progress steadily in this direction. Whether we see it in his growing appreciation of the Ultramontane or organic view of Catholicism, his articles on Comte in the 'Mémorial Catholique,' his personal relations with that philosopher, his acceptance of the principle that society is governed, not by those who seem to rule, but by *ideas generally prevalent, whose results may be calculated, just as in the material world the results of physical forces;* the classification of the sciences in his *Progrès de la Révolution*, or in the general tenor of the movement which bears his name, we cannot but be struck by this fact. Nor had this process of mental evolution come to an end at the period we have reached, and the letter quoted at the beginning of this chapter is but one out of innumerable evidences that he was still moving in the same direction.

Everything then tends to force us to the conclusion that, had this state of things continued, Comte's historic and scientific appreciation of Catholicism would have been propounded from a Catholic point of view, with the result that all later thought in religious matters would have been considerably modified.

It seems an irony of fate that the fulfilment of this idea should have become finally impossible at the very moment when it had almost reached maturity. For, in ceasing to be a Catholic, Lamennais had destroyed the only foundation on which a construction such as that which he had proposed to himself could be based, namely, an authority standing to ideas about the supernatural in the same relation as the criteria of any science to the facts of that science. In other words, he found himself in that fatal position so often and so graphically described in his writings: he was alone, and was compelled not only to live and to act alone, but to think alone, and he must have been painfully reminded of those terrible and closely reasoned denunciations which had characterised his early utterances.

Thus it happened that that great work on religion and society, the contents of which he had for so long been turning over in his mind, and which is so often hinted at in his correspondence, had now to be entirely altered in its scope and object. It is evident, from his own letters and from those of his friends, that while he was living with his little community at La Chênaie, the book was rapidly passing through its final stages; that men like Gerbet and Rohrbacher were co-operating in the work, and that a month or two would see it in the hands of the printers. It is for this reason, and because the years employed in its composition mark a period of transition in the author's mind, that I speak of it now, though its publication was inevitably postponed by the necessity of rewriting the greater part of it.

In fact, the first three volumes of the *Esquisse d'une Philosophie* were not published till 1841. It was not till five years later that the public were in possession of the fourth, and to these were added a supplementary volume, which is in reality little more than a sketch of the two concluding divisions of the subject, as originally planned out in the author's mind.

It is impossible to turn over the pages of these ponderous tomes without being deeply impressed by the profound change which has taken place, and by the painful evidences of a no less profound degeneration. And yet this falling off does not seem to lie so much in the man as in the circumstances in which he found himself. On the contrary, there is not a page in the *Esquisse* which does not bear traces of distinct mental development. There are signs of preciseness, of lucidity, and of consistency in thought which are almost altogether absent from the *Essay on Indifference*, while, even in the more imaginative portions of the book, he is less redundant, more economical, and therefore infinitely more vivid in his descriptions.

Indeed, I think that it is rather in the subject than in the author's treatment of it that the modern reader finds cause for irritation. Finding himself cut off from the only possible criterion, he saw no way out of the difficulty but to re-establish, one after the other, most of those propositions the futility of which he had triumphantly demonstrated in his earlier work. What, for instance, could be more devoid of philosophic meaning, and yet more poetically beautiful, than this passage from the sixth chapter of the first book?—

That which exists necessarily, that which is one, infinite, eternal, in a word, Being, is God. *He is He who is*; that is His Name, an incommunicable name, which, resounding from world to world, moves in the universe as life itself. It is uttered in every language, it is murmured in every sound. From the bosom of Creation, at the dawn of time, the voice of Eternity began to repeat it, and the stars, moved by celestial power, still write it through the realms of space in letters of fire.

Philosophers have vainly spent their lives, they have sounded the depths of reason to prove that God exists. What folly! God is by nature indemonstrable. Is it possible to demonstrate the existence of Being without presupposing it? This first notion, from which all others come, has no basis but itself. It cannot be deduced from anything anterior; and when we persuade ourselves that we are striving to reach it, we still assume it as our starting-point. For whence can we deduce a unity which is at once infinite and necessary? What we can prove is relative; the Absolute is beyond proof. Its foundation is in itself, and it is thus that it is the foundation of everything. For what is demonstration? It is the showing that a thing is contained in something else, that, if certain conditions are granted, it is relatively necessary. Therefore, what is absolutely necessary, that which contains everything and is contained by nothing, is obviously indemonstrable.

But if God cannot be proved, that does not justify us in denying His existence. Without this primitive idea of Being there could be no thought, no speech. Seen in our first thought, proclaimed in our earliest utterance, He is the foundation of our understanding. . . .

Starting from this, the author, making use of it as a skeleton, proceeds to develop his system of the universe, not however before he has committed himself to a further proposition, even more arbitrary and less tenable, if that were possible, than the first.

Assuming the existence of God in the sense here indicated, it was necessary that there should be present in the idea itself the possibility of creation, and, as it were, a divine shadowing forth or picturing of the whole scheme of the physical universe, from the simplest chemical combinations to human society. And so he was led to establish, on the unwarrantable basis of unfathomable mysticism, the fruitful hypothesis of a Trinity of divine persons, dividing and specialising the possible activities of the divine substance, breaking into and disturbing the eternal silence of a cold and lifeless unity.

And, in support of this, he makes use of an argument which bears a far off resemblance to the fundamental propositions of the 'Essay on Indifference,' but which, through the alteration in his circumstances, has entirely lost its force, even, I think, to the author himself.

So many men, he says, in the seventh chapter, whose names will be for ever great, cannot have lived and worked in vain; and society above everything, society, guided by a secret intuition of truth, which is the surest foundation . . . cannot, unless reason itself is a chimera, have been deceived by an illusion of eighteen centuries duration.

And he continues :—

. . . The notion of infinite Being necessarily includes that of three distinct properties co-existing in it, and therefore related to one another in an order, not of succession but of principle. Since, considered in its substance, infinite Being is an absolute unity, it follows that each of its properties is substantially the whole of Being, and, as these same properties are essentially distinct from one another, it follows . . . that *Power* is neither *Intelligence* nor *Love*, and is the whole of Being; that Intelligence is neither *Power* nor *Love*, and is the whole of Being; that Love is neither *Power* nor *Intelligence*, and is the whole of Being; in other words, that Power, Intelligence, Love are severally characterised, in the unity of absolute Being, by something which exclusively belongs to each of them, and consequently subsist in that unity, in a manner individually distinct from one another. Now, individuality which is at once intelligent, and determined by something essential and permanent, constitutes the notion of a person, and this in its turn presupposes a basis in substance, whence it draws its reality, its effective and radical being. Hence it follows that there are three persons in the unity of absolute Being; and these three persons, coexisting in the substance which is one and infinite, are God. . . .

Of these three divine Persons . . . we must conceive Power as the principle of the two others; for Power, or that by which everything that is is, necessarily precedes everything which exists only through it.

And since nothing precedes it, it draws from itself everything that owes to it its being, that is to say, it *gives birth* to it. . . . Intelligence in its relation to the efficient principle which produces its manifestation in God is then born of Power; whence it follows that Power stands to Intelligence as the *Father*, while manifested Intelligence, Light, the Word, &c., is the *Son*. For human language offers no better expression for the necessary relations of these two first Persons. Love, on the other hand, cannot be given birth to, for it implies two terms, reciprocally, equally active, the Father loving the Son, the Son loving the Father; it goes from the Father to the Son and from the Son to the Father; it *proceeds* from each of them. Its name, the only one which can describe its equal relation to the two first Persons, whose mutual bond it is, and the expression of their aspiration one towards the other, is the *Spirit*.

Thus he sets himself to establish, on what he considers a firmer basis, the time-honoured doctrines of Catholic Christianity; doctrines which, though fundamentally pregnant with useful results as the first utterances of an authoritative system, become, when propounded on their own authority, the basis of all possible forms of mystical extravagance the starting-point of unhealthy, futile speculations, in matters which are utterly beyond the domain of human reason.

But when we pass from these irritating subtleties to the practical application of the results to the phenomena of the physical universe, we cannot but be impressed by the power of thought and poetry which is manifested in the pages of this work, and we begin to realise what the world lost when Lamennais separated himself from the Catholic Church.

Leaving the uncertain ground of metaphysics, he now asks us to descend with him into the arena of actual fact, and bringing to bear on it all that was in him of deep learning, of thought, and of brilliant imagination, he slowly but systematically lays before us, in all its manifestations, the working out in all things of these three principles: the principle of power or force; the principle of intelligence or form, of light, of colour; and that other, which results from the relations of these two, the principle of love, affinity, which manifests itself in physical attraction, chemical combination, human sympathy, &c.

And it is in the second of these that he achieved his greatest success.

The volume which contains his speculations on this part of his subject has come down to us in a separate form, and will probably continue to live under its present title, *De l'Art et du Beau*. For this notion of the Second Person of the Trinity, the principle of intelligence, of form, of colour, found its highest expression in those things which men call beautiful in nature and in art.

And so it happens that after wearily making our way through those first dreary volumes, where science and mysticism are strangely mingled, we suddenly find ourselves transported to a beautiful dreamland, the meeting-ground of the creations of

God and man, where there is no fact, no picture, no criticism which does not compel us to admit that what is passing before us is the work of a master hand.

Architecture, sculpture, painting, dancing or rhythmic movement, music, poetry, &c., all are dealt with, and each has its place in the general plan by which, according to the author, all things have their origin and their fulfilment in God, and it follows from the same scheme of the universe that each of the arts, besides its own natural evolution, has its place in the separate periods of human history, and an epoch in which it reaches its highest point either in its own growth, or in relation to the other arts, a moment when it is the paramount expression of the religious instinct, which is the fundamental test of a civilisation.

Thus, for instance, sculpture reached its culminating point in the period of Greek ascendency, and gave rise to an architecture strictly subordinated to it; while, on the other hand, with the growth of Christianity this state of things was completely reversed. As with these, so also with all the others, and there is nothing among the possible productions of human genius which does not in some way mark all the progress of man from the more primitive to the more complicated forms of social organisation, and this is shown to have been a fact in the case of each of them in turn, from the art of dancing or rhythmic movement, which accompanied the earliest expressions of the religious aspiration, to that of oratory, which obtained its highest recognition in France at the time of the Revolution. His description of this last is, I think, worthy of quotation :—

Eloquence, which till then had been excluded from the political world, suddenly breaking into it, made of it its principal domain; it reigned there as a sovereign. Never before had the power of speech been so abundantly made manifest. It destroyed a civilisation and created a new one. None of those things which time had given strength to, or which custom, opinion, manners had made sacred, were able to stand before it. Government, laws, institutions were overthrown; it carried all before it as a torrent roaring along, and bounding over the steep broken sides of a mountain, carries away the hut which a shepherd has built by its banks. And as the old building crumbles away, a new one is raised on the site of it. Some plastic virtue seems to be hidden in the ruins. A mysterious breath moves among the social débris imbuing them with life, but in rising from the tomb it is completely changed. The peoples had advanced along the paths of civilisation bent under the yoke of servitude and egotistical privilege; they rise again in the name of liberty, of equality, of fraternity. The spirit of Christianity has revolted against the principles of paganism and has finally triumphed. . . .

At the distance of time from which we contemplate the instruments of Providence, in the fulfilment of its designs, the actors in that great drama assume superhuman proportions. Like to those giant beings whose battlings in the dark bosom of primitive creation are related in the poems of India, they appear to our dazzled imaginations in forms at once wild, colossal, and strange. To whom can we compare them? To what orators of preceding ages? No speech is like to theirs, ardent, impetuous, unrestrained; it flashes like lightning, roars as the tempest, overflows like the sea rising with the tidal wave, burns and devours as a fire. If we wish to picture to ourselves the effect of this extraordinary ebullition of the power of speech, we must not think of men, for each of them, however great, was but an echo; we must understand it in all its expressions and in all its contrasts, in its harmonies and its discords, its movements, so diverse, so sudden, so unexpected, the immensities of its ebb and flow, in its infinite variety and its formidable unity. But then, when its work was done, it sank once more into silence, and what has been heard since has been but a feeble, far-off echo of it.

On the other hand, nothing could be more delightful than the description of Arabesque architecture in the third chapter of this volume :—

Mahommetan peoples have never produced a religious architecture. Why is this? It is because their religion, which is pure deism, presupposes a fundamental separation between God and His works, and presents Him to the imagination neither in Himself nor in His relation to the creation, losing Him in the impenetrable darkness of absolute unity. . . .

But, if Islam has given birth to no religious architecture, if it has not been able to express a thought which is foreign to it, the civilised Arab has wrung from his native genius other monuments in which art, whatever it may have borrowed from Byzantium or from Hindostan, is turned into new channels. Born under a burning sky, in a country partly characterised by arid mountains and by sandy plains, broken only here and there by a rare oasis, this people owed to its climate, to the habits which resulted from it, and to the manners it gave birth to, the principal features which distinguish them. Living in tents, and too often driven to take from others by rapine what their climate denied them, wandering as they did from place to place, on horseback or on camels, without ever settling down, it was but natural that their national character should have been marked by a spirit of independence, by audacious courage, and by personal pride.

Knowing no bonds of union but those of the family and of the tribe, hospitality alone connected them with humanity, from which they were cut off by their isolated and nomadic existence. Roused to activity only on the day of battle . . . at all other times driven in upon himself, motionless under the folds of his woollen mantle, the Arab concentrated all his energies on the life of the soul. The very simplicity of that primitive state turned him from science. What remained to him then? Poetry: but a singular poetry, in harmony with his sun, his burning deserts. . . . Going where his fancy led him, he created, that he might dwell in them, regions at once beautiful and enchanting. His vivid imagination peopled the universe with invisible beings. . . . Nothing in the world around him suggested to him the great forces of nature. He substituted for them forces of another order, personified, arbitrary, free, independent of the fatal laws of inferior creation, and when, panting on the bare earth, in a burnt up atmosphere, he wandered through the by-paths of an unbridled fancy, he loved to picture to himself water and shade, a soft uncertain light, the rays of which, piercing the thick leafage on the banks of a limpid stream, lulled him into a dreamland of luxury and coolness. And this, for him, was the perfect type of beauty in nature.

These things it was which gave rise to Arabesque architecture. It is like a beautiful dream, shimmering at the caprice of genii through a network of stone, in those delicate cuttings, those light fringes, those fleeting lines, that lacework in which the eye is lost in pursuit of a symmetry which seems always near, but which ever eludes it in a perpetual graceful movement. These varied forms appear to us as a vegetation at once powerfully characterised and fantastic ; it is not nature, but it is a dream of it. The veiled light breaks in upon us in a series of colours gently mingling and producing the effect of an ethereal softness, born of this fairy world and increasing the illusion of it. In the murmuring rivulets, in the bubbling springs, there is a subtle influence which soothes the senses. If love, a love more passionate, more sensual than tender, breathes through all the intricacies of this magnificent palace, it is that the whole life of the Arab is there, pictured and idealised. Of a dogmatic explanation of things, of social thought, there is no sign. This delightful abode is destined only for the individual, and recalls only him. The hospitable customs of the sons of Ishmael have also their expression, but it is one which is more suited to a primitive state. On the dried-up roadways of the desert, wherever there is a spring and a few palm-trees, a hut is raised and a place of rest for the traveller.

But it is not till we arrive at a later part of this work that we begin to understand its real value as a fruitful theory of life. The Holy Spirit, or the principle of love, cohesion, chemical affinity, &c., offers in this respect the greatest scope for the author's constructive genius, and this in great measure accounts for the peculiar fascination which holds us, as we wander through the concluding volumes, the fourth of the 'Esquisse,' and the supplementary treatise of which I have already spoken. Indeed, the first of these owes so much of its interest to the wealth of scientific illustration brought to bear on the subject by the author, that it is with no small regret that I submit to the necessities of space and time and confine myself to the last, which is more immediate in its practical results.

For this supplementary volume, which is entitled *De la Société Première et de ses Lois*, or *De la Religion*, is but an application of the principles which hold good in chemistry and in the earlier sciences to the culminating science of society, which, if it completes, also presupposes the others; and it is here that it becomes evident, that if there are fundamental differences, there are many points in which he is in striking agreement with Comte.

And I think that in this a typical passage will best illustrate what I mean :—

The universe [he says in his first chapter] is but a vast society in which each being in unison with all the others, as a separate organ in a living body, exercises its own peculiar functions, which are necessary to the preservation and development of the whole; and thus society resolves itself into the principle of unity. . . . Nevertheless, it is not pure unity, but is derived from it; is the expression of it, and draws from it its essential character.

It is not pure unity, for pure unity which is absolute excludes all relations and consequently all society. Society implies multiplicity, for, if we are to be united, we must be many. It also implies diversity. Can we conceive a society of beings, numerically distinct but otherwise identical? Were this the case, each of them, imprisoned in itself, individually invariable in the plenitude of its being, incapable of receiving or of communicating anything, would be without bond of union with the others, being independent of them, as they of it, in the solitude of existence.

In its most general aspect then, *society* represents, in the multiplicity and diversity of beings, the principle which, according to the laws of their respective natures, draws them together, so that, little by little, they should be brought to that universal unity which, outside God, represents His internal, absolute, infinite oneness. These two being the elements from the combination of which results society, on the one hand unity, and on the other diversity and multiplicity, it is clear that the last should be subordinate to the first, for unity is the final end, while multiplicity and diversity is, if I may use the expression, only the material which unity has to bring under its laws, though without destroying it . . . since that would mean the destruction of society itself.

Thus, corresponding to the radical conditions of existence in its two modes, infinite and finite, everything presupposes it; it is necessary with the same necessity as being, although indefinitely variable in its manifestations in the bosom of creation, where, suiting itself to the differences of individual beings, it is modified in accordance with their nature, and reveals itself under as many forms as there are diversities in their nature. . . . Hence the separate legislations in each class, each genus, each species of beings; hence the growing complication as they ascend in the scale of organised life; and these fragmentary legislations, bound together by ties which order determines, form in their harmonious fulness the legislation of the universe.

Indeed, it is this idea of the universal necessity of society, whether seen in Nature or in God, that we must bear in mind, if we are to understand the religious inspiration of the later years of Lamennais' life. There is much in his treatment of the subject which forcibly suggests the thought and method of the founder of Positivism; while such phrases as *the growing complication as they ascend in the scale of organised life*, almost seem to be borrowed from the reasonings which led to the famous and much *abused classification of the sciences*. But it requires no very deep penetration to see that, in their basis, the two writers differ fundamentally from one another.

Lamennais, as we have seen, makes the God whom he has constructed with admirable subtlety the beginning and end of all things. It is true that he does face the actual problems of the universe, and that he challenges criticism in the domain of physical science; but we feel that these things are strictly subordinate, and that the author is hurrying us through our demonstration, hoping, when his God has been accepted, to lay these things aside, only holding to such facts of science as may be useful in illustration.

Comte, on the other hand, lays his greatest stress precisely on those facts which Lamennais made use of. To him they are everything; to the author of the 'Esquisse' they are merely stepping-stones to something else. The value of Comte's work lay in this, that he suggested a method by which religion might be brought under a scientific treatment, making it possible to predict the kind of religious expression which would be likely to appear under given circumstances of social evolution ; and, contrariwise, what social results would be likely to follow from predominance of certain forms of religious belief. That he pursued that method, and arrived at the conclusion that a normal state of society must be accompanied by a normal religion, that is to say, by a religion which has been evolved under similar circumstances, and which corresponds to it in all its details. The only system in modern times which, in my opinion, fulfils this condition, is the Catholic Church, which, for reasons I have already hinted at, is capable of expanding and developing without destroying itself.

The theory is certainly inconsistent with anything which is the work of the brain of a single man, as was the God of the *Esquisse d'une Philosophie*. And it is this which accounts for the fact that Lamennais' later religious opinions are now remembered by no one, though in his Catholic days, little as he knew it, he had destroyed an old world and created a new one. For the details of a religious system, the customs and doctrines which seem to some to obscure what men consider a central truth, are usually the only channels which connect such a system with the civilisations through which it has passed in the course of its evolution. To set these aside is to destroy the idea of which they may seem to be only the external setting, to deprive it of its meaning. Comte dwelt on the details, and he has been blamed for doing so. Perhaps he was right. At least the universal shipwreck of *purified* systems in modern times would seem to point to this conclusion.

But if Lamennais failed through the fact that he was no longer a Catholic, if he lost himself in the aimless wanderings of an unbridled mysticism, we are none the less forced to recognise the real speculative power which gave rise to this immense conception of an universal principle of evolution working itself out in the subject-matter of all the sciences, from the lowest to the highest, from the simplest to the most complicated. In his expression of this, and of that other idea, the manifestation of society in all phenomena, he leaves far behind him the foremost contemporary writers, not excluding Comte.

It is impossible, then, not to regret that all this depth and conciseness of thought should have been practically thrown away, made unpalatable and inadmissible to the modern reader, by the fact that it took as its starting-point a series of propositions which are not merely untenable, but which saturate with a mystical venom all that comes into contact with them, and *a fortiori*, all that is made to rest on them.

It is this which makes it difficult to deal with the concluding period of this extraordinary life. On the one hand, there is a perseverance, a consistency of purpose, and an almost heroic struggle for the realisation of an ideal; on the other, emptiness, anarchy, despondency; and, with all this, there is not a moment in which we cannot sympathise with him, hoping against hope that he will formulate his theory of life, and that he will do something towards the attainment of those objects which have now become paramount to him. But we instinctively feel that this cannot be, and that events are rapidly hurrying us to the closing scene of a terrible tragedy.

Before passing to the narration of these events, there is one circumstance which should be borne in mind. It will be remembered that in his Catholic days, when he was the recognised leader of the Ultramontane party, Lamennais had been on friendly terms with the founder of the Religion of Humanity, and that each had been inspired with the deepest respect for the other. When he severed his connection with the Church, a coldness sprang up between them, and it is stated by M. Lafitte that this increased as the former champion of Catholicism drifted further and further in the direction of the Revolution.

This chapter, then, may be fittingly concluded by an extract from a letter published by Mr. Wilfrid Ward in his volume on Dr. Ward and the Oxford movement. The circumstances which led to the writing of it were as follows:—

Shortly after the period at which we have arrived both Comte and Lamennais took part in a State trial, as advocates of the party which the Government was endeavouring to get legally condemned. After the conclusion of the proceedings, which had been marked by many stormy episodes, the two men met for the first time since the fundamental change I have described had come about in the opinions of the latter. 'So we have come to anarchy,' said the philosopher; and the ex-priest sadly nodded acquiescence.

About ten years later, in England, W. G. Ward became a convert to the Catholic faith, and he prepared his friends for the act by the publication of his *Ideal of a Christian Church*, in the course of which he spoke in praise both of J. S. Mill and of Auguste Comte, the last of whom he recognised as having surpassed the best Catholic writers in his appreciation of the historic position of Catholicism. Mill wrote to Comte to inform him of the fact, and the Frenchman answered in a letter which contains this remarkable passage:—

> At the outset of my philosophic career . . . in 1825 I was judged, almost as I have now been by Mr. Ward, by the too

famous Abbé de Lamennais, who was then in his true normal state as the upright and energetic leader of an avowed Catholic reaction. . . . You know what happened to my eminent antagonist, whom I met ten years ago on a characteristic occasion, when I was forced, having myself in no way changed, to recognise a shameful ally (*une sorte d'allié honteux*) in the man who had formerly seemed to me an estimable adversary. In the logical inconsequence which marks the present time, I should not be surprised if your new Catholic underwent, perhaps more quickly, a similar degeneration, though I sincerely hope that he will not do so.

Many of my readers will agree with me in rejecting Comte's statement that Catholicism is essentially retrograde, but this will not prevent a thorough appreciation of the full force of this interesting judgment, especially if we compare it with the fact, stated by M. Lafitte, on the authority of a personal friend both of himself and of Lamennais, that the latter never spoke of Positivism in his later years but in terms of contempt as *that philosophy*.

These things, I think, confirm what I have said of the philosophic results of Lamennais' lamentable fall from the principles he had defended in his earlier days.

CHAPTER X

A LIFE OF SUFFERING AND DEVOTION, '48

As the immediate result of the series of events which had marked the period following the condemnation of the *Avenir*, Lamennais had now completely changed his point of view, and he prepared, without reserve, to identify himself with the revolutionary movement.

The first steps in his new career were not at all encouraging, for his change of attitude involved the breaking of many of those ties of friendship which still bound him to the past, and increased his bitterness against those ideals which had been the occasion of their formation, and to which his own genius had given birth.

Lacordaire had already left him, but Montalembert still clung, with all the affection of which his ardent nature was capable, to the master to whom he owed everything which gave meaning and value to life. He still hoped that it might be possible to save him, and he seems to have been prepared to sacrifice everything rather than desert the man whom even now he looked upon as an inspired teacher of mankind. Lacordaire wrote to him, warning him of the danger of the course he was pursuing, but he seemed deaf to the pleadings of his former friend. Lamennais was bitter, sarcastic, and advised him never to sacrifice his freedom as a layman. Lacordaire was gentle and persuasive, and set before him, with that power and eloquence of which he alone was capable, the claims of the Catholic Church; yet he hesitated, and seemed inclined to identify himself with the stormy career which was now about to open for the unfortunate leader.

But time and reflection produced an effect which argument and entreaty had been powerless to accomplish, and years afterwards, writing on the career of that friend who had then passed away, leaving behind him a name to be for ever remembered, he was able to say:—

I was not a rebel, as might be supposed from these ardent remonstrances; I was only vacillating and troubled. Whilst obstinately resisting the pressing entreaties of Lacordaire, I was doing my best to persuade M. de Lamennais that silence and patience were his best course; and, to obtain this result, I could safely remind him of my faithful devotedness, as I was then the last to stand by him. But I was irritated at my younger and dearer friend for having taken a more public and decisive course. I rashly reproached him with his apparent forgetfulness of the liberal aspirations which had animated us both. When at last I yielded, it was but slowly, and not until I had made that generous heart bleed.

But Lamennais had a dearer friend and a truer disciple in the Abbé Gerbet, who had watched over him and nursed him in that terrible illness in 1827, when it was believed that his last moments had come, and who had stood by him through all the labours and misgivings which had accompanied the foundation of the Mennaisian School. He, too, was compelled for conscience sake to leave the master, but he did so in silence, and there was from him no word of public refutation, or bitter recrimination, to show the world that a rupture had taken place.

The Abbé Bruté, too, the friend of his young days, who had gone off to America about the time of his ordination, and who had not seen him since, after years of unrewarded missionary labour had at length been raised to the episcopal dignity and had come to France, where he had seen Lamennais. It appears that with greater zeal than tact he set about the conversion of his younger friend, and was not over prudent in the selecting of occasions for bemoaning his fall. On February 21, 1836, he wrote to him from Florence a letter conceived in the old mystical style which his correspondent knew so well. He says amongst other things :—

I come from the holy altar—the victim was there—the same who was on Calvary—whom you loved—who loves us —Dilexit ME! . . . Jesus Christ, the eternal Son, consubstantial, made man, your God and mine, loved us—loved Féli Lamennais and this poor Bruté, eighteen hundred years ago, so much that he died for them. You loved Him once! . . . Do you love Him still? . . . . Ah! how you did love Him in your ardent and tender soul! What letters those were in 1809, 1810, up to 1815 and later!—I have them still. . . . This sweet Saviour has not changed. He loves you. Who am I that I should cease to love you? that I should wish to wound you? No; such is not my intention. . . . These reproaches from your friend are but those of Jesus—those of Mary—those of Féli's guardian angel. You still believe in these, I hope. But how you forget and abandon them! . . .

And he continues in his own quaint way, alluding to the past, and reminding the ex-priest of those happy days on which he has now turned his back for ever. Under the circumstances it would have been impossible to imagine anything more exasperating, and the reply, if cruel, coming from the lips of an old friend, was not altogether undeserved :—

Monseigneur [he began], I am accustomed to most things, but I was, I confess, surprised at receiving a letter from you, after what I have heard from Paris, from many people, unknown to one another, about the zeal, as pious as it is indefatigable, with which you have insinuated things against me to those who have been so kind as to listen to you.

I do not know what it has pleased you to say about me; but this I do know :—

You came to see me as a friend; I received you as such. . . . You found me then, so far as you were concerned, just as you had known me twenty-five years ago. If, under the circumstances, I had expounded to you, in unsuspecting confidence, ideas, false in your opinion, perhaps wicked, anything that I said should have been sacred.

But I did not do so, for, seeing from the first moment that you intended to take upon yourself the functions of a *juge d'instruction*, I formally declared to you that I did not wish to explain myself on matters the very thought of which was distasteful to me. So that, whatever thoughts you may have attributed to me you owe to mere conjecture or to a kind of divination which, when it transforms itself into affirmation, becomes what I leave it to your conscience to describe.

And the letter ends with a refusal to hold further relations with a man who had shown himself incapable of conforming to the most ordinary rules of human intercourse.

But the saddest result of his change was his quarrel with his brother. Responsible as he was for innumerable institutions which owed their existence to him, the Abbé Jean was especially at the mercy of his ecclesiastical superiors. The publication of the 'Paroles' placed him in a position of considerable embarrassment. Hitherto he had identified himself in everything with the opinions of the author of the 'Essai sur l'Indifférence,' and it was but natural that outsiders should suppose that this state of things was now in no way altered. The Bishop of Rennes demanded an explanation of him, and it was agreed that he should write a letter repudiating the doctrines of the 'Paroles,' which could be shown privately whenever it was deemed necessary. Contrary to this agreement the letter was published, causing considerable scandal. As soon as the circumstances became known, Féli admitted that weakness was the most that could be laid to the charge of his brother, while the bishop sought to atone for his fault by an apology. But the harm had been done, and from this time the two brothers continued to draw steadily apart from one another.

It was not long before matters came to a crisis. In the unusually morbid state of his imagination, resulting from the catastrophe which had befallen him, Féli de Lamennais set himself to examine the events of his past life. Involuntarily he turned in thought to those months of anxious self-examinings which had preceded his ordination. Seen at so great a distance, through the intervening stages of an eventful career, the facts became clouded and dimmed, and the conviction gradually took possession of him that his brother had been mainly responsible for what now seemed to him a most fatal step.

What led to the final rupture it is not easy to say. A tradition tells us that a quarrel arose over their separate rights in La Chênaie and the books and other things which it contained. In any case it is certain that towards the close of the spring of 1836, Féli de Lamennais left his Breton home never to return. The two brothers had met for the last time.

From this time we find him living in Paris, a prey to the most abject misery. He had lost all his money in the failure or fraud of his publishers, and the pangs of starvation and cold were added to the other misfortunes which beset him. Indeed, nothing could be more heart-rending than those last terrible pages of his correspondence, from which no reader can turn away with a dry eye and without an aching heart, unless he be dead to every impulse of human feeling.

At one time he is saving up his food, at another he cannot work, for he has to remain in bed to avoid the necessity of a fire, which he cannot afford.

In one of his letters he tells us that he has been looking for lodgings, combining cheapness with a situation which may remind him of that life in the country which has now become impossible to him. He thought that he had found some, but the landlord was afraid of his name.

In the midst of all this it is pleasant to find that there were some of his friends who, in spite of considerable differences of opinion, did not desert him. Mme. de Senfft and M. de Coriolis continued a friendly correspondence with him during their lives. The most touching of the letters which have come down to us were written to an old St. Malo friend of his, M. Marion. The Abbé Houet, who died only a few years back, while holding the position of Superior of the Oratory of Rennes, never forgot the days of his discipleship, and remained to the last a devoted admirer, not to say worshipper, of his former master. And there were many others, but amongst them all none gave proof of a greater constancy or a truer devotion than the Baron de Vitrolles. At no time had he been in perfect agreement with Lamennais. Even during the most reactionary moods of the Ultramontane priest, the careful diplomatist had looked on him as a fantastic unpractical dreamer, and now there was no point of intellectual contact between them. Yet even now the ties of personal friendship were drawn closer, and it would be impossible to imagine a more touching picture than is offered by those weekly meetings in the baron's house, when the two old men came together for an evening chat.

But now as always, Lamennais found his chief consolation in his work. In 1836 he brought out his 'Affaires de Rome,' which is considered by some to be his masterpiece, and about which enough has been said already to give an idea both of its style and of its contents. He informed his readers that he wished it to be accepted as the last act in the Catholic period of his life.

He then began to look around him for a means of adapting his ideal to the altered circumstances in which he now stood, and it was not long before a solution presented itself to him.

In his Catholic days he had found a considerable portion of his doctrine of life ready to hand. The necessary weak points in any system of social reorganisation which may have suggested itself to him, had been naturally, and by an easy transition of thought, filled in and strengthened by the religion which he received in its entirety from the common consent of mankind; now that he had rejected that religion, it became imperatively necessary to find something to supply its place. It was probably while thinking on this that he came to a clear perception of the principle of attraction, chemical affinity, love, or society, working itself out in the world, which he afterwards elaborated into the third person of his philosophical Trinity.

Turning then to the human family as it existed around him, he clearly saw that the problem lay considerably deeper than had been anticipated by the majority of the editors of the *Avenir*. It was not merely political liberty, which had more than once been turned to the profit of the few, but the people, the material and spiritual wants of the toiling masses of the world of labour, which had to be dealt with.

Now as always he saw that the God of the majority of moderns was very different from the gods of the ancients, or the God of the middle ages. The thought suggested itself to him that what had once been a powerful principle had now been turned into an intangible metaphysical abstraction, more pernicious than otherwise whenever it was dragged forth from the obscurity of the schools; and that a venerable formula, originally pregnant with social meaning, had grown into a miserable parody of its former self—the Word was made gold and dwelt in Wall Street, and we have seen his glory, as the glory of the almighty dollar, full of power.

In the opinion of Lamennais the 'divine right' of the existing Government proceeded from this source, though the relations between the celestial powers and their *protégé* were not always very cordial.

In the need of the State [M. de Coriolis had written of the government of Louis XIV.] some one thought of Samuel Bernard. He was mentioned to the king, who was assured that a word from him would be sufficient to open Samuel's endless purse. It was arranged that the rich merchant should happen, as it were by chance, to be at Marly as the king was passing by. '*Good-morning, Monsieur Bernard, I am delighted to see you,*' said the latter. Samuel was so overcome that he said to Colbert: 'My whole fortune is at the service of his majesty.'

Lamennais answered on April 9, 1836:—

Your good Samuel Bernard was but a child, my dear friend; he would be hissed at the Bourse. Do you think that if Louis Philippe were to say to M. Rothschild: '*Monsieur Rothschild, I am delighted to see you,*' he in his joy would cry out: '*My whole fortune is at the service of Louis Philippe*'? By Solomon and his father David, the Jew would do nothing of the kind, and the Jew would be right. It is true that Louis Philippe is not Louis XIV.

But if this worship of wealth was laughable from one point of view, it was extremely serious in its effect on society at large, and as we advance through the pages of his published correspondence, it becomes painfully evident that such passages as this are very rare, and that when they appear they are but a cloak for a deep-rooted, gloomy pessimism which was slowly gaining possession of him.

Even before he had left La Chênaie he spoke of the approaching marriage between his niece, Augustine Blaize, and his young disciple, Élie de Kertanguy, in terms which, had they reached the young couple, would have clouded their happiness with the thought that they could not hope for sympathy from one who was very dear to them both. 'I shall not be present,' he wrote to M. Marion; 'such rejoicings are not for me; they have always, I do not know why, filled me with feelings of sadness.' Then nothing could be more hopeless than his comment on a proposed European Congress, which he mentions in a letter of August 19, 1836: 'If it takes place, it will lead to the result which always follows such assemblies, where the problem is this—to find a crime which all have an equal interest in committing.'

Filled with fear and loathing, he turned from the rulers to the people, and in the early weeks of the year 1837 he undertook the editorship of a democratic paper (the *Monde*), but a quarrel with the proprietor, who does not seem to have allowed him sufficient freedom, led to his resignation of this post after he had held it for little more than four months.

In the same year he published the *Livre du Peuple*, which may be considered as the first manifesto of his new opinions. It contains the earliest exposition of his mystical doctrine of society seen in every fact of the universe. It is frankly democratic, and if the author withholds his assent from anything like systematic Socialism, he is none the less in agreement with the Socialists in the objects which he has in view. If the book is inferior in style to the *Affaires de Rome*, and in warmth and brilliancy of imagination to the *Paroles*, it is more scientific in its methods than either of them, and may be looked upon as the first manifestation of that peculiar intellectual power which was afterwards revealed in the *Esquisse d'une Philosophie*.

Lamennais now so far concentrated his energies on that important work that the first three volumes were published in about the same number of years. But he was unable entirely to close his eyes to the countless evidences of approaching revolution which were daily borne in upon him.

He no longer contented himself with predicting an evil day for those in power. He had finally identified himself with the democracy, and it had become his duty to do his part in hastening the catastrophe. And this alteration in his point of view brought about a change in his estimate of the course of events. The ultimate downfall of the existing *régime* no longer seemed so near as when he had looked forward to it with a less certain hopefulness. Consequently his letters assume to the superficial reader an appearance of moderation which is altogether absent from those which were written in his Catholic days. All his energy is reserved for his public writings, his articles, and his pamphlets, written with a view to goading the authorities into acts of unconstitutional violence, and to preparing the people for the work which lay before them.

Thus it was that in October 1840 he published a violent denunciation of the Government, under the title 'Le Pays et le Gouvernement,' in which he compared the constitution of France to an Oriental despotism, a form of political organisation which could in no sense be dignified with the name of society. And he called on his fellow-countrymen to reject a yoke which was utterly degrading to human nature.

To the self-complacent courtiers of Louis Philippe this pamphlet seemed like an open incitement to armed sedition. A prosecution was resolved on, and Lamennais was summoned to appear before the representatives of the law. He did so, but not before he had received a striking testimony from a quarter whence his past career gave him little reason to expect it. It came in the form of a letter from Joseph Mazzini. Speaking in the name of the Italian workmen living in London who were members of the society of 'Young Italy,' the writer says:—

> They honour you for the genius God has given you; they love you for the use you have made of it.
> They know that during your whole career, even when you have seemed most hopelessly separated from the

apostles of the democracy, you have had but one inspiration—the love of the people; and one object—their moral, intellectual, and material good. In looking for the protectors and educators of the people you have knocked at every door. . . . Kings, popes, clergy, aristocracy all have failed you, anathematised you, deceived you.

You felt that God, who is at once intelligence and love, was not there . . . that you must penetrate the depths of society, to the bosom of that people which gave birth to Christ, and for which He died; and you came into our midst. . . . God and the people will not betray you . . . you will understand the religious meaning of the thought which is expressed on the envelope containing this letter: *God and Humanity*. One Master in Heaven, one interpreter of His law on the earth, such is the faith of those who now write to you. . . . May your powerful, your ardent pen be employed as a help to them, as their affection will follow you to the tomb.

Lamennais answered on December 8. After expressing his faith in the final triumph of *God and Humanity*, he says:—

I have seen Italy, and I could not see her without loving her, without believing that a great future was reserved to her. . . . May she prepare herself by a thorough and active self-education; may the thought of perfect unity free her from her fetters, and especially those which bind the soul, that they may the more easily subdue the body, local prejudices, and fatal national jealousies: are you not all brothers? May she arouse herself from the torpor of inertia; . . . mistress of herself, invincible, she will cease . . . to seek salvation from without; her salvation will be in her faith, in the firm resolution of each one of her children to die, if necessary, for her. All honour to the confessors, to the martyrs.

Perhaps, gentlemen, it will not be granted to me to see

any of you in this life, which passes as a shadow; but there is another where we shall meet.

Fortified by such expressions of a common sympathy, Lamennais prepared to face his judges. He was ably defended, and his influence in the country was immense. But the Government was determined to get him condemned, and he was undoubtedly guilty from a technical point of view. Such passages, for instance, as the following were quite sufficient to lead to a decision against him:—

Reform! Reform! such is the cry which should resound from one end of the country to the other, from Brest to Strasbourg, from Bayonne to Dunkerque.

Reform, a complete reform will free us from the egoistical race of cowards and of traitors, of money-grabbers who see in the people their legitimate prey.

France cannot perish, she is necessary to the world. If then—I say it to the timid—if you will not accept a peaceful reform, you shall have a violent one. *Choose!*

It was in vain that the newspapers ridiculed the idea of condemning for a breach of the laws against the press one of the foremost writers of the day. In vain did the counsel for the defence enlarge on the renown of the accused and the scandal which would result from an adverse decision. The very greatness of their opponent made it impossible for the Government to recede, and in spite of a short speech from Lamennais, in which he disclaimed any intention of instigating the people to violence, the Court condemned him to a fine of 2,000 francs and one year's imprisonment.

Fortunately he had just published the first three

volumes of the *Esquisse,* and his new misfortune and the bitterness resulting from it found no expression in the pages of that work.

On December 30 he wrote to Marion:—

Just a word, my dear friend, before I go to take possession of the rooms which have been got ready for me at Sainte-Pélagie. I think I shall go there the day after to-morrow, the sooner I go in the sooner I shall come out again. Besides, my imagination is in no way frightened by the prospect of a change in my life. It is pleasant to be where duty has led us, and my condemnation will be more useful to the holy cause . . . than my acquittal would have been. . . .

A fortnight later he describes his new quarters:—

My room is large enough, for I can walk nine paces from corner to corner. The height of the small windows from the ground and the bars on them make the place agreeably like a cellar. However, a few rays of sun get through, even at this time of year. My apartment faces two ways, to the west and to the south, and, as I am perched up under the roof, if I stand on a chair I get a pretty good view. From the brick floor, if I hold myself straight, I can touch the ceiling, not only with my hand but with my wrist. A small stove which I have had put in gives me some warmth. There is a little yard where I might walk with the others at certain times, but I do not go there, and shall never do so. I prefer to remain in my dungeon for more than one reason. It is comparatively easy to get permission to see me. My nephew, who is touching in his devotion to me, comes every day. As to letters, those which are addressed through the post are first brought to be read by the police. So I have made a declaration that, not wishing to have a hand in so infamous a proceeding, I shall receive none, no matter whence they come. At nine in the morning I make my coffee; four hours afterwards I eat a little bread and butter; at six they send me from a neighbouring restaurant two dishes for my dinner. The day goes on without my being bored, for one cannot be bored when one has books. But shall I be able to work? I cannot say yet; though I foresee that it will be difficult. I was forgetting one little ceremony. My door is held from within by a wooden latch, outside is a huge bolt . . . a warder draws this every evening. What I miss most is sleep. Perhaps that will come later. To sum up, I do not for a moment regret my position. I am where I ought to be . . . on account of the cause to which I have devoted my life.

The almost unbroken silence of this dreary solitude was often agreeably relieved by expressions of sympathy, both from personal friends and from different sections of that people for whom he offered up his sufferings to God. The luckless prisoner found too that he could sometimes work, and thus many a weary hour was usefully employed. But bad air and want of exercise gradually told on his health and spirits, and, after the first few months, a deep gloom seems to have settled down on him, filling his soul with bitterness. This accounts for that beautifully pathetic lamentation which runs through the last pages of his political allegory, the *Amschaspands et Darvands*. They were written in his cell at Sainte-Pélagie, and have since been published separately as *Une Voix de Prison*. One passage in particular gives evidence of the state of his mind at this time:—

It was an autumn evening: a warm breeze was blowing from the west, a gentle breath from the sleeping seas. The sun was suspended over the horizon in an ocean of transparent vapour. Dark blue clouds, ethereal flowers, spread around their borders corollas of a thousand forms, tinged with colours without number, whose mingling shades imperceptibly transformed themselves and were lost in a stream of gold. The seagull skimmed with its wing the smooth surface of the water, while over the sandy shore the martin sent forth its plaintive cry, and the only other sound was in the gentle murmur of the waves expiring at the foot of the rock. Overhead a black mass, a prison, threw around a gigantic shadow.

And little by little the air became as troubled water, and the twilight spread its veil of ever-deepening darkness over the cliff.

A voice went forth from the bosom of the waters, and rose up vague, immense, as the sighing of the spirit of the depths; and, from the summit of the solitary rock, another voice, mingling with that one, went out into the night and died away on the deserted shore.

And it said :—

They have bound the body, but the soul laughs at them, it is free!

Because I loved thee, oh my country! because I wished thee great, happy, those who betrayed thee have thrown me into this prison.

They have bound the body, but the soul laughs at them, it is free!

It is free, and it laughs at them, vile slaves of their own baseness, infamous serfs of fear, eternally buried in their cowardice, and walled up in their crimes.

. . . .

Can their bolts shut in my thought, my love? Can they withhold me from your midst, brothers; and is not your life mine?

When you suffer, I suffer with you; when you struggle, I struggle with you; there is, as it were, an invisible breath which passes from you to me, and from me to you. They may seize it if they can!

They have bound the body, but the soul laughs at them, it is free!

The voice was silent for a while, then it continued:—

Without, everything is silent, all things are at rest! In the midst of this silence something strikes the attentive ear; is it a sound or the dream of a sound?

Whilst earth, and air, and water in their sleep are peopled with dreams, whilst life is germinating in the bosom of sleep . . . old memories are awakened and lead me back to times which were and which will never be again.

How beautiful the sun was, how nature smiled on me! How keen, how gentle, how pure was the joy of the child lingering by the hedge of dog roses and of sweet-brier, listening to the soft murmur of the rustling leaves, watching the swaying of the young branches, or wandering in May in the thick underwood, torn by the brambles, or pursuing with outstretched hand, trembling and breathless, the insect with a long body and transparent wings among the rushes by the pond.

No regret for the past, no care for the future. Limpid horizons sometimes sprinkled with light clouds, which were soon blown away by the gentle winds.

My sister, do you remember our morning rambles over the dewy grass, our games in the woods, the nests which, with tears in your eyes, you forbade me to touch because of the poor mother?

Then days and years went by, and, thrown in upon itself, moved by unknown joys and sorrows, my soul spread out its mysterious wings over a new life about to be born.

And after the enchanting dreams, the ardours, the affections, the passions of my young days, came the severe duties of manhood, the great, the holy fight, in which to fall is to conquer, in which to die is to be born into life.

They are fallen and they have conquered, those whom I saw struck by the bullet or felled to the earth by the sword of the coward.

They, again, are fallen and they have conquered, who,

dying in long agony on prison straw, feebly murmured the name of their country.

Glorious band of brave men, you are near me, and I hear you say: 'Brother, listen! the martyrs are calling us from on high!' Crowned in splendour, divine messengers, they go from sphere to sphere, singing the song of the future.

A virtue goes out from them, it penetrates the hearts of the people, they beat faster, the earth and the heavens tremble, and the worlds, palpitating in the bosom of immensity, say one to another: 'A great act of justice is about to be done; did you not feel the breath of God?'

Once more the voice was silent as if lost in the immensity of space. Then, all at once, vibrating with renewed force:—

'They have bound the body but the soul laughs at them, it is free!'

When Lamennais left his prison at the end of 1841 he was utterly broken down in health, but he was buoyed up by the hope that he would have something to do with the approaching overthrow of the existing *régime*. After a short visit to his friend Marion, in Brittany, he settled down sadly to his work. On March 7, 1842, he wrote to his host:—

I was not so tired after the return journey as I was after getting down to your place. I am not yet quite myself, but I am better. I am slowly getting accustomed to my new rooms, which are comfortable and which suit me. . . . I was so happy with you, my dear friend, that I am filled with sadness at the thought that it will not be easy to renew such visits. It is sad to be so far apart, to be so old, to find travelling so difficult. Why am I not twenty years younger? Then the journey would be nothing. But we should take life as it is. We do not do so, and it defeats us after a certain time. But I do not complain. Why should one wish to strike deeper root in the mud on which we vegetate?

But if this life in Paris was hopeless in the isolation and misery to which it condemned the unfortunate ex-priest, it none the less gave rise from time to time to amusing episodes. One of these took place about two years before the imprisonment at Sainte-Pélagie.

Providence [he wrote] condemns me to live alone, and more than ever now that I have got rooms at one of the extremities of Paris, about three-quarters of a league from the centre. Over my head I have a fat English woman, with whom I am at open war. In spite of the messages I have sent her by the porter, she persists in waking me at about ten or eleven o'clock by the noise she makes, and I cannot sleep the rest of the night. Seeing which, one hour after she has got into bed, I get up and pay her back in full. The woman is furious, and so far I cannot say how the matter will end. One thing is certain, I shall not yield.

Soon afterwards we learn that the lady is not English, but French, and that he is looking for rooms elsewhere.

It is true that his isolation was not absolute, that in leaving his old friends he had opened the way for an acquaintance with many who were held in high honour in various paths of life, and that his reputation and his destiny became interwoven with such names as those of George Sand, Béranger, Arago, O'Connell, Mazzini, &c., but there is no evidence in the case of any of these that intellectual sympathy ever ripened into a warmer feeling, or that he found in his new surroundings any response to the natural longings of his affectionate nature. In his letters to Marion he constantly speaks of his loneliness, and, with the exception of the Baron de Vitrolles, it is hard to find anyone among his Parisian acquaintance who, in the true sense of the word, could be called his friend. 'As for me,' he says on one occasion, 'I have no one to love me: I am alone; so I watch the time go by, as the traveller, seated on a bare rock by the side of a river, waits till it is low enough that he may cross over and come to his evening resting-place.'

Then nothing could be more hopelessly pessimistic than many of the thoughts in his 'Discussions critiques et Pensées diverses,' concluded in prison. I select a few of them:—

Lie there, my people, and bleat for joy, for you have a master who loves you, a father rather than a pastor. Oh, dear people! return love for love; give me your wool, for I am cold; your blood, for I am thirsty; your flesh, for I am hungry.

Oh, God! they have turned Thy temple into a sepulchre where the priest crawls and disputes their impure food with the worms.

They say that there have been cannibals in the world. I do not deny it, but it cannot have been for long; they must have died of poisoning.

What is it that they call the lustre of old families? It is the shining track which snails leave behind them as they crawl.

Some one was asked what number France contained of ministers, general directors, préfets, sous-préfets, in a word, of Government officials. He answered: 'When I meet a corpse on the road I do not amuse myself by counting the worms which are moving in it!'

If misfortune weighs upon you, fly to the desert. The tears of man are received only in the bosom of his mother, Nature, or of his father, God.

Could anything be more terrible than this? Could any more striking expression be found for the most utter misery and despair. It is not surprising that reports of the state of his mind should have reached his Breton home, and that vague, uncertain rumours should have got to the ears of the Abbé Jean, who had been trying to drown his grief in the performance of the duties of his office, and of that labour of love to which he had devoted his life. The two brothers had not spoken since that fatal day in 1836, when they had turned their backs on one another for ever, and even now he did not dare to disturb the sullen solitude of Féli, but he wrote to the elder Blaize on July 8, 1842:—

I beg of you to ask Ange to tell Féli from me that I make over to him the full, entire, and absolute right to La Chênaie without the smallest reserve; he may dispose of it as he will, and as if I were no longer in the world! The only thing to which I will not consent is that I should receive a centime in payment for it. . . . Poor Féli, how happy I should be if I knew that he was near, even though I should be condemned never to tell him, face to face, how I have always loved him, and how I love him still.

The answer, which was sent through Marion, was indeed cruel. The offer was refused, and the writer added:—

I know how difficult it is to get the individual in question to terminate a business which he thinks he has an interest in prolonging.
It is true that his hands are full with other things; he is travelling in Lower Brittany. Perhaps he is gone on a pilgrimage to Saint Yves.

To realise the deep pathos of the situation, it is not necessary to blame an act which may have been justified by the circumstances.

Turning from his private to his public life, the outlook at this period is hardly more hopeful.

'To whom can we turn to-day?' he says in one letter. 'What can we stir up but filth, and that of the foulest?' He still believed that the existing *régime* was doomed, but he seems to have come to the conclusion that the final crash might be indefinitely postponed in the prevailing corruption. This it is which gives a theoretical colouring to his two well-known political pamphlets, *Du Passé et de l'Avenir du Peuple*, and *De l'Esclavage moderne*, and it was this which made him concentrate his energies on the completing of the fourth volume of the *Esquisse*, which appeared in 1846, and on his beautiful translation of the Gospels which preceded it at no very great distance, and in which the founder of Christianity is represented as the type of the persecuted people.

Hence the interest with which we read what remains of his correspondence with various friends of his among the working classes, most of which, and especially the letters to his tailor, M. Dessoliaire, are directed to the promoting of a belief in the future. One of these, selected at random from Blaize, will serve to give an idea of the rest. It is dated September 28, 1846:—

Many thanks, my dear M. Dessoliaire, for having thought of my winter clothing, but I shall not want anything this year; I have two waistcoats and two pairs of trousers, one of them old and the other new, and that will be enough. As to the overcoat, I have that too ; it is true it was not made for me, but it will do well enough when it has been shortened a little and taken in. I have also had a present made me of a dressing-gown.

My health is not good; I suffer nearly every night from fever. Great family misfortunes have come upon me. One of my nieces, after having lost one of her children, has lost her husband.[1] . . . He has died . . . . leaving behind him five poor little orphans. Providence will watch over them as it will watch over you, whatever persecutions may be directed against you. The power of the wicked has its limits, which God does not allow it to transgress. Walk in uprightness, in justice, and in love, pitying those whose errors or evil passions turn them from the path, for they are truly to be pitied; and in the remorse and suffering which hatred engenders in them, they begin here below to reap the fruit of their works. Without in any way abandoning the truth and its holy cause, keep yourself from a too ardent zeal, which would raise up enemies against you without profit to those whom it is your mission to instruct. Jesus Christ told His disciples to combine the wisdom of the serpent with the simplicity of the dove. The man who moves too quickly falls; he who walks reaches the goal. . . .

Tell your friends that I remember them, and that from the bottom of my heart I pray to the Heavenly Father for His blessing on them.—Yours very affectionately . . .

And again : 'This year will be a hard one for the poor. How much less evil would result from it if each man acted as he ought! Let us work together to hasten the time when these things will be.'

Lamennais never recovered from the physical

[1] Élie de Kertanguy.

weakness brought on by age and by his year of prison life. 'For the last six weeks,' he wrote to Marion in March 1845, 'I have suffered much from my head and my stomach. About a week ago this resulted in a long syncope. Fortunately, this accident, which, as you know, is no new thing with me, has led to nothing serious, but I have to be careful.' And in June: 'I am still suffering, not only in my leg, but in my side from the hip. It is very inconvenient, and I see no hope of getting cured, so I am letting things go as they may. . . . The disease and its treatment would make two evils: I am content with one.' Again, in October: 'Whilst you were on the wing, I was in bed with a fever; I simply waited without seeing a doctor or taking any medicine, and, in the end, the fever went away of itself.' And on April 27, 1846: 'My health is of the worst; I have hardly any strength left, and I never sleep. After excessive fatigue in more than one direction, rest is absolutely necessary to me, but I cannot get it. The old horse must trot, trot, till he falls by the roadside.'

It would be difficult to imagine anything sadder than the spectacle of this old man, after a life at once more active and more violent in its contrasts than falls to the lot of ordinary mortals, compelled in his declining years ever to go forward on a seemingly endless journey. What was the cause of this terrible infliction of a ruthless destiny? Was it the result of a diseased imagination, of the tyranny of an idea? Must its victim be looked upon as a fugitive from the insatiable hunger of a maddened conscience?

You remember [he wrote a fortnight later to Marion], you remember the invalid of whom I spoke to you two months ago, when I spent three weeks by his bedside, and got so tired that I had no strength left. Having been sent for by him in a fresh crisis, I have now been with him for eight days, during which time I have not left him for a moment, and I am writing this in his room. So you see it is not my literary labours which are killing me. On the contrary, I foresee that I shall lose the summer on which I had counted for getting on with the *Esquisse*. It would take too long if I were to attempt to describe all the embarrassments and cares of every kind, resulting from my functions as *garde-malade* to a man who is touchy, fantastic to a degree, and whose distressing whims often border on insanity. But I have taken the thing up, so I must go through with it, and I shall do so if my strength permits.

I should like to continue this chat with you . . . but the sick man will not leave me a quarter of an hour's peace. . . .

So days, and weeks, and months went by, and the old man gave no sign that he suspected the near approach of a revolution which was to shake to their foundations the constitutions of all the leading countries of Europe. Up to the last moment he seems to have contented himself with sowing the seeds of moderation and fraternity among his working friends, without apparently any hope of himself being alive to witness the results. So late as June 31, 1847, he wrote to Dessoliaire :—

I am very much touched by the affectionate things you write to me, both in your own name and in that of your friends, on the occasion of my birthday. Will you thank in particular Hivern and Camus, who have been so good as personally to send messages to me in your letter. The true bond of union with souls, and the foundation of all hope in the future, is that holy love which, coming from God and returning to Him, makes of men so many brothers, and destroys, with egoism, the principle of evil on the earth. Such is the true law which the good should first put into practice, and then defend against the wicked, whose kingdom should not be allowed to prevail against that of God. The time will come when it will be necessary to fight; let each one prepare himself beforehand.

A few months later we find him in the midst of the determined agitation for reform which marked the last months of the year 1847.

The history of the Revolution of 1848 has already been written, in as far as it can be written, at the comparatively short distance of time which as yet separates us from it. The situation at the close of the reign of Louis Philippe has been well summed up by Lamartine :—

The people is not scientific in its methods, but it has a vague political sense. It had quickly perceived that the nation was being sacrificed to the interests . . . of the dynasty, in our relations with foreign powers; that Louis Philippe made peace humiliating; that his alliance at any price with London sometimes made him appear in Europe as the viceroy of England on the continent; that the treaties of 1815, a natural but momentary reaction from the unjust conquests of the Empire, were becoming, with his dynasty, the recognised state of things with regard to France's position in Europe. . . . An opinion, uttered or unexpressed, of the masses accused the reign of Louis Philippe of having betrayed the Revolution in the country itself, by adopting, one by one, the traditions of monarchy by divine right, instead of conforming to the democratic principle which had created the elective monarchy of 1830.

'A parliamentary oligarchy seemed to be the ideal of this prince, formed in the political atmosphere of Great Britain. That oligarchy was itself swamped in the mechanism of government. A Chamber of Peers . . . deprived of its independence by the absence of the hereditary principle, was but the mockery of a senate,' at the mercy of the king. 'A Chamber of Deputies crammed with public officials, &c.'

Such was the state of things which, when crowned by an unpopular diplomatico-matrimonial move on the part of the family of Orleans, produced the Revolution of 1848.

The movement began by a series of political banquets, organised as an occasion for protesting against existing abuses. There is a letter in the collection published by Blaize, dated November 18, 1847, in which Lamennais declines to be present at one of these meetings, on account of his health, and he adds :—

Let them know, in any case, that at heart I shall be with them; that with them I shall protest with my whole soul against the corruption, the meanness, the hypocrisy of a system, retrograde to the extent of wishing to establish despotism . . . that with them I shall demand that in accordance with justice and reason . . . the question should be seriously gone into, how it is possible, in the distribution of the fruits of labour, to do away with the revolting anomalies which crush under their weight the most numerous portion of the human family.

After a rapid succession of events, including the attempted suppression of the banquets, the invasion of the Chamber by the people of Paris, the abdication of the king, and the formation of a provisional government by Lamartine and his friends, the Republic was proclaimed from the Hôtel de Ville on February 24, 1848.

In the excitement which followed, during which the inmates of the Hôtel de Ville were compelled to withstand the repeated assaults of an angry and unreasoning populace, the fate of the young Republic was for some time held in the balance. The struggle has been graphically described by Lamartine, and it is needless here to go over the ground which has already been covered by him. But there is one fact in his work which calls for notice here; he speaks of Lamennais as of a man on whom he had relied to moderate the violence of the extreme parties in Paris, and he tells us that he was disappointed in him, and that he found him a ruthless demagogue, one of those who contributed most to the failure of the Republic.

From the letters I have quoted we should hardly have expected this, and perhaps the opinion is a little exaggerated. But it is undoubted that the famous writer was dragged into the vortex of the storm which then raged over France, carrying all before it.

When the machinery for the approaching elections to a constituent assembly had been set in motion, he became editor of an uncompromising Republican paper, the *Peuple Constituant*; but still his attitude seems to have been all that could be desired from the point of view of the party of order. On March 17, 1848, he wrote to Dessoliaire:—

I snatch a moment at the beginning of a fourteen hours day to write you this note. Go on getting ready for the approaching elections. Send us convinced and honest Republicans, friends of order and of liberty. The Communist sects have done much harm among the workmen. They are beset by extravagant dreams, and they loiter in the streets instead of going to work. But, God be praised, reasonable people are in a majority.

Perhaps we may see in a letter of May 6 an indication of the kind of thing which led to the adverse judgment of Lamartine:—

I have not a moment to myself, and I am utterly tired out. The justice of God is come; a better future opens before us. . . . Get ready for the elections, every one is going to vote; may there be a general agreement to elect only right-minded men, men of honour and probity, sincerely attached to the Republic, which alone can save us. Other things will follow if we make sure of that. Beware of cunning, of intriguers of every kind; of *all those who have had anything to do with public affairs, there is hardly one of them who is not more or less corrupted.*

The last clause may have been personally disagreeable to more than one member of the provisional government, but that it meant nothing more terrible may be seen in his next letter to the same group of political friends:—

The Communists and the Terrorists have done us a great deal of harm; they have been, and still are, the truest supporters of the factions, through the fear they inspire, and the disorder into which they have thrown the workmen, who have determined to remain idle.

But there was one friend who was sincerely troubled at the doings of Féli de Lamennais. The

Baron de Vitrolles had remained true to him through all the vicissitudes of his life, and the greatest differences of opinion had never raised a barrier between them. The excitement of the political agitation had now put a stop to their intercourse, and the old diplomatist seems to have been horrified at the rumours which reached him. On May 11 he wrote :—

Judging by myself, my dear friend, I have a firm belief in your wishing that we could meet, at least for a few minutes; and, in spite of your occupations, I cannot understand that it should be absolutely impossible, for I can think of many who have even more to do—as it has been with me at certain periods of my life—who know how to find quarters of an hour for friendship.

M. Scheffer has discouraged me from going to look for you in the offices of your paper. He says that he was badly received, and that he was evidently a cause of embarrassment to you. Writing to you would not quite satisfy me, and then I am not good at it. I see by your answers that you do not understand me, or that you have not time to read my letters. In this perplexity, and that I may have some one who can speak to me of you, and to whom I can speak, would it be indiscreet to ask if I could see your nephew? If I knew his address I should have gone to look him up, or asked him to come round for a moment to me.

You see I am determined, my dear friend, and they will never get me to believe that you are not as anxious as I am.

Lamennais answered next day :—

I have been suffering all night from fever. It is now six o'clock; they have just brought me your letter with several others. This is my life : on jumping out of bed the most important letters of the preceding evening to answer.

Article to write. At twelve, room. On coming back dozens of letters to open, read, &c. Next day's issue of the paper to look over, articles to correct, &c. My dinner of a quarter of an hour never goes by without interruption. I have then to myself only Sunday afternoons; I put off till then all my interviews, which are subject, as you may imagine, to considerable accumulation. It is on that day, from one to five, that we might meet; come then, for you may be sure I desire it as much as you. There is not a word of truth in what Ary Scheffer told you. He is an excellent man, but very sensitive. I have not time for more. Ever yours, &c.

When the constituent assembly came together after the elections, the supporters of Lamartine were in a majority, and Lamennais, who took up his position on the Extreme Left, found himself seated on the same benches with Lacordaire, who wore the habit of the Dominican order. He was not a success in the chamber, for he was entirely wanting in the gifts of oratory, but he was elected a member of the committee appointed to draw up the constitution. Yet, even here, success did not await him, for his naturally dogmatic temperament had become exaggerated by age and misfortune, and he found it impossible to compromise matters with his more practical colleagues.

Meanwhile the ultra moderate tendencies of the assembly, which bordered on reaction, led to considerable ill-feeling among the people of Paris. The unemployed, of whom Lamennais spoke in writing to Dessoliaire, became a formidable source of danger to the assembly. Already in May an organised outbreak had been with difficulty suppressed by the energy of Lamartine and his friends, and towards the end of June the streets of the capital were once more handed over to the mercies of an insurrectionary mob. The struggle began on the 23rd; it raged for three days in spite of the military operations carried on against the insurgents under the dictatorship of General Cavaignac, and it was only at the end of that time that the last of the barricades were finally carried, through the combined effect of a bombardment of mortars, which set fire to the surrounding houses, the pushing of a mine under the ground occupied by the revolutionists, and a flank attack on their position by General Lamoricière.

As the immediate result of the suppression of this movement, a powerful reaction set in in the assembly, which now adopted measures with which men like Lamennais could not possibly agree. Even before the outbreak, the editor of the *Peuple Constituant* had begun to differ from his colleagues in the Chamber:—

Things are looking very bad here [he had written to Dessoliaire on June 9]. . . . The Government is powerless or worse. It has just got a law passed on gatherings in the streets, placards, seditious cries, &c., which is more revolting than anything imagined by Louis Philippe. Something serious will happen.

And now that something had happened; the Government was victorious, and those who, like Lamennais, had shown sympathy for the people, were compelled to suffer. On June 28 he wrote to his nephew Blaize:—

I shall not speak of the sad events of the last few days now that the battle is over, the battle but not the war; the factions, who for two months have been moving heaven and earth to get it to take place, have reaped the benefit, inaugurating their advent to power by proscriptive laws, based, they say, in imitation of '93, on general security and public safety. I passed a part of last night at the assembly, wishing to protest by my vote against these execrable measures. My paper has not been suppressed, but the police are confiscating it as it is distributed. If this kind of thing goes on, the censorship will soon be re-established, and then the stamp. For my part, I am resolved to do my duty to the bitter end; so long as it is possible to write, I shall write.

He kept his word. During the four months which followed the outbreak of June he continued to defend, with his still powerful pen, the threatened interests of the young Republic and the cause of the starving people, and during that time he welcomes in his correspondence any signs of relaxation in the general tension, and of the gradual return of the unemployed to work. Then suddenly we come upon a letter to Dessoliaire, dated October 27, in which he says:—

The *Peuple Constituant* was condemned yesterday by a magistrate and a jury appointed under Louis Philippe. M. Veyron-Lacroix is to go to prison for a month, while I am to pay, including costs, about 1,200 francs for having defended the Republic, the principles of order, and the poor people, outlawed *en masse*, because they asked for bread.

They are going to nominate a president. Louis Bonaparte and Cavaignac are running against one another, and, in different ways, they are both equally worthy. . . . True Republicans will vote for Ledru-Rollin. Get this known, and see that every one agrees in supporting his candidature.

Then he threw himself with all his remaining energy into this final struggle, striving to the utmost to arouse the flagging enthusiasm of his fellow citizens of the republic of labour, and thus to make impossible the success of their twofold enemy, the representative of the Empire, and the man whose hand was red with the blood of their comrades.

It was a hopeless undertaking, and may possibly have contributed to the defeat of the candidate who, at least, was a sincere Republican. And it would be useless to enter into the details of a campaign which ended in the utter defeat of the democratic party. Suffice it to say that the election of Louis Bonaparte was followed by a series of measures directed against those elements in society which were opposed to the new *régime*.

The *Peuple Constituant* was crippled by a tax which made such literature possible only to the rich, and Lamennais was reluctantly compelled to withdraw it. In an article which reminds us of his former days, he took leave of his readers, reminding them that he, too, was poor, and that, like them, a member of the proletariat, he was deprived of the rights of citizenship, bidding them hope in the future, which was in the hands of God. And then, seeing around him the ruins of his dearest hopes, utterly disappointed, he turned his back for ever on public life.

CHAPTER XI

CLOSING SCENES

GOOD-BYE, be careful of your health, and do not, through your own fault, bring on a relapse, although, to tell the truth, the best course, as Tertullian says, is to get out of this sad world as soon as possible, provided always that one is certain that duty does not require one's presence in it.

Thus ended a short correspondence which, in the summer of 1848, had broken the long silence which, since their rupture at La Chênaie, had separated Féli de Lamennais from Abbé Jean. The former had heard that his brother was seriously ill, and had written to him. Indeed, he even appears to have thought of a more decisive move, for, on the same day, June 28, 1848, he had written to Ange Blaize :—

Make them get on, I beg of you, with the work at La Chênaie. When the walls are finished, and the earth is laid down, they must plant the espaliers and other fruit trees. I am anxious about these things, whether I am to see them or not. It is possible under certain circumstances that I may decide to return to La Chênaie; the contrary is also possible. Who knows to-day what the morrow will bring? It would be better to live in exile than in one's country if it is to remain in the hands of those who have been allowed to gain the upper hand.

But the hope had never been fulfilled, and

Lamennais had remained in Paris, absorbed in the struggle to which he had devoted what remained of his former power.

Now that his political ideal had failed him, at the very moment when it had seemed about to be realised, that he had finally quitted the arena of public life, he began to feel the full meaning of the isolation in which he stood. He would have liked to retire to the country, there to end his days in peaceful seclusion, but he could not afford it. He might have returned to La Chênaie, but he did not wish to meet his brother, or to bring about a reconciliation with him, and so he was compelled to live on amid the noise and bustle of the capital, making himself as comfortable as might be in different lodgings, none of which he kept for long, being compelled to leave them, either through unsuitability of the neighbourhood or stress of poverty.

He tried for a time to find solace in his correspondence with his political friends, wishing to inspire them with hopes which he himself seems hardly to have shared, but he does not appear to have been always successful in submitting to the self-restraint which was necessary for this. In July, for instance, 1850, he wrote to one of them :—

How resist the profound grief inspired by the spectacle which now presents itself to us ? Never did the world see anything like it, and I know nothing so terrifying as crime combined with imbecility. The men who, in their blind passion, are hurrying France to its destruction, do not suspect that they are preparing their own punishment, a terrible punishment, for unmeasured oppression will lead to unmeasured revenge. In closing the way to peaceful progress, they are causing to germinate in the bosom of the masses thoughts of violence and anger. . . . A bad spirit of jacquerie is fermenting among the peasantry of a part of France. They had consoled themselves in their misery by the hope of a better future, to be created by universal suffrage. Now that they are deprived of their right, declared to be outside society, they will appeal to force, and will arm themselves with their iron tools, as did the slaves in the time of Spartacus. That is where those madmen are leading us . . . who have taken possession of the machinery of government, hideous worms who, squeezing themselves through the cracks in the great tomb which is called the past, try to draw the people after them, that they may feed on them in the lonely silence of the night. . . .

M. Barbet sends you all sorts of messages. He is feeling pretty well in spite of the heat, which does not suit him.

From about this time till the day of his death this M. Barbet seems to have been constantly with him. We shall meet him again presently.

In the midst of his solitude it was well for Lamennais that some of his old friends continued to visit him. Many of them had passed away. The Marquis de Coriolis, Mme. de Senfft, and Marion, to whom he had poured out his inmost thoughts in his letters, had quitted the arena of life, the last only in '48, and in 1844 he had received a heart-rending letter from Mlle. de Villiers, whom he had known at the Feuillantines, who lay on her death-bed, and who wrote to him that she offered her last prayers and her sufferings for his conversion.

He tried to comfort himself in speaking words of

kindness to his friends. In January 1852 he wrote to Dessoliaire: 'We must not be sorry for those who go away at the present time. Think of this, and you will be consoled for the loss of your father. Some sooner, some later; we shall all meet in a better world.' But he felt that he was alone, and he could not bear the thought of living on and gradually dwindling away in the midst of old associations. 'If my health,' he wrote in the same month to Blaize, 'if my health made it possible for me to stand the fatigues of a voyage, and I could arrange my affairs in such a way as to give myself sufficient security, if not that I could live in easy circumstances, at least that I could be assured of the bare necessaries, it is possible that I might decide to end, far from this country, a life which is already too long.'

But he could not escape from Paris, and he was compelled, to the end, to drag out a weary existence in the midst of surroundings which were anything but cheerful. Shortly before the death of Marion, Lamennais had written to him:—

I see no hope of getting out of these depressing lodgings before two years. I should have to get some one to take my tenancy from me; that would be a stroke of fortune I dare not count upon. . . . Two more winters in this ice-house! It is hard!

Make the most, my dear friend, of your pure air, of your beautiful river, of your quiet garden. It is at least pleasant to think that those whom one loves have found in life a less thorny path than that up which one has been oneself compelled to climb.

After years of wandering from district to district

in a vain search after lodgings combining comfort with a rent which he could afford, Lamennais finally settled down in an apartment in the Rue du Grand Chantier, No. 12. It was probably while there that he received a visit which is mentioned by M. Roussel:—

One day M. Houet, who was then in Paris, went to see his unfortunate master, whom he found living in a room more than modest, situated on the fourth or fifth floor. It was winter. During the conversation, Lamennais noticed that his former disciple often looked sadly at the cold hearth. 'Well, yes,' he said, with a smile, 'there is no fire; it is an economy necessitated by my financial position. But it does not prevent me from beginning my day early; I wrap myself in this travelling coat which you see here, and so protect myself to some extent from the cold. If a ray of sun pays me a visit, it is always welcome. The important thing, my dear Houet, is to do one's duty; everything lies in that.'

But what duty was it possible for him to fulfil? The long dreaded *coup d'état* had come and gone; France was no longer, even in name, a Republic, and those whom he might have influenced were counted for nothing in the existing constitution. In former days he would have gone about among the poor, or watched by the bedsides of the sick and dying; but now he was too old, too broken in health, and he but seldom left his room. In fact, Barbet was his only constant companion, for his older friends, men who, like Vitrolles, could have drawn him from himself, wandering with him in imagination through the memories of the past, were old and feeble as he was, and were rarely able to visit him, while men of the generation of Houet were tied by their work to posts in the country, generally far from Paris. Sometimes he relieved himself by working at his translation of Dante, which was not destined to see the light during his lifetime; but even such a palliative was not always possible, for his imagination was no longer characterised by its former vividness, and when, as sometimes happened, it showed signs of re-awakening, it was not for long.

This it is which gives a peculiar tone of sadness to his last letters. The sudden bursts of brilliant sarcasm which have so often roused us to thoughts of life and hope, in the midst of the gloomiest periods, are now almost entirely absent. He constantly speaks of the health of his companion, of his own failing strength, of the mental and bodily ills which result from it, of old age, of isolation, and through all there is a kind of longing for death, the one true friend of those who are utterly alone in the world. Who would not feel the terrible pathos of the letter, almost the last in their correspondence, which he wrote to Vitrolles on September 14, 1853?—

I went, about ten days ago, to the Zoological Gardens, and saw there, lying in the sun, that monstrous beast which they call a hippopotamus; the crowd stood round it, joyful, happy. One would have said that it was a family feast. For my part, dreaming, I retired into those long deserted alleys, bordered by beds of flowers, autumn flowers, without perfume, as those of life in its decline. Then I felt the awakening within me, faint, sad, the love of nature, formerly so strong in me; I heard the voices of the past, as a far-off echo, and my thoughts floated vaguely in a mingling of memories and sensations, almost indistinguishable.

Little more than four months later Lamennais was on his death-bed. The Abbé Jean received the news from a friend in Paris, and he forwarded the letter to Houet, with the words 'Read, and with me weep and pray.'

From the first it was evident that the sick man was watched by Barbet and other of his later friends, who were anxious to protect him from visits which, besides irritating him, might cause him, in a moment of weakness, to revert to his former opinions.

'M. de Vitrolles,' said the correspondent of the Abbé Jean, 'is furious with these people, who even wished to prevent him from coming, which he did in spite of them. M. Martin did not dare to go, for he heard that M. Féli had said that he did not wish to see him.' And the writer added in a postscript: 'We think that if Augustine were to come it would be useful, for then these strangers would no longer be masters.'

Accordingly, at the beginning of February 1854, Augustine de Kertanguy, Lamennais' niece, the widow of his former disciple, arrived in Paris. On the 3rd of that month the same correspondent informed the Abbé Jean that she had gone with his sister to see Féli, and in a postscript to the same letter he added: 'My sister [Madame de Grandville] has just come back. I open my letter to tell you that she has seen our dear invalid, who is steadily getting better, but she found him terribly changed, and it was on condition that she should not speak to him that they allowed her to come in. Augustine is not to see him till to-morrow.'

About a fortnight later Madame de Kertanguy herself wrote to her uncle, describing her first visit: 'I wished to speak to him a little about God, and this is how I began: "Féli, my children want you to know that they are thinking of you, that they are praying for you, that they have gone to communion and are having Masses said for your intention."' And she concludes by saying that she has protected him from a visit from two priests.

On the 20th she describes a longer interview:—

I found my uncle better. . . . He spoke to me of my property in Lower Brittany, and then of his health, which seems to trouble him. He said to me: 'I feel that the end has come, I must resign myself to the will of God; I shall be happy when I am at rest with Him.' I answered: 'Yes, my dear Féli, God's will be done; we are only happy when we are with Him, but you are better.' And I tried to reassure him, but he said: 'Do not speak so.' . . . Then there was a moment of silence, after which, my good uncle, I took upon myself to speak of your longing to be near your brother, a longing the fulfilment of which was beyond your strength, and I told him how your friends had prevented you from setting out for Paris, and Uncle Féli said: 'I am glad he did not come.' I answered that it would have shocked you to see him so ill. 'Yes,' he said, 'write to him that I have been worse than I am to-day.' . . . I asked him whether he would allow me to send you a message from him; he did not answer, and I said: 'My dear Féli, my Uncle Jean is broken down with grief; for some nights he has not been able to sleep, a word from you would do him so much good.' . . . He pulled himself together and said, as he would have done formerly: 'Send it him.' I continued: 'I shall give my Uncle Jean all kinds of messages from you.' 'Yes,' he said affectionately, and then I left him.'

But the reconciliation was never completed. The Abbé Jean was persuaded by his friends that his post of duty was at the bedside of his brother. With touching devotion, in defiance both of age and failing health, he started on the journey to Paris; but he got no further than Rennes, where it was recognised that further exertion would be fatal to him. Augustine de Kertanguy continued to do her utmost for her uncle, but she was practically alone, for those who sympathised with her were rarely admitted to the room of the dying man, and she herself was often unable to overcome the opposition of those who jealously guarded him.

On the 23rd she wrote to Jean: 'On Saturday, I shall send you news; to-morrow I shall know nothing; one cannot put any trust in what M. Barbet says.' And two days later: 'I am sick at heart, the more so that I know that this will break yours. Yesterday I went to my uncle's house. I saw only M. Barbet, who told me that our dear Féli was losing strength, and that he did not dare to go into his room. I asked him if my uncle knew that I was still in Paris; he answered: '*No, and I do not feel disposed to tell him.*'

On the evening of the 26th she managed to get to her uncle's room. She was shocked by his altered appearance, and she said, '*Féli, would you like to see a priest? You would like to see a priest?*' Lamennais answered: '*No.*' His niece went on: '*Reflect,*

I beseech you.' But he pulled himself together, and said in a firmer tone : ' *No, no, no, leave me in peace.*' This scene is related in the procès-verbal, drawn up and signed by those who watched over him through his illness.

Next day a letter was written by one of his little grand-nephews, who had been left in Brittany with his brothers :—

My dear good Uncle Féli,—

My brothers and I have been gladdened by a letter from my mother, who says that you are better, and I hope that God will soon bring you back to health. He is so good that He will not refuse your recovery to the prayers, feeble though they are, which we are always offering for you. I should like to be with you, to help my mother in taking care of you ; but, since it is God's will that I should remain here, I offer Him, for your health, the unpleasantness I feel at being so far from you, able to help you only by my feeble prayers.

Good-bye, my dear Uncle Féli, you know you can always rely on the increasing friendship of your grand-nephew,

ÉLIE DE KERTANGUY.

This touching letter never reached him. It came, when all was over, into the hands of the broken-hearted niece and mother, who forwarded it to the Abbé Jean with the words : ' The poor children are doing all they can to soften my grief.'

On the 26th it became evident to all who were near him that the end was approaching. Towards evening he intimated that he wished to speak with Emile Forgues, to whom he had entrusted the publication of his correspondence and of his translation of Dante.

He had sent for me [says that writer] when he realised that his last hour was at hand. Bending over him, I had received his last farewell to his old friend M. de Vitrolles, and a recommendation not to allow myself to be turned . . . from the duty he had confided in me. When he had heard my solemn promise, he seemed relieved. . . .

A profound silence reigned in the room where his life was slowly ebbing away. Not a murmur and, so to speak, not a movement was heard. With the exception of the nurse, no one was there but his niece and one of her friends. . . . M. Barbet came and went between this room and the study, where a few friends were passing the evening. At about eleven o'clock there were only three or four of us, and the rest of the night passed thus.

At about two in the morning Barbet came to Forgues and told him that Lamennais had tried to speak, that he had heard something about *papers*, but that he had been unable to understand anything more. Seeing this, with a sign of helpless irritation, Lamennais had turned his face to the wall. Once more there was silence, and my tired eyes followed on the clock the inexorable march of time.

The day was already come when I heard, for the last time, the voice of the dying man, who was then alone with the nurse. The servant was called. His friends gathered round the bed. He was raised up, but he fainted in the effort.

The agony was prolonged. I turned my eyes from the cruel sight, and went to the window. I could see from it the little gardens enclosed by houses, the dark skeletons of leafless trees, the blackened pathways surrounding plots of withered grass. The pale winter sun, piercing the morning mist, threw over the melancholy scene a brightness which was damp and veiled.

Tired out by watching and anxiety, Augustine de Kertanguy had gone away with her friend. After taking a little food, she had gone to Mass, and was now in a neighbouring church praying for her uncle, whom she had seen alive for the last time.

That last fond farewell, faintly uttered on the previous evening, had been brought to the Baron de Vitrolles, and he hurried, on this morning of the 27th, to the bedside of his friend.

It was nine o'clock when he got to the room. 'I found,' he afterwards said, 'that my unfortunate friend had lost consciousness. In vain I twice laid my hand on his breast. His respiration was quick and uncertain; and, at the end of about twenty-five minutes, or half an hour, we knew that he had breathed his last.'

Lamennais had gone to his rest. '*Ce sont les bons moments*,' he had said wearily, as he laid himself down to his last sleep. Then all had become silent, and there was no sign of recognition, no word of greeting for his old friend, his true companion in every period of his stormy life, bound to him by a sympathy which no difference of opinion or ideal had been able to alter. As the old man stood by the bedside of him to whom an irony of fate had given the name of *Félicité* de Lamennais, he must have felt that he, too, was now alone in the world, that the feeble chain which still bound him to life had been severed, a chain of friendship, consecrated by mutual suffering, sorrow, and disappointment; he must have longed for some sign which, awakening in him a sad echo of the dreary past, might beckon him to that bed of rest for which he also yearned, and to which he was soon to follow. And if an old tradition is to be believed, that sign was vouchsafed to him; for it is said that when the dying man had ceased to speak, when all around him had become silent, when every outward expression of life was gone, his eye became moist, and a tear rolled down his cheek, worn and furrowed by care and pain.

He was buried on March 1, 1854. In his will he had said: ' I wish to be buried with the poor, and as the poor. There must be nothing to mark my tomb, not even a simple stone.' To the recently established government of Louis Napoleon he appeared greater in death than in life. Measures were taken to prevent a demonstration. The streets on the way to Père la Chaise were guarded by police, as were the gates of the cemetery itself, and even the space round the grave. One of the intimate friends who were allowed to be present at this last sad scene has described it in words which I borrow from Forgues: ' The coffin was let down into one of those long unsightly ditches in which the people are buried. When the earth had been thrown in upon it, a workman asked, "*Do you want a cross?*" M. Barbet answered, "No." M. de Lamennais had said, " Nothing must mark my grave." Not a word was spoken over the tomb.'

Some months later, says a contemporary writer, quoted by M. Spuller, ' in June 1854, a carriage drew up one evening before the door of the little chapel at

La Chênaie. An old priest, broken down more by sorrow than by age, got out of it, and kneeling on the pavement, bowing his head covered with grey hairs, before a deserted altar, while his eyes were filled with warm tears, he prayed long and fervently. . . . Then he got up and came out.

'Hardly had he advanced a few paces when his eye fell upon one of the windows of the house, and, raising his arms, as if to reach a form which he alone could see, he cried out: "*Féli, Féli! my brother.*" . . .

'It was the Abbé Jean de Lamennais.'

www.ingramcontent.com/pod-product-compliance
Lightning Source LLC
Chambersburg PA
CBHW032357230426
43672CB00007B/733